BREAD FOR THE DAY

DAILY BIBLE READINGS AND PRAYERS

2021

Minneapolis

BREAD FOR THE DAY 2021
Daily Bible Readings and Prayers

Editors: Dennis Bushkofsky, Laurie Hanson
Cover design: Laurie Ingram
Cover art: Christina Saj
Interior art: Gertrud Mueller Nelson

Contributors to the weekday prayers:
Jennifer M. Manis, Raleigh, North Carolina (January); David L. Miller, Naperville, Illinois (February); Melinda A. Quivik, Saint Paul, Minnesota (March); Stacey Nalean-Carlson, Decorah, Iowa (April); Kurt Lammi, Dayton, Ohio (May); Scott A. Moore, Erfurt, Germany (June); Matthew Ian Fleming, Eden Prairie, Minnesota (July); Becca Ajer Frantz, Gettysburg, Pennsylvania (August); James Rowe, Denton, Texas (September); Richard J. Bruesehoff, Lac Du Flambeau, Wisconsin (October); Elle Dowd, Chicago, Illinois (November); Linnéa K. Clark, Somerset, New Jersey (December)

ACKNOWLEDGMENTS
Scripture quotations are from the New Revised Standard Version Bible © 1989 Division of Christian Education of the National Council of the Churches of Christ in the United States of America. Used by permission.

Hymn suggestions and prayers of the day for Sundays and festivals are from *Evangelical Lutheran Worship*, copyright © 2006 Evangelical Lutheran Church in America.

Materials prepared by the Consultation on Common Texts (CCT), published in *Revised Common Lectionary* © 1992 and *Revised Common Lectionary Daily Readings* © 2005. Used by permission.

"Table prayer for the season of Lent," "Table prayer for summer," "A prayer to begin the work day," "A prayer to begin the school day," "Morning blessing," and "Evening blessing" are from *Reformation 500 Sourcebook: Anniversary Resources for Congregations* © 2016 Augsburg Fortress.

Materials prepared by the English Language Liturgical Consultation (ELLC), published in *Praying Together* © 1988: "Blessed are you, Lord" and "My soul proclaims the greatness of the Lord." Used by permission.

ISBN 978-1-5064-4982-1
Manufactured in the USA

Contents

Foreword

Beloved of God,

For generations, the living word has sustained God's people. In times of prosperity and turmoil, joy and sorrow, the church has found hope and consolation in scripture.

The Evangelical Lutheran Church in America has embraced the initiative called Book of Faith. In it we have committed ourselves to deepening our fluency in the first language of faith, holy scripture. *Bread for the Day* is a wonderful resource for your daily encounter with the word. You will be nourished, encouraged, and sustained, as have the saints before you.

As the Conference of Bishops, we invite you to join us, and this whole church, in persistent attentiveness to the word. Your faith will be deepened, your witness empowered, and your church enriched. God bless your journey in faith.

Conference of Bishops
Evangelical Lutheran Church in America

For more about Book of Faith, visit www.bookoffaith.org.

Introduction

Daily prayer is an essential practice for those who seek to hear God's voice and cultivate an inner life. Whether you pray alone or with others, with brevity or in sustained meditation, the rhythm of daily prayer reveals the life-sustaining communion to which God invites all human beings. Such prayer is a serene power silently at work, drawing us into the ancient yet vital sources of faith, hope, and love.

The guiding principle of the selection of daily readings in *Bread for the Day* is their relationship to the Sunday readings as presented in the Revised Common Lectionary (a system of readings in widespread use across denominations). The readings are chosen so that the days leading up to Sunday (Thursday through Saturday) prepare for the Sunday readings. The days flowing out from Sunday (Monday through Wednesday) reflect on the Sunday readings.

How this book is organized

- Each day's page is dated and named in relationship to the church's year. Lesser festivals are listed along with the date as part of the day heading. Commemorations are listed just below in smaller type. Notes on those commemorated can be found on pages 407–416.
- Several verses of one of the appointed scripture texts are printed. The full text citation is provided for those who would like to reflect on the entire text. In addition, two or three additional reading citations with short descriptions are provided.
- Two psalms are appointed for each week: one psalm for Monday through Wednesday and a second psalm for Thursday through Saturday. In this way the days leading up to Sunday or flowing out from Sunday have a distinct relationship with one another in addition to their relationship with the Sunday readings.

- Following the printed scripture text is a hymn suggestion from *Evangelical Lutheran Worship* and a prayer that incorporates a theme present in one or more of the readings.
- Household prayers and blessings appropriate to the changing seasons are placed throughout the book. Simplified forms of morning and evening prayer, morning and evening blessings, and prayers with children can be found on pages 424–431.

How to use this book

- Use the weekday readings to prepare for and reflect on the Sunday readings.
- Use the questions printed on page 432 to guide your reflection on the scripture texts.
- Use the resources for household prayer placed throughout the book. See the Contents on pages 3–4 for a complete list.
- Use the page at the beginning of each month to record prayer requests.
- In addition to being used to guide individual prayer, this book may be used to guide family prayer, prayer in congregational or other settings during the week, prayer with those who are sick or homebound, or prayer with other groups.

Even though Christians gather on the Lord's day, Sunday, for public worship, much of our time is spent in the home. We first learn the words, gestures, and songs of faith in the home. We discover our essential identity as a community of faith and mark significant transitions of life in the home. To surround and infuse the daily rhythm of sleeping and waking, working, resting, and eating with the words and gestures of Christian prayer is to discover the ancient truth of the gospel: the ordinary and the human can reveal the mystery of God and divine grace. Like planets around the sun, our daily prayer draws us to the Sunday assembly where we gather for the word and the breaking of the bread in the changing seasons of the year. From the Sunday assembly, our daily prayer flows into the week.

Prayer List for January

_____

_____

_____

_____

_____

_____

_____

_____

_____

_____

Friday, January 1, 2021
Name of Jesus

Numbers 6:22-27
The Aaronic blessing

The LORD spoke to Moses, saying: Speak to Aaron and his sons, saying,
Thus you shall bless the Israelites: You shall say to them,
    The LORD bless you and keep you;
    the LORD make his face to shine upon you, and be gracious to you;
    the LORD lift up his countenance upon you, and give you peace.
So they shall put my name on the Israelites, and I will bless them.
(Num. 6:22-27)

Psalm
Psalm 8
How exalted is your name

Additional Readings
Galatians 4:4-7
We are no longer slaves

Luke 2:15-21
The child is named Jesus

Hymn: Jesus, the Very Thought of You, ELW 754

Eternal Father, you gave your incarnate Son the holy name of Jesus to be a sign of our salvation. Plant in every heart the love of the Savior of the world, Jesus Christ our Lord, who lives and reigns with you and the Holy Spirit, one God, now and forever.

Saturday, January 2, 2021
Week of Christmas 1

Johann Konrad Wilhelm Loehe, renewer of the church, died 1872

Psalm 148
God's splendor is over earth and heaven

Kings of the earth and all peoples,
>   princes and all rulers of the earth!
Young men and women alike,
>   old and young together!

Let them praise the name of the LORD,
>   for his name alone is exalted;
>   his glory is above earth and heaven.
He has raised up a horn for his people,
>   praise for all his faithful,
>   for the people of Israel who are close to him.
Praise the LORD! (Ps. 148:11-14)

Additional Readings
Proverbs 1:1-7
Grow in wisdom and knowledge

James 3:13-18
The wisdom from above

Hymn: Where Charity and Love Prevail, ELW 359

King of kings, your glory surpasses heaven and earth. Fill us with wonder as we encounter the Word made flesh, your son, Jesus Christ. Transform us into a people who embody your love with our whole lives.

Sunday, January 3, 2021
Second Sunday of Christmas

John 1:[1-9] 10-18

God with us

He was in the world, and the world came into being through him; yet the world did not know him. He came to what was his own, and his own people did not accept him. But to all who received him, who believed in his name, he gave power to become children of God, who were born, not of blood or of the will of the flesh or of the will of man, but of God.

And the Word became flesh and lived among us, and we have seen his glory, the glory as of a father's only son, full of grace and truth. (John 1:10-14)

Psalm

Psalm 147:12-20
Praising God in Zion

Additional Readings

Jeremiah 31:7-14
Joy as God's scattered flock gathers

Ephesians 1:3-14
The will of God made known in Christ

Hymn: Of the Father's Love Begotten, ELW 295

O God our redeemer, you created light that we might live, and you illumine our world with your beloved Son. By your Spirit comfort us in all darkness and turn us toward the light of Jesus Christ our Savior, who lives and reigns with you and the Holy Spirit, one God, now and forever.

Monday, January 4, 2021
Week of Christmas 2

Psalm 110
Prayers for the king

The LORD sends out from Zion
>	your mighty scepter.
>	Rule in the midst of your foes.

Your people will offer themselves willingly
>	on the day you lead your forces
>	on the holy mountains.

From the womb of the morning,
>	like dew, your youth will come to you.

The LORD has sworn and will not change his mind,
>	"You are a priest forever according to the order of Melchizedek."

(Ps. 110:2-4)

Additional Readings

Proverbs 3:1-12
Trust in God with all your heart

James 4:11-17
Our plans for our time are in God's hands

Hymn: Abide, O Dearest Jesus, ELW 539

Speak anew your wisdom, eternal Lord. Open the leaders of every nation to the vision of your justice. Empower peacemakers. Protect military personnel and bring with haste the day war is no more and peace reigns.

Tuesday, January 5, 2021
Week of Christmas 2

Luke 6:27-31

Do to others as you would have them do to you

[Jesus said to his disciples,] "But I say to you that listen, Love your enemies, do good to those who hate you, bless those who curse you, pray for those who abuse you. If anyone strikes you on the cheek, offer the other also; and from anyone who takes away your coat do not withhold even your shirt. Give to everyone who begs from you; and if anyone takes away your goods, do not ask for them again. Do to others as you would have them do to you." (Luke 6:27-31)

Psalm
Psalm 110
Prayers for the king

Additional Reading
Proverbs 22:1-9
The generous are blessed

Hymn: Angels, from the Realms of Glory, ELW 275

Love Divine, your grace endures from generation to generation. You love us abundantly, yet we struggle to love ourselves and our neighbors. Equip us to give and receive compassion for ourselves and our neighbors.

Blessing for a Home at Epiphany

Matthew writes that when the magi saw the shining star stop overhead, they were filled with joy. "On entering the house, they saw the child with Mary his mother" (Matt. 2:10-11). In the home, Christ is met in family and friends, in visitors and strangers. In the home, faith is shared, nurtured, and put into action. In the home, Christ is welcome.

Twelfth Night (January 5), Epiphany of Our Lord (January 6), or another day during the time after Epiphany offers an occasion for gathering with friends and family members for a blessing for the home. Someone may lead the greeting and blessing, while another person may read the scripture passage. Following an eastern European tradition, a visual blessing may be inscribed with white chalk above the main door; for example, 20 + CMB + 21. The numbers change with each new year. The three letters stand for either the ancient Latin blessing *Christe mansionem benedicat,* which means, "Christ, bless this house," or the legendary names of the magi (Caspar, Melchior, and Balthasar).

Greeting

Peace to this house and to all who enter here.
By wisdom a house is built,
and through understanding it is established;
through knowledge its rooms are filled
with rare and beautiful treasures. *(Prov. 24:3-4)*

Reading

As we prepare to ask God's blessing on this household,
let us listen to the words of scripture.
In the beginning was the Word,
and the Word was with God, and the Word was God.
He was in the beginning with God.
All things came into being through him,
and without him not one thing came into being.

What has come into being in him was life,
and the life was the light of all people.
The Word became flesh and lived among us, and we have seen his glory,
the glory as of a father's only son, full of grace and truth.
From his fullness we have all received, grace upon grace.
(John 1:1-4, 14, 16)

Inscription

This inscription may be made with chalk above the entrance:

20 + C M B + 21

Write the appropriate character (left) while speaking the text (right).

The magi of old, known as

C   Caspar,

M   Melchior, and

B   Balthasar,

followed the star of God's Son who came to dwell among us

20   two thousand

21   and twenty-one years ago.

+   Christ, bless this house,

+   and remain with us throughout the new year.

Prayer of Blessing

O God,
you revealed your Son to all people by the shining light of a star.
We pray that you bless this home and all who live here
with your gracious presence.
May your love be our inspiration, your wisdom our guide,
your truth our light, and your peace our benediction;
through Christ our Lord. Amen.

Then everyone may walk from room to room, blessing the house with incense or by sprinkling with water, perhaps using a branch from the Christmas tree.

Wednesday, January 6, 2021
Epiphany of Our Lord

Matthew 2:1-12

Christ revealed to the nations

In the time of King Herod, after Jesus was born in Bethlehem of Judea, wise men from the East came to Jerusalem, asking, "Where is the child who has been born king of the Jews? For we observed his star at its rising, and have come to pay him homage." When King Herod heard this, he was frightened, and all Jerusalem with him; and calling together all the chief priests and scribes of the people, he inquired of them where the Messiah was to be born. They told him, "In Bethlehem of Judea; for so it has been written by the prophet." (Matt. 2:1-5)

Psalm
Psalm 72:1-7, 10-14
All shall bow down

Additional Readings
Isaiah 60:1-6
Nations come to the light

Ephesians 3:1-12
The gospel's promise for all

Hymn: Brightest and Best of the Stars, ELW 303

Everlasting God, the radiance of all faithful people, you brought the nations to the brightness of your rising. Fill the world with your glory, and show yourself to all the world through him who is the true light and the bright morning star, your Son, Jesus Christ, our Savior and Lord, who lives and reigns with you and the Holy Spirit, one God, now and forever.

Time after Epiphany

On the Epiphany of Our Lord (January 6), the household joins the church throughout the world in celebrating the manifestation, the "epiphany," of Christ to the world. The festival of Christmas is thus set within the context of outreach to the larger community; it possesses an outward movement. The festival of the Epiphany asks the Christian household: How might our faith in Christ the Light be shared with friends and family, with our neighbors, with the poor and needy in our land, with those who live in other nations?

Table Prayer for Epiphany and the Time after Epiphany (January 6–February 16)

Generous God,
you have made yourself known in Jesus, the light of the world.
As this food and drink give us refreshment,
so strengthen us by your Spirit,
that as your baptized sons and daughters
we may share your light with all the world.
Grant this through Christ our Lord.
Amen.

Thursday, January 7, 2021
Time after Epiphany

Psalm 29
The voice of God upon the waters

Ascribe to the LORD, O heavenly beings,
    ascribe to the LORD glory and strength.
Ascribe to the LORD the glory of his name;
    worship the LORD in holy splendor.

The voice of the LORD is over the waters;
    the God of glory thunders,
    the LORD, over mighty waters.
The voice of the LORD is powerful;
    the voice of the LORD is full of majesty. (Ps. 29:1-4)

Additional Readings
1 Samuel 3:1-21   **Acts 9:10-19a**
Samuel called by God as a prophet   *Saul is baptized*

Hymn: Oh, Worship the King, ELW 842

How majestic is your voice, Holy One! You spoke all creation into being.
Speak to us now. Open our ears. Open our hearts. Speak, for your servants
are listening. Tell us how to be your light.

Friday, January 8, 2021
Time after Epiphany

1 Timothy 4:11-16

Gift of prophecy with laying on of hands

These are the things you must insist on and teach. Let no one despise your youth, but set the believers an example in speech and conduct, in love, in faith, in purity. Until I arrive, give attention to the public reading of scripture, to exhorting, to teaching. Do not neglect the gift that is in you, which was given to you through prophecy with the laying on of hands by the council of elders. Put these things into practice, devote yourself to them, so that all may see your progress. Pay close attention to yourself and to your teaching; continue in these things, for in doing this you will save both yourself and your hearers. (1 Tim. 4:11-16)

Psalm

Psalm 29
The voice of God upon the waters

Additional Reading

1 Samuel 16:1-13
David anointed king by Samuel

Hymn: Holy God, We Praise Your Name, ELW 414

God of every age, you equip us, young and old, with gifts for sharing your gospel. Create boldness within us to share our gifts and an openness to the ways your gospel is revealed.

Saturday, January 9, 2021
Time after Epiphany

1 Kings 2:1-4, 10-12

Solomon is designated king by David

When David's time to die drew near, he charged his son Solomon, saying: "I am about to go the way of all the earth. Be strong, be courageous, and keep the charge of the LORD your God, walking in his ways and keeping his statutes, his commandments, his ordinances, and his testimonies, as it is written in the law of Moses, so that you may prosper in all that you do and wherever you turn. Then the LORD will establish his word that he spoke concerning me: 'If your heirs take heed to their way, to walk before me in faithfulness with all their heart and with all their soul, there shall not fail you a successor on the throne of Israel.'" (1 Kings 2:1-4)

Psalm

Psalm 29
The voice of God upon the waters

Additional Reading

Luke 5:1-11
Jesus calls Simon, James, and John

Hymn: Faith of Our Fathers, ELW 812/813

God our creator and redeemer, in you we are born and in you we die. Empower us to share your teaching with every generation. Raise us up with all the saints and all creation into life eternal.

Sunday, January 10, 2021
Baptism of Our Lord

Mark 1:4-11

Jesus revealed as God's servant

John the baptizer appeared in the wilderness, proclaiming a baptism of repentance for the forgiveness of sins. And people from the whole Judean countryside and all the people of Jerusalem were going out to him, and were baptized by him in the river Jordan, confessing their sins. Now John was clothed with camel's hair, with a leather belt around his waist, and he ate locusts and wild honey. He proclaimed, "The one who is more powerful than I is coming after me; I am not worthy to stoop down and untie the thong of his sandals. I have baptized you with water; but he will baptize you with the Holy Spirit." (Mark 1:4-8)

Psalm

Psalm 29
The voice of God upon the waters

Additional Readings

Acts 19:1-7
Baptized in the name of Jesus

Genesis 1:1-5
God creates light

Hymn: When Jesus Came to Jordan, ELW 305

Holy God, creator of light and giver of goodness, your voice moves over the waters. Immerse us in your grace, and transform us by your Spirit, that we may follow after your Son, Jesus Christ, our Savior and Lord, who lives and reigns with you and the Holy Spirit, one God, now and forever.

Monday, January 11, 2021
Time after Epiphany

Psalm 69:1-5, 30-36
God will save through water

Save me, O God,
> for the waters have come up to my neck.
I sink in deep mire,
> where there is no foothold;
I have come into deep waters,
> and the flood sweeps over me.
I am weary with my crying;
> my throat is parched.
My eyes grow dim
> with waiting for my God. (Ps. 69:1-3)

Additional Readings
Genesis 17:1-13
Circumcision a covenant sign

Romans 4:1-12
God makes righteous apart from works

Hymn: Rock of Ages, Cleft for Me, ELW 623

Steadfast Lord, you never leave us. When the waters rise, when the winds blow strong, when tears fall like rain, you are our stronghold. You are our comfort. Be with us and all who cry out when life overwhelms.

Tuesday, January 12, 2021
Time after Epiphany

Acts 22:2-16
Paul describes his own baptism

[Paul spoke about his own conversion,] "A certain Ananias, who was a devout man according to the law and well spoken of by all the Jews living there, came to me; and standing beside me, he said, 'Brother Saul, regain your sight!' In that very hour I regained my sight and saw him. Then he said, 'The God of our ancestors has chosen you to know his will, to see the Righteous One and to hear his own voice; for you will be his witness to all the world of what you have seen and heard. And now why do you delay? Get up, be baptized, and have your sins washed away, calling on his name.'" (Acts 22:12-16)

Psalm
Psalm 69:1-5, 30-36
God will save through water

Additional Reading
Exodus 30:22-38
Anointing a sign of holiness

Hymn: All Who Believe and Are Baptized, ELW 442

Righteous One, your mercy never ends. Thank you for all who accompany us in healing our physical, mental, and spiritual wounds. Thank you for calling us and claiming us in baptism. Let nothing separate us from you.

Wednesday, January 13, 2021
Time after Epiphany

Isaiah 41:14-20

God gives water in the desert

When the poor and needy seek water,
>   and there is none,
>   and their tongue is parched with thirst,
I the LORD will answer them,
>   I the God of Israel will not forsake them.
I will open rivers on the bare heights,
>   and fountains in the midst of the valleys;
I will make the wilderness a pool of water,
>   and the dry land springs of water. . . .
so that all may see and know,
>   all may consider and understand,
that the hand of the LORD has done this,
>   the Holy One of Israel has created it. (Isa. 41:17-18, 20)

Psalm

Psalm 69:1-5, 30-36
God will save through water

Additional Reading

John 1:29-34
John's account of Jesus' baptism

Hymn: Crashing Waters at Creation, ELW 455

Beautiful Savior, you spoke over the waters and they moved. Many cry out for clean and accessible water. Hear their pleas. Move us to advocate and act for clean water for all people. Pour out your Holy Spirit on us.

Thursday, January 14, 2021
Time after Epiphany

Psalm 139:1-6, 13-18
You have searched me out

O LORD, you have searched me and known me.
You know when I sit down and when I rise up;
    you discern my thoughts from far away.
You search out my path and my lying down,
    and are acquainted with all my ways.
Even before a word is on my tongue,
    O LORD, you know it completely. (Ps. 139:1-4)

Additional Readings

Judges 2:6-15
Uncertain times after Joshua's death

2 Corinthians 10:1-11
Corinthian behavior during Paul's absence

Hymn: Borning Cry, ELW 732

Holy One, you are from everlasting to everlasting. Blessed are you for loving us and knowing us completely. Blessed are you for your never-ending mercy. Grant us your grace abundantly to share our whole life long.

Friday, January 15, 2021
Time after Epiphany

Martin Luther King Jr., renewer of society, martyr, died 1968

Acts 13:16-25
Leaders prior to Christ's coming

[Paul spoke:] "God has brought to Israel a Savior, Jesus, as he promised; before his coming John had already proclaimed a baptism of repentance to all the people of Israel. And as John was finishing his work, he said, 'What do you suppose that I am? I am not he. No, but one is coming after me; I am not worthy to untie the thong of the sandals on his feet.'" (Acts 13:23-25)

Psalm
Psalm 139:1-6, 13-18
You have searched me out

Additional Reading
Judges 2:16-23
God calls forth the judges

Hymn: Soli Deo Gloria, ELW 878

God of justice, you equip the saints of every age to embody your love. Embolden your church to be faithful to our baptismal calling. Give us courage to proclaim your truth. Make all we do reveal your glory.

Saturday, January 16, 2021
Time after Epiphany

1 Samuel 2:21-25

Eli's sons sin

And the Lord took note of Hannah; she conceived and bore three sons and two daughters. And the boy Samuel grew up in the presence of the Lord.

Now Eli was very old. He heard all that his sons were doing to all Israel, and how they lay with the women who served at the entrance to the tent of meeting. He said to them, "Why do you do such things? For I hear of your evil dealings from all these people. No, my sons; it is not a good report that I hear the people of the Lord spreading abroad. If one person sins against another, someone can intercede for the sinner with the Lord; but if someone sins against the Lord, who can make intercession?" But they would not listen to the voice of their father; for it was the will of the Lord to kill them. (1 Sam. 2:21-25)

Psalm
Psalm 139:1-6, 13-18
You have searched me out

Additional Reading
Matthew 25:1-13
Wise and foolish bridesmaids

Hymn: Lord Jesus, Think on Me, ELW 599

Gracious Lord, you created us to be in relationship with one another and relationships are hard. Sometimes we hurt one another with our words and actions. Forgive us and help us to forgive those who have hurt us.

Sunday, January 17, 2021
Second Sunday after Epiphany

Antony of Egypt, renewer of the church, died around 356
Pachomius, renewer of the church, died 346

John 1:43-51
The calling of the first disciples

The next day Jesus decided to go to Galilee. He found Philip and said to him, "Follow me." Now Philip was from Bethsaida, the city of Andrew and Peter. Philip found Nathanael and said to him, "We have found him about whom Moses in the law and also the prophets wrote, Jesus son of Joseph from Nazareth." Nathanael said to him, "Can anything good come out of Nazareth?" Philip said to him, "Come and see." (John 1:43-46)

Psalm
Psalm 139:1-6, 13-18
You have searched me out

Additional Readings
1 Samuel 3:1-10
[11-20]
The calling of Samuel

1 Corinthians 6:12-20
Glorify God in your body

Hymn: The Son of God, Our Christ, ELW 584

Thanks be to you, Lord Jesus Christ, most merciful redeemer, for the countless blessings and benefits you give. May we know you more clearly, love you more dearly, and follow you more nearly, day by day praising you, with the Father and the Holy Spirit, one God, now and forever.

Monday, January 18, 2021
Confession of Peter

Week of Prayer for Christian Unity begins

Matthew 16:13-19

Peter confesses, You are the Messiah

[Jesus] said to [his disciples], "But who do you say that I am?" Simon Peter answered, "You are the Messiah, the Son of the living God." And Jesus answered him, "Blessed are you, Simon son of Jonah! For flesh and blood has not revealed this to you, but my Father in heaven. And I tell you, you are Peter, and on this rock I will build my church, and the gates of Hades will not prevail against it. I will give you the keys of the kingdom of heaven, and whatever you bind on earth will be bound in heaven, and whatever you loose on earth will be loosed in heaven." (Matt. 16:15-19)

Psalm

Psalm 18:1-6, 16-19
My God, my rock, worthy of praise

Additional Readings

Acts 4:8-13
Salvation is in no one other than Jesus

1 Corinthians 10:1-5
Drinking from the spiritual rock of Christ

Hymn: Oh, Praise the Gracious Power, ELW 651

Almighty God, you inspired Simon Peter to confess Jesus as the Messiah and Son of the living God. Keep your church firm on the rock of this faith, so that in unity and peace it may proclaim one truth and follow one Lord, your Son, Jesus Christ our Savior, who lives and reigns with you and the Holy Spirit, one God, now and forever.

Tuesday, January 19, 2021
Time after Epiphany

Henry, Bishop of Uppsala, martyr, died 1156

Acts 5:1-11
Ananias and Sapphira judged

But a man named Ananias, with the consent of his wife Sapphira, sold a piece of property; with his wife's knowledge, he kept back some of the proceeds, and brought only a part and laid it at the apostles' feet. "Ananias," Peter asked, "why has Satan filled your heart to lie to the Holy Spirit and to keep back part of the proceeds of the land? While it remained unsold, did it not remain your own? And after it was sold, were not the proceeds at your disposal? How is it that you have contrived this deed in your heart? You did not lie to us but to God!" Now when Ananias heard these words, he fell down and died. And great fear seized all who heard of it. (Acts 5:1-5)

Psalm
Psalm 86
Walking in God's way

Additional Reading
1 Samuel 15:10-31
Samuel rebukes King Saul

Hymn: I Want to Walk as a Child of the Light, ELW 815

God of abundance, you call us into community to care for one another. Scarcity calls us too, to hoard all that you give us. Help us to give as we receive and to ask as we have need.

Wednesday, January 20, 2021
Time after Epiphany

Luke 18:15-17
Jesus blesses little children

People were bringing even infants to [Jesus] that he might touch them; and when the disciples saw it, they sternly ordered them not to do it. But Jesus called for them and said, "Let the little children come to me, and do not stop them; for it is to such as these that the kingdom of God belongs. Truly I tell you, whoever does not receive the kingdom of God as a little child will never enter it." (Luke 18:15-17)

Psalm
Psalm 86
Walking in God's way

Additional Reading
Genesis 16:1-14
Hagar sees God and is blessed

Hymn: Cradling Children in His Arm, ELW 444

Eternal Father, you sent your son to reveal the boundless nature of your love. Forgive us when we put limits on your love. Teach us to embody the grace you give freely. Equip us to love like Jesus.

Thursday, January 21, 2021
Time after Epiphany

Agnes, martyr, died around 304

Psalm 62:5-12
In God is my safety and my honor

For God alone my soul waits in silence,
> for my hope is from him.
He alone is my rock and my salvation,
> my fortress; I shall not be shaken.
On God rests my deliverance and my honor;
> my mighty rock, my refuge is in God. (Ps. 62:5-7)

Additional Readings
Jeremiah 19:1-15
Jeremiah announces disaster

Revelation 18:11-20
Lament over a fallen city

Hymn: He Comes to Us as One Unknown, ELW 737

O God, our rock and our salvation, in you is refuge from the storm. Deliver us from the ways of sin. Heal us from the pain of shame. Fill us with your hope and surround us with your compassionate spirit.

Friday, January 22, 2021
Time after Epiphany

2 Peter 3:1-7

Scoffers doubt God's message

First of all you must understand this, that in the last days scoffers will come, scoffing and indulging their own lusts and saying, "Where is the promise of his coming? For ever since our ancestors died, all things continue as they were from the beginning of creation!" They deliberately ignore this fact, that by the word of God heavens existed long ago and an earth was formed out of water and by means of water, through which the world of that time was deluged with water and perished. But by the same word the present heavens and earth have been reserved for fire, being kept until the day of judgment and destruction of the godless. (2 Peter 3:3-7)

Psalm

Psalm 62:5-12
In God is my safety and my honor

Additional Reading

Jeremiah 20:7-13
Jeremiah denounces his persecutors

Hymn: O God of Light, ELW 507

Eternal covenant maker, you keep your promises. Place us in communities open to being part of your promise and its fulfillment in every age. Make us bold to work for peace and justice in all creation until your kingdom comes.

Saturday, January 23, 2021
Time after Epiphany

Luke 10:13-16

Woe to those who reject God's messengers

[The Lord said,] "Woe to you, Chorazin! Woe to you, Bethsaida! For if the deeds of power done in you had been done in Tyre and Sidon, they would have repented long ago, sitting in sackcloth and ashes. But at the judgment it will be more tolerable for Tyre and Sidon than for you. And you, Capernaum,

> will you be exalted to heaven?
>> No, you will be brought down to Hades.

"Whoever listens to you listens to me, and whoever rejects you rejects me, and whoever rejects me rejects the one who sent me." (Luke 10:13-16)

Psalm

Psalm 62:5-12
In God is my safety and my honor

Additional Reading

Jeremiah 20:14-18
Jeremiah curses the day of his birth

Hymn: Listen, God Is Calling, ELW 513

God of the prophets, you send messengers in every age to speak your truth. Open our hearts to receive your word. Empower us to be compassionate prophets who share your truth in love for the good of all creation.

Sunday, January 24, 2021
Third Sunday after Epiphany

Mark 1:14-20

The calling of the disciples at the sea

Now after John was arrested, Jesus came to Galilee, proclaiming the good news of God, and saying, "The time is fulfilled, and the kingdom of God has come near; repent, and believe in the good news."

As Jesus passed along the Sea of Galilee, he saw Simon and his brother Andrew casting a net into the sea—for they were fishermen. And Jesus said to them, "Follow me and I will make you fish for people." And immediately they left their nets and followed him. As he went a little farther, he saw James son of Zebedee and his brother John, who were in their boat mending the nets. Immediately he called them; and they left their father Zebedee in the boat with the hired men, and followed him. (Mark 1:14-20)

Psalm

Psalm 62:5-12
In God is my safety and my honor

Additional Readings

Jonah 3:1-5, 10
Repentance at Nineveh

1 Corinthians 7:29-31
Living in the end times

Hymn: You Have Come Down to the Lakeshore, ELW 817

Almighty God, by grace alone you call us and accept us in your service. Strengthen us by your Spirit, and make us worthy of your call, through Jesus Christ, our Savior and Lord.

Monday, January 25, 2021
Conversion of Paul

Galatians 1:11-24
Paul receives a revelation of Christ

You have heard, no doubt, of my earlier life in Judaism. I was violently persecuting the church of God and was trying to destroy it. I advanced in Judaism beyond many among my people of the same age, for I was far more zealous for the traditions of my ancestors. But when God, who had set me apart before I was born and called me through his grace, was pleased to reveal his Son to me, so that I might proclaim him among the Gentiles, I did not confer with any human being, nor did I go up to Jerusalem to those who were already apostles before me, but I went away at once into Arabia, and afterwards I returned to Damascus. (Gal. 1:13-17)

Psalm
Psalm 67
Let all the peoples praise you, O God

Additional Readings
Acts 9:1-22
Saul is converted to Christ

Luke 21:10-19
The end times will require endurance

Hymn: For by Grace You Have Been Saved, ELW 598

O God, by the preaching of your apostle Paul you have caused the light of the gospel to shine throughout the world. Grant that we may follow his example and be witnesses to the truth of your Son, Jesus Christ, our Savior and Lord, who lives and reigns with you and the Holy Spirit, one God, now and forever.

Tuesday, January 26, 2021
Time after Epiphany

Timothy, Titus, and Silas, missionaries

Genesis 45:25—46:7

God calls Jacob to go to Egypt

When Israel set out on his journey with all that he had and came to Beer-sheba, he offered sacrifices to the God of his father Isaac. God spoke to Israel in visions of the night, and said, "Jacob, Jacob." And he said, "Here I am." Then he said, "I am God, the God of your father; do not be afraid to go down to Egypt, for I will make of you a great nation there. I myself will go down with you to Egypt, and I will also bring you up again; and Joseph's own hand shall close your eyes." (Gen. 46:1-4)

Psalm
Psalm 46
The God of Jacob is our stronghold

Additional Reading
Acts 5:33-42
The apostles are tried and flogged

Hymn: O God of Every Nation, ELW 713

God of the journey, you are with us everywhere we go. When we don't know where to go, guide us. When we are afraid to start an adventure, speak to us. When we doubt the way, make your presence known.

Wednesday, January 27, 2021
Time after Epiphany

Lydia, Dorcas, and Phoebe, witnesses to the faith

Proverbs 8:1-21
Wisdom calls the people

Does not wisdom call,
>   and does not understanding raise her voice?
On the heights, beside the way,
>   at the crossroads she takes her stand;
beside the gates in front of the town,
>   at the entrance of the portals she cries out:
"To you, O people, I call,
>   and my cry is to all that live.
O simple ones, learn prudence;
>   acquire intelligence, you who lack it." (Prov. 8:1-5)

Psalm
Psalm 46
The God of Jacob is our stronghold

Additional Reading
Mark 3:13-19a
Jesus appoints the twelve

Hymn: O Holy Spirit, Root of Life, ELW 399

Gracious God, you call to us with wisdom and understanding. Sin beckons to us with worldly power and fleeting wealth. Whisper your wisdom in our ears. Sing your understanding in our souls. Keep us attuned to your voice.

Thursday, January 28, 2021
Time after Epiphany

Thomas Aquinas, teacher, died 1274

Psalm 111
The beginning of wisdom

Praise the Lord!
I will give thanks to the Lord with my whole heart,
    in the company of the upright, in the congregation.
Great are the works of the Lord,
    studied by all who delight in them.
Full of honor and majesty is his work,
    and his righteousness endures forever.
He has gained renown by his wonderful deeds;
    the Lord is gracious and merciful. (Ps. 111:1-4)

Additional Readings
Deuteronomy 3:23-29
Moses sees Canaan from afar

Romans 9:6-18
God's mercy cannot be controlled

Hymn: My God, How Wonderful Thou Art, ELW 863

Creative Lord, wonderful are your works. For the laughter of children and the wisdom of elders, we thank you. For the mystery of the universe and the wonder of salvation, we worship you. For all you are, we praise you.

Friday, January 29, 2021
Time after Epiphany

Deuteronomy 12:28-32
Warnings against idolatry

When the LORD your God has cut off before you the nations whom you are about to enter to dispossess them, when you have dispossessed them and live in their land, take care that you are not snared into imitating them, after they have been destroyed before you: do not inquire concerning their gods, saying, "How did these nations worship their gods? I also want to do the same." You must not do the same for the LORD your God, because every abhorrent thing that the LORD hates they have done for their gods. They would even burn their sons and their daughters in the fire to their gods. You must diligently observe everything that I command you; do not add to it or take anything from it. (Deut. 12:29-32)

Psalm
Psalm 111
The beginning of wisdom

Additional Reading
Revelation 2:12-17
Idolatrous behavior is condemned

Hymn: Baptized and Set Free, ELW 453

Redeeming God, in your law is life. Forgive us when we twist it to fulfill selfish desires. Turn us to receive the wisdom of your law embodied in Christ Jesus. Reconcile us to you and to one another.

Saturday, January 30, 2021
Time after Epiphany

Deuteronomy 13:1-5
Beware of false prophets

If prophets or those who divine by dreams appear among you and promise you omens or portents, and the omens or the portents declared by them take place, and they say, "Let us follow other gods" (whom you have not known) "and let us serve them," you must not heed the words of those prophets or those who divine by dreams; for the LORD your God is testing you, to know whether you indeed love the LORD your God with all your heart and soul. The LORD your God you shall follow, him alone you shall fear, his commandments you shall keep, his voice you shall obey, him you shall serve, and to him you shall hold fast. But those prophets or those who divine by dreams shall be put to death for having spoken treason against the LORD your God—who brought you out of the land of Egypt and redeemed you from the house of slavery. (Deut. 13:1-5)

Psalm
Psalm 111
The beginning of wisdom

Additional Reading
Matthew 8:28—9:1
Jesus heals the Gadarene demoniacs

Hymn: O Jesus, I Have Promised, ELW 810

God of exodus, you lead your people from slavery into freedom. Lead on. Guide us each day and give us wisdom to discern false from true prophets, for we seek to love you with all our hearts.

Sunday, January 31, 2021
Fourth Sunday after Epiphany

Mark 1:21-28

The healing of one with an unclean spirit

[Jesus and the disciples] went to Capernaum; and when the sabbath came, [Jesus] entered the synagogue and taught. They were astounded at his teaching, for he taught them as one having authority, and not as the scribes. Just then there was in their synagogue a man with an unclean spirit, and he cried out, "What have you to do with us, Jesus of Nazareth? Have you come to destroy us? I know who you are, the Holy One of God." But Jesus rebuked him, saying, "Be silent, and come out of him!" (Mark 1:21-25)

Psalm

Psalm 111
The beginning of wisdom

Additional Readings

Deuteronomy 18:15-20
The prophet speaks with God's authority

1 Corinthians 8:1-13
Limits to liberty

Hymn: O Christ, Our Light, O Radiance True, ELW 675

Compassionate God, you gather the whole universe into your radiant presence and continually reveal your Son as our Savior. Bring wholeness to all that is broken and speak truth to us in our confusion, that all creation will see and know your Son, Jesus Christ, our Savior and Lord.

Prayer List for February

_____

_____

_____

_____

_____

_____

_____

_____

_____

Monday, February 1, 2021
Time after Epiphany

Psalm 35:1-10

God is our salvation

Contend, O Lᴏʀᴅ, with those who contend with me;
>   fight against those who fight against me!
Take hold of shield and buckler,
>   and rise up to help me!
Draw the spear and javelin
>   against my pursuers;
say to my soul,
>   "I am your salvation." (Ps. 35:1-3)

Additional Readings

Numbers 22:1-21
King Balak asks Balaam to curse Israel

Acts 21:17-26
Rules for Gentile converts

Hymn: A Mighty Fortress Is Our God, ELW 503/504/505

Fears arise that steal our breath and sap our strength, Holy One, but you do not abandon us and never will. Speak peace in the depths of our hearts that knowing your love we may live with quiet courage.

Tuesday, February 2, 2021
Presentation of Our Lord

Luke 2:22-40
The child is brought to the temple

Simeon took [Jesus] in his arms and praised God, saying,
"Master, now you are dismissing your servant in peace,
according to your word;
for my eyes have seen your salvation,
which you have prepared in the presence of all peoples,
a light for revelation to the Gentiles
and for glory to your people Israel." (Luke 2:28-32)

Psalm

Psalm 84
How dear to me is your dwelling, O God

Additional Readings

Malachi 3:1-4
My messenger, a refiner and purifier

Hebrews 2:14-18
Jesus shares human flesh and sufferings

Hymn: In His Temple Now Behold Him, ELW 417

Almighty and ever-living God, your only-begotten Son was presented this day in the temple. May we be presented to you with clean and pure hearts by the same Jesus Christ, our great high priest, who lives and reigns with you and the Holy Spirit, one God, now and forever.

Wednesday, February 3, 2021
Time after Epiphany

Ansgar, Bishop of Hamburg, missionary to Denmark and Sweden, died 865

Jeremiah 29:1-14

Jeremiah speaks God's word

Thus says the LORD of hosts, the God of Israel, to all the exiles whom I have sent into exile from Jerusalem to Babylon: Build houses and live in them; plant gardens and eat what they produce. Take wives and have sons and daughters; take wives for your sons, and give your daughters in marriage, that they may bear sons and daughters; multiply there, and do not decrease. But seek the welfare of the city where I have sent you into exile, and pray to the LORD on its behalf, for in its welfare you will find your welfare. For thus says the LORD of hosts, the God of Israel: Do not let the prophets and the diviners who are among you deceive you, and do not listen to the dreams that they dream, for it is a lie that they are prophesying to you in my name; I did not send them, says the LORD. (Jer. 29:4-9)

Psalm
Psalm 35:1-10
God is our salvation

Additional Reading
Mark 5:1-20
Jesus heals a man with a demon

Hymn: Let the Whole Creation Cry, ELW 876

You labor in love to share your life in every place and with every person we shall ever meet. Grant us the joy of sharing your holy work this day that we may rest in peace when evening falls.

Thursday, February 4, 2021
Time after Epiphany

Psalm 147:1-11, 20c
The Lord heals the brokenhearted

Praise the LORD!
How good it is to sing praises to our God;
    for he is gracious, and a song of praise is fitting.
The LORD builds up Jerusalem;
    he gathers the outcasts of Israel.
He heals the brokenhearted,
    and binds up their wounds.
He determines the number of the stars;
    he gives to all of them their names.
Great is our LORD, and abundant in power;
    his understanding is beyond measure. (Ps. 147:1-5)

Additional Readings
Proverbs 12:10-21
The tongue of the wise brings healing

Galatians 5:2-15
The nature of Christian freedom

Hymn: Come, Ye Disconsolate, ELW 607

How shall we praise you, dearest friend? You touch our lives and fill our hearts with the love you are. May we see you in every love and grace, and delight in the joy of knowing you.

Friday, February 5, 2021
Time after Epiphany

The Martyrs of Japan, died 1597

1 Corinthians 9:1-16

An apostle's life

This is my defense to those who would examine me. Do we not have the right to our food and drink? . . .

Nevertheless, we have not made use of this right, but we endure anything rather than put an obstacle in the way of the gospel of Christ. Do you not know that those who are employed in the temple service get their food from the temple, and those who serve at the altar share in what is sacrificed on the altar? In the same way, the Lord commanded that those who proclaim the gospel should get their living by the gospel. (1 Cor. 9:3-4, 12b-14)

Psalm
Psalm 147:1-11, 20c
The Lord heals the brokenhearted

Additional Reading
Job 36:1-23
God's goodness is exalted

Hymn: Lord, You Give the Great Commission, ELW 579

You are the love who frees us from our pride and anxious self-assertion. Fill our every emptiness, that our hearts may spring open to receive you and enter the joyful communion of all who praise the love you are.

Saturday, February 6, 2021
Time after Epiphany

Isaiah 46:1-13
Who is equal to God?

Listen to me, O house of Jacob,
    all the remnant of the house of Israel,
who have been borne by me from your birth,
    carried from the womb;
even to your old age I am he,
    even when you turn gray I will carry you.
I have made, and I will bear;
    I will carry and will save.

To whom will you liken me and make me equal,
    and compare me, as though we were alike?
(Isa. 46:3-5)

Psalm
Psalm 147:1-11, 20c
The Lord heals the brokenhearted

Additional Reading
Matthew 12:9-14
A healing on the sabbath

Hymn: Be Thou My Vision, ELW 793

Our heavy hearts are never too much for you, Holy One. From childhood play to days of age, you cradle our lives in loving care. Carry us through this day and into the joy of knowing you.

Sunday, February 7, 2021
Fifth Sunday after Epiphany

Mark 1:29-39
The healing of Peter's mother-in-law

As soon as [Jesus and the disciples] left the synagogue, they entered the house of Simon and Andrew, with James and John. Now Simon's mother-in-law was in bed with a fever, and they told him about her at once. He came and took her by the hand and lifted her up. Then the fever left her, and she began to serve them. (Mark 1:29-31)

Psalm
Psalm 147:1-11, 20c
The Lord heals the brokenhearted

Additional Readings
Isaiah 40:21-31
The Creator cares for the powerless

1 Corinthians 9:16-23
A servant of the gospel

Hymn: God, Whose Almighty Word, ELW 673

Everlasting God, you give strength to the weak and power to the faint. Make us agents of your healing and wholeness, that your good news may be made known to the ends of your creation, through Jesus Christ, our Savior and Lord.

Monday, February 8, 2021
Time after Epiphany

Psalm 102:12-28
Prayer for healing

Let this be recorded for a generation to come,
>   so that a people yet unborn may praise the LORD:
that he looked down from his holy height,
>   from heaven the LORD looked at the earth,
to hear the groans of the prisoners,
>   to set free those who were doomed to die;
so that the name of the LORD may be declared in Zion,
>   and his praise in Jerusalem,
when peoples gather together,
>   and kingdoms, to worship the LORD. (Ps. 102:18-22)

Additional Readings
2 Kings 4:8-17, 32-37
Elisha raises the Shunammite child

Acts 14:1-7
Resistance to the message of the apostles

Hymn: I'm So Glad Jesus Lifted Me, ELW 860

Fierce is your love, O Lord, a mother's endless passion for her beloved. Look upon the pains of your people and release every captive to fear and death, injustice and hardship that we may rise to serve and praise you.

Tuesday, February 9, 2021
Time after Epiphany

2 Kings 8:1-6
The Shunammite widow's land restored

Now the king was talking with Gehazi the servant of the man of God, saying, "Tell me all the great things that Elisha has done." While he was telling the king how Elisha had restored a dead person to life, the woman whose son he had restored to life appealed to the king for her house and her land. Gehazi said, "My lord king, here is the woman, and here is her son whom Elisha restored to life." When the king questioned the woman, she told him. So the king appointed an official for her, saying, "Restore all that was hers, together with all the revenue of the fields from the day that she left the land until now." (2 Kings 8:4-6)

Psalm
Psalm 102:12-28
Prayer for healing

Additional Reading
Acts 15:36-41
Paul and Barnabas separate

Hymn: By Gracious Powers, ELW 626

Your divine heart burns for those who bear the burdens of injustice. Shake us from sleep to share the struggles of the hungry and poor, the refugee and those oppressed that the light of your kingdom may shine among us.

Wednesday, February 10, 2021
Time after Epiphany

Mark 3:7-12
Jesus heals many people

Jesus departed with his disciples to the sea, and a great multitude from Galilee followed him; hearing all that he was doing, they came to him in great numbers from Judea, Jerusalem, Idumea, beyond the Jordan, and the region around Tyre and Sidon. He told his disciples to have a boat ready for him because of the crowd, so that they would not crush him; for he had cured many, so that all who had diseases pressed upon him to touch him. Whenever the unclean spirits saw him, they fell down before him and shouted, "You are the Son of God!" But he sternly ordered them not to make him known. (Mark 3:7-12)

Psalm
Psalm 102:12-28
Prayer for healing

Additional Reading
Job 6:1-13
Job's lament at misfortune

Hymn: O Christ, What Can It Mean for Us, ELW 431

Love and fear bring us to you, loving God. As you touched the crowds through the healing presence of your son, touch us this day that our fears may be relieved and our hearts healed.

Thursday, February 11, 2021
Time after Epiphany

Psalm 50:1-6
God shines forth in glory

Our God comes and does not keep silence,
>   before him is a devouring fire,
>   and a mighty tempest all around him.
He calls to the heavens above
>   and to the earth, that he may judge his people:
"Gather to me my faithful ones,
>   who made a covenant with me by sacrifice!"
The heavens declare his righteousness,
>   for God himself is judge. (Ps. 50:3-6)

Additional Readings
1 Kings 11:26-40
Ahijah prophesies to Jeroboam

2 Corinthians 2:12-17
God spreads the fragrance of life in Christ

Hymn: Blessing and Honor, ELW 854

You are just, O Lord, when you judge us wanting. We wander from the path of compassion and justice, lost in self-absorbed lives. Judge our waywardness and save us from ourselves that tasting your mercy we may live your love.

Friday, February 12, 2021
Time after Epiphany

1 Timothy 1:12-20
Gratitude for mercy

I am grateful to Christ Jesus our Lord, who has strengthened me, because he judged me faithful and appointed me to his service, even though I was formerly a blasphemer, a persecutor, and a man of violence. But I received mercy because I had acted ignorantly in unbelief, and the grace of our Lord overflowed for me with the faith and love that are in Christ Jesus. The saying is sure and worthy of full acceptance, that Christ Jesus came into the world to save sinners—of whom I am the foremost. But for that very reason I received mercy, so that in me, as the foremost, Jesus Christ might display the utmost patience, making me an example to those who would come to believe in him for eternal life. (1 Tim. 1:12-16)

Psalm
Psalm 50:1-6
God shines forth in glory

Additional Reading
1 Kings 14:1-18
Ahijah receives Jeroboam's wife

Hymn: Amazing Grace, How Sweet the Sound, ELW 779

Gracious God, you delight to show mercy to the sinner, calling the most broken and lost to know you. Open our eyes to the wonder of your grace that we may live in daily gratitude.

Saturday, February 13, 2021
Time after Epiphany

Luke 19:41-44
The time of God's visitation

As [Jesus] came near and saw the city, he wept over it, saying, "If you, even you, had only recognized on this day the things that make for peace! But now they are hidden from your eyes. Indeed, the days will come upon you, when your enemies will set up ramparts around you and surround you, and hem you in on every side. They will crush you to the ground, you and your children within you, and they will not leave within you one stone upon another; because you did not recognize the time of your visitation from God." (Luke 19:41-44)

Psalm
Psalm 50:1-6
God shines forth in glory

Additional Reading
1 Kings 16:1-7
Jehu warns King Baasha

Hymn: Lord Christ, When First You Came to Earth, ELW 727

You are our peace, faithful and loving God. Your presence quiets our hearts and fans our hope for every tomorrow. Grant us eyes to see you in every small grace and beauty that our hearts may rest in you.

Sunday, February 14, 2021
Transfiguration of Our Lord

Cyril, monk, died 869; Methodius, bishop, died 885; missionaries to the Slavs

Mark 9:2-9

Christ revealed as God's beloved Son

Six days later, Jesus took with him Peter and James and John, and led them up a high mountain apart, by themselves. And he was transfigured before them, and his clothes became dazzling white, such as no one on earth could bleach them. And there appeared to them Elijah with Moses, who were talking with Jesus. Then Peter said to Jesus, "Rabbi, it is good for us to be here; let us make three dwellings, one for you, one for Moses, and one for Elijah." He did not know what to say, for they were terrified. (Mark 9:2-6)

Psalm

Psalm 50:1-6
God shines forth in glory

Additional Readings

2 Kings 2:1-12
Elijah taken up to heaven

2 Corinthians 4:3-6
God's light seen in Christ

Hymn: Jesus on the Mountain Peak, ELW 317

Almighty God, the resplendent light of your truth shines from the mountaintop into our hearts. Transfigure us by your beloved Son, and illumine the world with your image, through Jesus Christ, our Savior and Lord, who lives and reigns with you and the Holy Spirit, one God, now and forever.

Monday, February 15, 2021
Time after Epiphany

Psalm 110:1-4
A priest forever

The LORD sends out from Zion
>your mighty scepter.
>Rule in the midst of your foes.
Your people will offer themselves willingly
>on the day you lead your forces
>on the holy mountains.
From the womb of the morning,
>like dew, your youth will come to you.
The LORD has sworn and will not change his mind,
>"You are a priest forever according to the order of Melchizedek."
(Ps. 110:2-4)

Additional Readings
Exodus 19:7-25
Moses meets God on the mountain

Hebrews 2:1-4
Do not neglect so great a salvation

Hymn: Oh, Wondrous Image, Vision Fair, ELW 316

Our land suffers division and mistrust for want of wisdom, O Lord. Lift up leaders of truth and understanding, and save us from the discord of party spirit that your will may be known and loved among us.

Tuesday, February 16, 2021
Time after Epiphany

Job 19:23-27
Job will see God

[Job said:]
"O that my words were written down!
     O that they were inscribed in a book!
O that with an iron pen and with lead
     they were engraved on a rock forever!
For I know that my Redeemer lives,
     and that at the last he will stand upon the earth;
and after my skin has been thus destroyed,
     then in my flesh I shall see God,
whom I shall see on my side,
     and my eyes shall behold, and not another.
     My heart faints within me!" (Job 19:23-27)

Psalm
Psalm 110:1-4
A priest forever

Additional Reading
1 Timothy 3:14-16
The mystery of our religion

Hymn: I Know That My Redeemer Lives! ELW 619

Grant that we may see you, O Lord, amid winter's gray, for our hearts are hungry to know you near. Embrace us in the golden rays of your presence and warm us in the fullness of your love.

Lent

Lent is a forty-day journey to Easter. Christians keep company with Noah and his family, who were in the ark for forty days; with the Hebrews, who journeyed through the desert for forty years; and with Moses, Elijah, and Jesus, who fasted for forty days before they embarked on the tasks God had prepared for them.

During Lent Christians journey with those who are making final preparations for baptism at Easter. Together, Christians struggle with the meaning of their baptismal promises: Do you reject evil? Do you believe in God the Father, the Son, and the Holy Spirit? Do you believe in the church, the forgiveness of sins, the resurrection of the dead?

The disciples of the Lord Jesus are called to contend against everything that leads them away from love of God and neighbor. Fasting, prayer, and works of love—the disciplines of Lent—help the household rejoice in the gifts of baptism: God's forgiveness and mercy.

Table Prayer for the Season of Lent

Blessed are you, O God, giver of all.
You adorn our tables with food
and give companionship for our journeys.
Be present with us as we are fed in body and spirit
that our sharing this meal is a sign of your life
broken and shared for the world.
In Jesus' name we pray.
Amen.

Matthew 6:1-6, 16-21

The practice of faith

[Jesus said,] "Do not store up for yourselves treasures on earth, where moth and rust consume and where thieves break in and steal; but store up for yourselves treasures in heaven, where neither moth nor rust consumes and where thieves do not break in and steal. For where your treasure is, there your heart will be also." (Matt. 6:19-21)

Psalm

Psalm 51:1-17
Plea for mercy

Additional Readings

Joel 2:1-2, 12-17
Return to God

2 Corinthians
5:20b—6:10
Now is the day of salvation

Hymn: Savior, When in Dust to You, ELW 601

Gracious God, out of your love and mercy you breathed into dust the breath of life, creating us to serve you and our neighbors. Call forth our prayers and acts of kindness, and strengthen us to face our mortality with confidence in the mercy of your Son, Jesus Christ, our Savior and Lord, who lives and reigns with you and the Holy Spirit, one God, now and forever.

Thursday, February 18, 2021
Week before Lent 1

Martin Luther, renewer of the church, died 1546

Psalm 25:1-10
Your paths are love and faithfulness

To you, O LORD, I lift up my soul.
O my God, in you I trust;
> do not let me be put to shame;
> do not let my enemies exult over me.
Do not let those who wait for you be put to shame;
> let them be ashamed who are wantonly treacherous.

Make me to know your ways, O LORD;
> teach me your paths.
Lead me in your truth, and teach me,
> for you are the God of my salvation;
> for you I wait all day long. (Ps. 25:1-5)

Additional Readings
Daniel 9:1-14
Daniel prays for the people's forgiveness

1 John 1:3-10
The apostolic message of forgiveness

Hymn: O Master, Let Me Walk with You, ELW 818

You are our hope when every strength fades and our hearts tremble within. Shelter us in the arms of your mercy when troubles come that knowing your care we may face our days with confident and courageous hearts.

Friday, February 19, 2021
Week before Lent 1

2 Timothy 4:1-5
Apostolic and pastoral advice for Timothy

In the presence of God and of Christ Jesus, who is to judge the living and the dead, and in view of his appearing and his kingdom, I solemnly urge you: proclaim the message; be persistent whether the time is favorable or unfavorable; convince, rebuke, and encourage, with the utmost patience in teaching. For the time is coming when people will not put up with sound doctrine, but having itching ears, they will accumulate for themselves teachers to suit their own desires, and will turn away from listening to the truth and wander away to myths. As for you, always be sober, endure suffering, do the work of an evangelist, carry out your ministry fully. (2 Tim. 4:1-5)

Psalm
Psalm 25:1-10
Your paths are love and faithfulness

Additional Reading
Daniel 9:15-25a
An angel speaks to Daniel

Hymn: How Clear Is Our Vocation, Lord, ELW 580

We thank you, O Lord, for faithful guides who love your word and share your grace. Stir your spirit within us that we may listen with eager hearts and hear your voice through their witness.

Saturday, February 20, 2021
Week before Lent 1

Matthew 9:2-13

Jesus forgives sin and calls sinners to service

And as [Jesus] sat at dinner in the house, many tax collectors and sinners came and were sitting with him and his disciples. When the Pharisees saw this, they said to his disciples, "Why does your teacher eat with tax collectors and sinners?" But when he heard this, he said, "Those who are well have no need of a physician, but those who are sick. Go and learn what this means, 'I desire mercy, not sacrifice.' For I have come to call not the righteous but sinners." (Matt. 9:10-13)

Psalm
Psalm 25:1-10
Your paths are love and faithfulness

Additional Reading
Psalm 32
God forgives sin

Hymn: Lord, Whose Love in Humble Service, ELW 712

You do not despise us for our sins but invite us to come and rest, rapt in the immensity of your love. Heal us from the guilt we carry and banish the burden of shame that haunts our hearts.

Mark 1:9-15
The temptation of Jesus

In those days Jesus came from Nazareth of Galilee and was baptized by John in the Jordan. And just as he was coming up out of the water, he saw the heavens torn apart and the Spirit descending like a dove on him. And a voice came from heaven, "You are my Son, the Beloved; with you I am well pleased."

And the Spirit immediately drove him out into the wilderness. He was in the wilderness forty days, tempted by Satan; and he was with the wild beasts; and the angels waited on him.

Now after John was arrested, Jesus came to Galilee, proclaiming the good news of God, and saying, "The time is fulfilled, and the kingdom of God has come near; repent, and believe in the good news." (Mark 1:9-15)

Psalm
Psalm 25:1-10
Your paths are love and faithfulness

Additional Readings
Genesis 9:8-17
The rainbow, sign of God's covenant

1 Peter 3:18-22
Saved through water

Hymn: O Lord, throughout These Forty Days, ELW 319

Holy God, heavenly Father, in the waters of the flood you saved the chosen, and in the wilderness of temptation you protected your Son from sin. Renew us in the gift of baptism. May your holy angels be with us, that the wicked foe may have no power over us, through Jesus Christ, our Savior and Lord, who lives and reigns with you and the Holy Spirit, one God, now and forever.

Monday, February 22, 2021
Week of Lent 1

Psalm 77

Prayer for God to remember us

I cry aloud to God,
>aloud to God, that he may hear me.
In the day of my trouble I seek the Lord;
>in the night my hand is stretched out without wearying;
>my soul refuses to be comforted.
I think of God, and I moan;
>I meditate, and my spirit faints. (Ps. 77:1-3)

Additional Readings

Job 4:1-21
Eliphaz speaks of sin

Ephesians 2:1-10
The death of sin, the gift of grace

Hymn: What a Friend We Have in Jesus, ELW 742

Hear us, O Lord, when we sink beneath the restless waves that wash over us. Speak tenderly in the depth of our souls. Quiet the tempest within that we may trust your unfailing love when storms overwhelm.

Tuesday, February 23, 2021
Week of Lent 1

Polycarp, Bishop of Smyrna, martyr, died 156

1 Peter 3:8-18a
About suffering

Now who will harm you if you are eager to do what is good? But even if you do suffer for doing what is right, you are blessed. Do not fear what they fear, and do not be intimidated, but in your hearts sanctify Christ as Lord. Always be ready to make your defense to anyone who demands from you an accounting for the hope that is in you; yet do it with gentleness and reverence. Keep your conscience clear, so that, when you are maligned, those who abuse you for your good conduct in Christ may be put to shame. For it is better to suffer for doing good, if suffering should be God's will, than to suffer for doing evil. For Christ also suffered for sins once for all, the righteous for the unrighteous, in order to bring you to God. (1 Peter 3:13-18a)

Psalm
Psalm 77
Prayer for God to remember us

Additional Reading
Job 5:8-27
Seek God

Hymn: When We Are Living, ELW 639

Your voice echoes across the ages, blessed Lord, "Do not be afraid." Grant us the courage of Christ Jesus that with quiet confidence we may be who we are, blessed and beloved, sharing your mercy and living your justice.

Wednesday, February 24, 2021
Week of Lent 1

Proverbs 30:1-9

Plea to be safe from temptation

Two things I ask of you;
> do not deny them to me before I die:
Remove far from me falsehood and lying;
> give me neither poverty nor riches;
> feed me with the food that I need,
or I shall be full, and deny you,
> and say, "Who is the LORD?"
or I shall be poor, and steal,
> and profane the name of my God. (Prov. 30:7-9)

Psalm
Psalm 77
Prayer for God to remember us

Additional Reading
Matthew 4:1-11
Matthew's account of Jesus' temptation

Hymn: If You But Trust in God to Guide You, ELW 769

You know our weakness, gracious God. Wipe clean the hidden guilt that clings and accuses, and save us from the sins that tempt us so we may live with a free conscience in the light of your presence.

Thursday, February 25, 2021
Week of Lent 1

Elizabeth Fedde, deaconess, died 1921

Psalm 22:23-31

All the earth shall turn to God

All the ends of the earth shall remember
     and turn to the LORD;
and all the families of the nations
     shall worship before him.
For dominion belongs to the LORD,
     and he rules over the nations.

To him, indeed, shall all who sleep in the earth bow down;
     before him shall bow all who go down to the dust,
     and I shall live for him.
Posterity will serve him;
     future generations will be told about the Lord,
and proclaim his deliverance to a people yet unborn,
     saying that he has done it. (Ps. 22:27-31)

Additional Readings

Genesis 15:1-6, 12-18
God covenants with Abraham

Romans 3:21-31
Righteousness through faith

Hymn: Shout to the Lord, ELW 821

All shall bow before you and worship, living God, for you raise your beloved from death into life. Lift us from the dust into which we fall that we may join the song of resurrection.

Friday, February 26, 2021
Week of Lent 1

Genesis 16:1-6

Ishmael born to Abram and Hagar

Now Sarai, Abram's wife, bore him no children. She had an Egyptian slave-girl whose name was Hagar, and Sarai said to Abram, "You see that the LORD has prevented me from bearing children; go in to my slave-girl; it may be that I shall obtain children by her." And Abram listened to the voice of Sarai. . . . He went in to Hagar, and she conceived; and when she saw that she had conceived, she looked with contempt on her mistress. Then Sarai said to Abram, "May the wrong done to me be on you! I gave my slave-girl to your embrace, and when she saw that she had conceived, she looked on me with contempt. May the LORD judge between you and me!" But Abram said to Sarai, "Your slave-girl is in your power; do to her as you please." Then Sarai dealt harshly with her, and she ran away from her. (Gen. 1-2, 4-6)

Psalm
Psalm 22:23-31
All the earth shall turn to God

Additional Reading
Romans 4:1-12
Abraham counted righteous by God for his faith

Hymn: The God of Abraham Praise, ELW 831

Blessed God, you perform your saving work through the lives of imperfect people. Grant us faith to trust that you are working out your loving purpose through our lives, even though we may never see or know how.

Saturday, February 27, 2021
Week of Lent 1

Mark 8:27-30
Peter's confession

Jesus went on with his disciples to the villages of Caesarea Philippi; and on the way he asked his disciples, "Who do people say that I am?" And they answered him, "John the Baptist; and others, Elijah; and still others, one of the prophets." He asked them, "But who do you say that I am?" Peter answered him, "You are the Messiah." And he sternly ordered them not to tell anyone about him. (Mark 8:27-30)

Psalm
Psalm 22:23-31
All the earth shall turn to God

Additional Reading
Genesis 16:7-15
An angel comforts Hagar at a spring of water

Hymn: O Christ the Same, ELW 760

We thank you for those moments when our hearts, filled with love, know the love you are for us and all that is. Awaken true knowledge of you throughout your church that we may confess the wonder of your grace.

Sunday, February 28, 2021
Second Sunday in Lent

Mark 8:31-38
The passion prediction

[Jesus] called the crowd with his disciples, and said to them, "If any want to become my followers, let them deny themselves and take up their cross and follow me. For those who want to save their life will lose it, and those who lose their life for my sake, and for the sake of the gospel, will save it. For what will it profit them to gain the whole world and forfeit their life? Indeed, what can they give in return for their life? Those who are ashamed of me and of my words in this adulterous and sinful generation, of them the Son of Man will also be ashamed when he comes in the glory of his Father with the holy angels." (Mark 8:34-38)

Psalm
Psalm 22:23-31
All the earth shall turn to God

Additional Readings
Genesis 17:1-7, 15-16
God blesses Abraham and Sarah

Romans 4:13-25
The promise to those of Abraham's faith

Hymn: Come, Follow Me, the Savior Spake, ELW 799

O God, by the passion of your blessed Son you made an instrument of shameful death to be for us the means of life. Grant us so to glory in the cross of Christ that we may gladly suffer shame and loss for the sake of your Son, Jesus Christ, our Savior and Lord, who lives and reigns with you and the Holy Spirit, one God, now and forever.

Prayer List for March

_____

_____

_____

_____

_____

_____

_____

_____

_____

_____

_____

Monday, March 1, 2021
Week of Lent 2

George Herbert, hymnwriter, died 1633

Psalm 105:1-11, 37-45
God promises life to Abraham

O give thanks to the LORD, call on his name,
    make known his deeds among the peoples.
Sing to him, sing praises to him;
    tell of all his wonderful works.
Glory in his holy name;
    let the hearts of those who seek the LORD rejoice.
Seek the LORD and his strength;
    seek his presence continually.
Remember the wonderful works he has done,
    his miracles, and the judgments he uttered,
O offspring of his servant Abraham,
    children of Jacob, his chosen ones. (Ps. 105:1-6)

Additional Readings
Genesis 21:1-7
God gives Abraham and Sarah a son

Hebrews 1:8-12
The Son whose years will never end

Hymn: My God, How Wonderful Thou Art, ELW 863

We give you thanks this day, giver of marvelous deeds. We praise you for creating the universe and earth with all its bounty, and for our neighbors, friends, and families in whom we see your goodness. Make us always grateful.

Tuesday, March 2, 2021
Week of Lent 2

John Wesley, died 1791; Charles Wesley, died 1788; renewers of the church

Hebrews 11:1-3, 13-19
By faith Abraham obeyed God

By faith Abraham, when put to the test, offered up Isaac. He who had received the promises was ready to offer up his only son, of whom he had been told, "It is through Isaac that descendants shall be named for you." He considered the fact that God is able even to raise someone from the dead—and figuratively speaking, he did receive him back. (Heb. 11:17-19)

Psalm
Psalm 105:1-11, 37-45
God promises life to Abraham

Additional Reading
Genesis 22:1-19
God asks Abraham to sacrifice Isaac

Hymn: Give Thanks for Saints, ELW 428

Holy God, you never fail to show us your saving help, revealing to us new pathways when we do not know where to turn. Give us the faith of Abraham whenever we are most in need.

Wednesday, March 3, 2021
Week of Lent 2

Jeremiah 30:12-22
God will restore Israel

Thus says the LORD:
I am going to restore the fortunes of the tents of Jacob,
    and have compassion on his dwellings;
the city shall be rebuilt upon its mound,
    and the citadel set on its rightful site.
Out of them shall come thanksgiving,
    and the sound of merrymakers.
I will make them many, and they shall not be few;
    I will make them honored, and they shall not be disdained.
Their children shall be as of old,
    their congregation shall be established before me;
    and I will punish all who oppress them. . . .
And you shall be my people,
    and I will be your God. (Jer. 30:18-20, 22)

Psalm
Psalm 105:1-11, 37-45
God promises life to Abraham

Additional Reading
John 12:36-43
The unbelief of the people

Hymn: Oh, Happy Day When We Shall Stand, ELW 441

Compassionate God who hears our cries when we have lost our stability, heed now the prayers of all who look to you for reassurance. We bring before you all those who suffer today and crave your loving care.

Thursday, March 4, 2021
Week of Lent 2

Psalm 19

The commandments give light to the eyes

The law of the LORD is perfect,
>   reviving the soul;
the decrees of the LORD are sure,
>   making wise the simple;
the precepts of the LORD are right,
>   rejoicing the heart;
the commandment of the LORD is clear,
>   enlightening the eyes;
the fear of the LORD is pure,
>   enduring forever;
the ordinances of the LORD are true
>   and righteous altogether.
(Ps. 19:7-9)

Additional Readings

Exodus 19:1-9a
Preparation for the giving of the commandments

1 Peter 2:4-10
You are God's own people

Hymn: O Christ, Your Heart, Compassionate, ELW 722

Holy Wisdom, you give to all your people the way of righteousness, lighting for us the path of peace. Open our hearts to see our neighbors through your eyes, with the vision to do as you would have us do.

Friday, March 5, 2021
Week of Lent 2

Exodus 19:9b-15
Preparation for the giving of the commandments

When Moses had told the words of the people to the LORD, the LORD
said to Moses: "Go to the people and consecrate them today and
tomorrow. Have them wash their clothes and prepare for the third day,
because on the third day the LORD will come down upon Mount Sinai in
the sight of all the people. You shall set limits for the people all around,
saying, 'Be careful not to go up the mountain or to touch the edge of it.
Any who touch the mountain shall be put to death. No hand shall touch
them, but they shall be stoned or shot with arrows; whether animal
or human being, they shall not live.' When the trumpet sounds a long
blast, they may go up on the mountain." So Moses went down from the
mountain to the people. He consecrated the people, and they washed
their clothes. And he said to the people, "Prepare for the third day; do
not go near a woman." (Exod. 19:9b-15)

Psalm
Psalm 19
The commandments give light to the eyes

Additional Reading
Acts 7:30-40
God spoke to Moses at Mount Sinai

Hymn: Lord Jesus, Think on Me, ELW 599

*All-powerful God, who sets boundaries for the seas and sets the stars in the
skies, lifts up mountains and levels the plains, you show us limits for our
own good. Give us the discipline to abide by your commands.*

Saturday, March 6, 2021
Week of Lent 2

Exodus 19:16-25
Preparation for the giving of the commandments

Then the LORD said to Moses, "Go down and warn the people not to break through to the LORD to look; otherwise many of them will perish. Even the priests who approach the LORD must consecrate themselves or the LORD will break out against them." Moses said to the LORD, "The people are not permitted to come up to Mount Sinai; for you yourself warned us, saying, 'Set limits around the mountain and keep it holy.'" The LORD said to him, "Go down, and come up bringing Aaron with you; but do not let either the priests or the people break through to come up to the LORD; otherwise he will break out against them." So Moses went down to the people and told them. (Exod. 19:21-25)

Psalm
Psalm 19
The commandments give light to the eyes

Additional Reading
Mark 9:2-8
Moses with Elijah and Jesus on a mountain

Hymn: Before You, Lord, We Bow, ELW 893

Holy God, our only home, you call to your people from the mountain through the prophets and teach us where to stand and listen. Give us ears to hear and hearts to follow where you lead.

Sunday, March 7, 2021
Third Sunday in Lent

Perpetua and Felicity and companions, martyrs at Carthage, died 202

John 2:13-22
The cleansing of the temple

The Passover of the Jews was near, and Jesus went up to Jerusalem. In the temple he found people selling cattle, sheep, and doves, and the money changers seated at their tables. Making a whip of cords, he drove all of them out of the temple, both the sheep and the cattle. He also poured out the coins of the money changers and overturned their tables. He told those who were selling the doves, "Take these things out of here! Stop making my Father's house a marketplace!" (John 2:13-16)

Psalm

Psalm 19
The commandments give light to the eyes

Additional Readings

Exodus 20:1-17
The commandments given at Sinai

1 Corinthians 1:18-25
Christ crucified, the wisdom of God

Hymn: Holy God, Holy and Glorious, ELW 637

Holy God, through your Son you have called us to live faithfully and act courageously. Keep us steadfast in your covenant of grace, and teach us the wisdom that comes only through Jesus Christ, our Savior and Lord, who lives and reigns with you and the Holy Spirit, one God, now and forever.

Monday, March 8, 2021
Week of Lent 3

Psalm 84
How lovely is God's dwelling place

How lovely is your dwelling place,
     O LORD of hosts!
My soul longs, indeed it faints
     for the courts of the LORD;
my heart and my flesh sing for joy
     to the living God.

Even the sparrow finds a home,
     and the swallow a nest for herself,
     where she may lay her young,
at your altars, O LORD of hosts,
     my King and my God.
Happy are those who live in your house,
     ever singing your praise. (Ps. 84:1-4)

Additional Readings
1 Kings 6:1-4, 21-22
Solomon builds the temple

1 Corinthians 3:10-23
You are God's temple

Hymn: In Heaven Above, ELW 630

The dwelling place you have made for us, Lord, is beauty and peace where we find rest and joy in your presence. Meet us in every hour of our lives with the blessings that keep us in your steadfast love.

Tuesday, March 9, 2021
Week of Lent 3

Hebrews 9:23-28
Christ as priest and once-for-all sacrifice

Thus it was necessary for the sketches of the heavenly things to be purified with these rites, but the heavenly things themselves need better sacrifices than these. For Christ did not enter a sanctuary made by human hands, a mere copy of the true one, but he entered into heaven itself, now to appear in the presence of God on our behalf. Nor was it to offer himself again and again, as the high priest enters the Holy Place year after year with blood that is not his own; for then he would have had to suffer again and again since the foundation of the world. But as it is, he has appeared once for all at the end of the age to remove sin by the sacrifice of himself. And just as it is appointed for mortals to die once, and after that the judgment, so Christ, having been offered once to bear the sins of many, will appear a second time, not to deal with sin, but to save those who are eagerly waiting for him. (Heb. 9:23-28)

Psalm
Psalm 84
How lovely is God's dwelling place

Additional Reading
2 Chronicles 29:1-11, 16-19
Hezekiah cleanses the temple

Hymn: Lord of Glory, You Have Bought Us, ELW 707

Glorious Lord, you come to all who are eager to know you. You place yourself into human life through Christ Jesus who suffered as we do. Give us courage and strength like Jesus so that we remain faithful to his love.

Wednesday, March 10, 2021
Week of Lent 3

Harriet Tubman, died 1913; Sojourner Truth, died 1883; renewers of society

Mark 11:15-19
Jesus cleanses the temple

Then [Jesus and his disciples] came to Jerusalem. And he entered the temple and began to drive out those who were selling and those who were buying in the temple, and he overturned the tables of the money changers and the seats of those who sold doves; and he would not allow anyone to carry anything through the temple. He was teaching and saying, "Is it not written,

> 'My house shall be called a house of prayer for all the nations'?
>> But you have made it a den of robbers."

And when the chief priests and the scribes heard it, they kept looking for a way to kill him; for they were afraid of him, because the whole crowd was spellbound by his teaching. And when evening came, Jesus and his disciples went out of the city. (Mark 11:15-19)

Psalm
Psalm 84
How lovely is God's dwelling place

Additional Reading
Ezra 6:1-16
King Darius orders the temple rebuilt

Hymn: Open Now Thy Gates of Beauty, ELW 533

God of righteousness, you see our sin, know our weaknesses, and drive out of us all that is not worthy of your gifts. Open our minds to what is missing in our lives. Turn us toward you with bold prayers.

Thursday, March 11, 2021
Week of Lent 3

Psalm 107:1-3, 17-22
God delivers from distress

Some were sick through their sinful ways,
    and because of their iniquities endured affliction;
they loathed any kind of food,
    and they drew near to the gates of death.
Then they cried to the LORD in their trouble,
    and he saved them from their distress;
he sent out his word and healed them,
    and delivered them from destruction.
Let them thank the LORD for his steadfast love,
    for his wonderful works to humankind. (Ps. 107:17-21)

Additional Readings

Genesis 9:8-17
The covenant with Noah

Ephesians 1:3-6
Blessed be God, who chose us in Christ

Hymn: O God, My Faithful God, ELW 806

Our greed, resentment, and lack of compassion, O Lord, take away our health and joy. May all your gifts to us each day lead us from despair to gratitude. Give us peace and merciful hearts.

Friday, March 12, 2021
Week of Lent 3

Gregory the Great, Bishop of Rome, died 604

Ephesians 1:7-14
We live to the praise of God's glory

In Christ we have also obtained an inheritance, having been destined according to the purpose of him who accomplishes all things according to his counsel and will, so that we, who were the first to set our hope on Christ, might live for the praise of his glory. In him you also, when you had heard the word of truth, the gospel of your salvation, and had believed in him, were marked with the seal of the promised Holy Spirit; this is the pledge of our inheritance toward redemption as God's own people, to the praise of his glory. (Eph. 1:11-14)

Psalm
Psalm 107:1-3, 17-22
God delivers from distress

Additional Reading
Daniel 12:5-13
The people will be purified

Hymn: How Great Thou Art, ELW 856

Your will, Holy God, is for your people to live in assurance of your love, showered with plenty, made content with what we have been given. Help us each day to begin and end our waking hours in praise of you.

Saturday, March 13, 2021
Week of Lent 3

Numbers 20:22-29
The death of Aaron

Then the LORD said to Moses and Aaron at Mount Hor, on the border of the land of Edom, "Let Aaron be gathered to his people. For he shall not enter the land that I have given to the Israelites, because you rebelled against my command at the waters of Meribah. Take Aaron and his son Eleazar, and bring them up Mount Hor; strip Aaron of his vestments, and put them on his son Eleazar. But Aaron shall be gathered to his people, and shall die there." (Num. 20:23-26)

Psalm
Psalm 107:1-3, 17-22
God delivers from distress

Additional Reading
John 3:1-13
Jesus and Nicodemus

Hymn: Guide Me Ever, Great Redeemer, ELW 618

Almighty God, life and death are in your hands. Give us water in the desert, guidance through the wilderness, and leaders who are wise and faithful. When we fail, lead us toward your more excellent way.

Sunday, March 14, 2021
Fourth Sunday in Lent

John 3:14-21
The lifting up of the Son of Man

[Jesus said to Nicodemus,] ". . . as Moses lifted up the serpent in the wilderness, so must the Son of Man be lifted up, that whoever believes in him may have eternal life.

"For God so loved the world that he gave his only Son, so that everyone who believes in him may not perish but may have eternal life." (John 3:14-16)

Psalm
Psalm 107:1-3, 17-22
God delivers from distress

Additional Readings
Numbers 21:4-9
The lifting up of the serpent

Ephesians 2:1-10
Alive in Christ

Hymn: God Loved the World, ELW 323

O God, rich in mercy, by the humiliation of your Son you lifted up this fallen world and rescued us from the hopelessness of death. Lead us into your light, that all our deeds may reflect your love, through Jesus Christ, our Savior and Lord, who lives and reigns with you and the Holy Spirit, one God, now and forever.

Monday, March 15, 2021
Week of Lent 4

Psalm 107:1-16

God gives food and light

Some wandered in desert wastes,
>   finding no way to an inhabited town;
hungry and thirsty,
>   their soul fainted within them.
Then they cried to the LORD in their trouble,
>   and he delivered them from their distress;
he led them by a straight way,
>   until they reached an inhabited town.
Let them thank the LORD for his steadfast love,
>   for his wonderful works to humankind.
For he satisfies the thirsty,
>   and the hungry he fills with good things. (Ps. 107:4-9)

Additional Readings

Exodus 15:22-27
God gives the people water

Hebrews 3:1-6
The faithfulness of Moses

Hymn: All Who Hunger, Gather Gladly, ELW 461

Author of life, we give you thanks for the many ways you satisfy our yearnings. Make us aware of how we might best use our gifts to answer the needs of our neighbors. Give us courage to grow in faith.

Tuesday, March 16, 2021
Week of Lent 4

1 Corinthians 10:6-13
God is faithful

Now these things occurred as examples for us, so that we might not desire evil as they did. Do not become idolaters as some of them did; as it is written, "The people sat down to eat and drink, and they rose up to play." We must not indulge in sexual immorality as some of them did, and twenty-three thousand fell in a single day. We must not put Christ to the test, as some of them did, and were destroyed by serpents. And do not complain as some of them did, and were destroyed by the destroyer. These things happened to them to serve as an example, and they were written down to instruct us, on whom the ends of the ages have come. (1 Cor. 10:6-11)

Psalm
Psalm 107:1-16
God gives food and light

Additional Reading
Numbers 20:1-13
God gives water from the rock

Hymn: Goodness Is Stronger than Evil, ELW 721

Giver of bounty beyond our understanding, you set limits before us to school our vision and we thank you. Without your guideposts we would lose our way. Send your Holy Spirit to keep us moored to your compassionate will.

Wednesday, March 17, 2021
Week of Lent 4

Patrick, bishop, missionary to Ireland, died 461

Isaiah 60:15-22
God is our light

The sun shall no longer be
　　your light by day,
nor for brightness shall the moon
　　give light to you by night;
but the Lord will be your everlasting light,
　　and your God will be your glory.
Your sun shall no more go down,
　　or your moon withdraw itself;
for the Lord will be your everlasting light,
　　and your days of mourning shall be ended.
Your people shall all be righteous;
　　they shall possess the land forever.
(Isa. 60:19-21)

Psalm
Psalm 107:1-16
God gives food and light

Additional Reading
John 8:12-20
Christ the light of the world

Hymn: Glorious Things of You Are Spoken, ELW 647

Everlasting light, our morning star, you shine within us to bathe our sorrows in a brightness that illuminates the goodness we cannot always see. Quell our fears and dispel our loneliness in the joy and gladness you plant in us.

Thursday, March 18, 2021
Week of Lent 4

Psalm 51:1-12
Create in me a clean heart

Create in me a clean heart, O God,
    and put a new and right spirit within me.
Do not cast me away from your presence,
    and do not take your holy spirit from me.
Restore to me the joy of your salvation,
    and sustain in me a willing spirit. (Ps. 51:10-12)

Additional Readings

Isaiah 30:15-18
God's gifts of returning and rest

Hebrews 4:1-13
God promises an eternal sabbath rest

Hymn: Change My Heart, O God, ELW 801

Ruler of time, you make us new every morning and guard us all night long. Let your spirit invigorate us so that in adversity or celebration we may see your world as a place to give and receive joy.

Friday, March 19, 2021
Joseph, Guardian of Jesus

Matthew 1:16, 18-21, 24a

The Lord appears to Joseph in a dream

Now the birth of Jesus the Messiah took place in this way. When his mother Mary had been engaged to Joseph, but before they lived together, she was found to be with child from the Holy Spirit. Her husband Joseph, being a righteous man and unwilling to expose her to public disgrace, planned to dismiss her quietly. But just when he had resolved to do this, an angel of the Lord appeared to him in a dream and said, "Joseph, son of David, do not be afraid to take Mary as your wife, for the child conceived in her is from the Holy Spirit. She will bear a son, and you are to name him Jesus, for he will save his people from their sins." (Matt. 1:18-21)

Psalm

Psalm 89:1-29
The Lord's steadfast love is established forever

Additional Readings

2 Samuel 7:4, 8-16
God makes a covenant with David

Romans 4:13-18
The promise to those who share Abraham's faith

Hymn: Our Father, by Whose Name, ELW 640

O God, from the family of your servant David you raised up Joseph to be the guardian of your incarnate Son and the husband of his blessed mother. Give us grace to imitate his uprightness of life and his obedience to your commands, through Jesus Christ, our Savior and Lord, who lives and reigns with you and the Holy Spirit, one God, now and forever.

Saturday, March 20, 2021
Week of Lent 4

John 12:1-11
Jesus is anointed for his coming death

Mary took a pound of costly perfume made of pure nard, anointed Jesus' feet, and wiped them with her hair. The house was filled with the fragrance of the perfume. But Judas Iscariot, one of his disciples (the one who was about to betray him), said, "Why was this perfume not sold for three hundred denarii and the money given to the poor?" (He said this not because he cared about the poor, but because he was a thief; he kept the common purse and used to steal what was put into it.) Jesus said, "Leave her alone. She bought it so that she might keep it for the day of my burial. You always have the poor with you, but you do not always have me." (John 12:3-8)

Psalm
Psalm 51:1-12
Create in me a clean heart

Additional Reading
Habakkuk 3:2-13
God will save the anointed

Hymn: Tree of Life and Awesome Mystery, ELW 334

Defender of the persecuted, God of love divine, you embrace those who are friendless and lonely by standing beside all who need help. Wherever there is hurt and misunderstanding, shed light upon what is worthy to correct what is wrong.

Sunday, March 21, 2021
Fifth Sunday in Lent

Thomas Cranmer, Bishop of Canterbury, martyr, died 1556

John 12:20-33

The grain of wheat dying in the earth

Jesus answered [the Greeks who came to see him], "The hour has come for the Son of Man to be glorified. Very truly, I tell you, unless a grain of wheat falls into the earth and dies, it remains just a single grain; but if it dies, it bears much fruit. Those who love their life lose it, and those who hate their life in this world will keep it for eternal life. Whoever serves me must follow me, and where I am, there will my servant be also. Whoever serves me, the Father will honor." (John 12:23-26)

Psalm

Psalm 51:1-12
Create in me a clean heart

Additional Readings

Jeremiah 31:31-34
A new covenant written on the heart

Hebrews 5:5-10
Through suffering Christ saves

Hymn: As the Sun with Longer Journey, ELW 329

O God, with steadfast love you draw us to yourself, and in mercy you receive our prayers. Strengthen us to bring forth the fruits of the Spirit, that through life and death we may live in your Son, Jesus Christ, our Savior and Lord, who lives and reigns with you and the Holy Spirit, one God, now and forever.

Monday, March 22, 2021
Week of Lent 5

Jonathan Edwards, teacher, missionary to American Indians, died 1758

Psalm 119:9-16
I treasure your promise in my heart

How can young people keep their way pure?
>   By guarding it according to your word.
With my whole heart I seek you;
>   do not let me stray from your commandments.
I treasure your word in my heart,
>   so that I may not sin against you. (Ps. 119:9-11)

Additional Readings
Isaiah 43:8-13   2 Corinthians 3:4-11
God is our savior   *God's glory in Christ*

Hymn: Lord, Keep Us Steadfast in Your Word, ELW 517

Holy Wisdom, voice of truth, you call us to abide in your commands. Stir us to heed your word, for you are the author of our will to obey. Help us guard ourselves for goodness' sake.

Tuesday, March 23, 2021
Week of Lent 5

Acts 2:14-24

Peter proclaims the crucified Christ to be alive

[Peter addressed the crowd,] "You that are Israelites, listen to what I have to say: Jesus of Nazareth, a man attested to you by God with deeds of power, wonders, and signs that God did through him among you, as you yourselves know—this man, handed over to you according to the definite plan and foreknowledge of God, you crucified and killed by the hands of those outside the law. But God raised him up, having freed him from death, because it was impossible for him to be held in its power." (Acts 2:22-24)

Psalm
Psalm 119:9-16
I treasure your promise in my heart

Additional Reading
Isaiah 44:1-8
God gives life to the people

Hymn: Come to Me, All Pilgrims Thirsty, ELW 777

Holy Word, by whose power death has been defeated and by whose love we are made in your image, open our hearts and minds to hear the astonishing promise of new life and freedom in the name of Christ Jesus.

Wednesday, March 24, 2021
Week of Lent 5

Oscar Arnulfo Romero, Bishop of El Salvador, martyr, died 1980

Haggai 2:1-9, 20-23
God promises future blessings

The word of the LORD came a second time to Haggai on the twenty-fourth day of the month: Speak to Zerubbabel, governor of Judah, saying, I am about to shake the heavens and the earth, and to overthrow the throne of kingdoms; I am about to destroy the strength of the kingdoms of the nations, and overthrow the chariots and their riders; and the horses and their riders shall fall, every one by the sword of a comrade. On that day, says the LORD of hosts, I will take you, O Zerubbabel my servant, son of Shealtiel, says the LORD, and make you like a signet ring; for I have chosen you, says the LORD of hosts. (Hag. 2:20-23)

Psalm
Psalm 119:9-16
I treasure your promise in my heart

Additional Reading
John 12:34-50
God gives eternal life

Hymn: If God My Lord Be for Me, ELW 788

God of power and life, you have made your people your chosen ones and clothed us with righteousness that never lets go. Give courage to those who face the sword and food to those who are made hungry by it.

Thursday, March 25, 2021
Annunciation of Our Lord

Luke 1:26-38
The angel greets Mary

In the sixth month the angel Gabriel was sent by God to a town in Galilee called Nazareth, to a virgin engaged to a man whose name was Joseph, of the house of David. The virgin's name was Mary. And he came to her and said, "Greetings, favored one! The Lord is with you." But she was much perplexed by his words and pondered what sort of greeting this might be. The angel said to her, "Do not be afraid, Mary, for you have found favor with God. And now, you will conceive in your womb and bear a son, and you will name him Jesus." (Luke 1:26-31)

Psalm
Psalm 45
Your name will be remembered

Additional Readings
Isaiah 7:10-14
A young woman will bear a son

Hebrews 10:4-10
The offering of Jesus' body sanctifies us

Hymn: Signs and Wonders, ELW 672

Pour your grace into our hearts, O God, that we who have known the incarnation of your Son, Jesus Christ, announced by an angel, may by his cross and passion be brought to the glory of his resurrection; for he lives and reigns with you, in the unity of the Holy Spirit, one God, now and forever.

Friday, March 26, 2021
Week of Lent 5

Philippians 2:12-18
Shine like stars in the world

Do all things without murmuring and arguing, so that you may be blameless and innocent, children of God without blemish in the midst of a crooked and perverse generation, in which you shine like stars in the world. It is by your holding fast to the word of life that I can boast on the day of Christ that I did not run in vain or labor in vain. But even if I am being poured out as a libation over the sacrifice and the offering of your faith, I am glad and rejoice with all of you—and in the same way you also must be glad and rejoice with me. (Phil. 2:14-18)

Psalm
Psalm 118:1-2, 19-29
Blessed is the one who comes

Additional Reading
Jeremiah 33:1-9
God will restore and cleanse from sin

Hymn: Day by Day, ELW 790

God whose love is never-ending, we give you thanks that you teach us daily how to live as your children and make us shine like stars in a world that darkens our days. Be the light for our paths.

Saturday, March 27, 2021
Week of Lent 5

Jeremiah 33:10-16

In a place of desolation, God will bring gladness

Thus says the LORD of hosts: In this place that is waste, without human beings or animals, and in all its towns there shall again be pasture for shepherds resting their flocks. In the towns of the hill country, of the Shephelah, and of the Negeb, in the land of Benjamin, the places around Jerusalem, and in the towns of Judah, flocks shall again pass under the hands of the one who counts them, says the LORD.

The days are surely coming, says the LORD, when I will fulfill the promise I made to the house of Israel and the house of Judah. In those days and at that time I will cause a righteous Branch to spring up for David; and he shall execute justice and righteousness in the land. In those days Judah will be saved and Jerusalem will live in safety. And this is the name by which it will be called: "The LORD is our righteousness." (Jer. 33:12-16)

Psalm
Psalm 118:1-2, 19-29
Blessed is the one who comes

Additional Reading
Mark 10:32-34, 46-52
Jesus approaches Jerusalem

Hymn: Bless Now, O God, the Journey, ELW 326

Holy and life-giving God, we thank you that you have promised to send us rest from our labors, relief from want, and reunion for those who have wandered. Bless your people with hope now and forever.

Holy Week

On the Sunday of the Passion, Christians enter into Holy Week. This day opens before the Christian community the final period of preparation before the celebration of the Three Days of the Lord's passion, death, and resurrection.

In many churches, palm branches will be given to worshipers for the procession into the worship space. Following an ancient custom, many Christians bring their palms home and place them in the household prayer center, behind a cross or sacred image, or above the indoor lintel of the entryway.

At sunset on Maundy Thursday, Lent comes to an end as the church begins the celebration of the events through which Christ has become the life and the resurrection for all who believe.

Prayer for Placing Palms in the Home

Use this blessing when placing palms in the home after the Palm Sunday liturgy.

Blessed is the One who comes in the name of the Lord!
May we who place these palms receive Christ into our midst
with the joy that marked the entrance to Jerusalem.
May we hold no betrayal in our hearts,
but peacefully welcome Christ
who lives and reigns with you and the Holy Spirit,
one God, now and forever. Amen.

Sunday, March 28, 2021
Sunday of the Passion / Palm Sunday

Mark 14:1—15:47

The passion and death of Jesus

When it was noon, darkness came over the whole land until three in the afternoon. At three o'clock Jesus cried out with a loud voice, "Eloi, Eloi, lema sabachthani?" which means, "My God, my God, why have you forsaken me?" When some of the bystanders heard it, they said, "Listen, he is calling for Elijah." And someone ran, filled a sponge with sour wine, put it on a stick, and gave it to him to drink, saying, "Wait, let us see whether Elijah will come to take him down." Then Jesus gave a loud cry and breathed his last. And the curtain of the temple was torn in two, from top to bottom. Now when the centurion, who stood facing him, saw that in this way he breathed his last, he said, "Truly this man was God's Son!" (Mark 15:33-39)

Psalm
Psalm 31:9-16
I commend my spirit

Additional Readings
Isaiah 50:4-9a
The servant submits to suffering

Philippians 2:5-11
Death on a cross

Hymn: My Song Is Love Unknown, ELW 343

O God of mercy and might, in the mystery of the passion of your Son you offer your infinite life to the world. Gather us around the cross of Christ, and preserve us until the resurrection, through Jesus Christ, our Savior and Lord, who lives and reigns with you and the Holy Spirit, one God, now and forever.

Monday, March 29, 2021
Monday in Holy Week

Hans Nielsen Hauge, renewer of the church, died 1824

Psalm 36:5-11
Refuge under the shadow of your wings

How precious is your steadfast love, O God!
    All people may take refuge in the shadow of your wings.
They feast on the abundance of your house,
    and you give them drink from the river of your delights.
For with you is the fountain of life;
    in your light we see light. (Ps. 36:7-9)

Additional Readings

Isaiah 42:1-9
The servant brings forth justice

Hebrews 9:11-15
The blood of Christ redeems for eternal life

John 12:1-11
Mary of Bethany anoints Jesus

Hymn: Alas! And Did My Savior Bleed, ELW 337

O God, your Son chose the path that led to pain before joy and to the cross before glory. Plant his cross in our hearts, so that in its power and love we may come at last to joy and glory, through Jesus Christ, our Savior and Lord, who lives and reigns with you and the Holy Spirit, one God, now and forever.

Tuesday, March 30, 2021
Tuesday in Holy Week

1 Corinthians 1:18-31

The cross of Christ reveals God's power and wisdom

For since, in the wisdom of God, the world did not know God through wisdom, God decided, through the foolishness of our proclamation, to save those who believe. For Jews demand signs and Greeks desire wisdom, but we proclaim Christ crucified, a stumbling block to Jews and foolishness to Gentiles, but to those who are the called, both Jews and Greeks, Christ the power of God and the wisdom of God. For God's foolishness is wiser than human wisdom, and God's weakness is stronger than human strength. (1 Cor. 1:21-25)

Psalm

Psalm 71:1-14
From my mother's womb you have been my strength

Additional Readings

Isaiah 49:1-7
The servant brings salvation to earth's ends

John 12:20-36
Jesus speaks of his death

Hymn: Seed That in Earth Is Dying, ELW 330

Lord Jesus, you have called us to follow you. Grant that our love may not grow cold in your service, and that we may not fail or deny you in the time of trial, for you live and reign with the Father and the Holy Spirit, one God, now and forever.

Wednesday, March 31, 2021
Wednesday in Holy Week

John Donne, poet, died 1631

Isaiah 50:4-9a
The servant is vindicated by God

The Lord GOD helps me;
> therefore I have not been disgraced;
therefore I have set my face like flint,
> and I know that I shall not be put to shame;
> he who vindicates me is near.
Who will contend with me?
> Let us stand up together.
Who are my adversaries?
> Let them confront me.
It is the Lord GOD who helps me;
> who will declare me guilty? (Isa. 50:7-9a)

Psalm
Psalm 70
Be pleased, O God, to deliver me

Additional Readings
Hebrews 12:1-3
Look to Jesus, who endured the cross

John 13:21-32
Jesus foretells his betrayal

Hymn: Ah, Holy Jesus, ELW 349

Almighty God, your Son our Savior suffered at human hands and endured the shame of the cross. Grant that we may walk in the way of his cross and find it the way of life and peace, through Jesus Christ, our Savior and Lord, who lives and reigns with you and the Holy Spirit, one God, now and forever.

Prayer List for April

_____

_____

_____

_____

_____

_____

_____

_____

_____

The Three Days

As the sun sets on Maundy Thursday, so Lent ends and the Three Days begin, ending with sunset on Easter Day. During these central days, Christians prepare to celebrate God's gift of new life given in baptism. Indeed, the readings of the Three Days move toward the baptismal font where new brothers and sisters are born of water and the Spirit, and where the baptized renew their baptismal promises.

In the home and in the church community, special attention is given to these days through prayer and keeping greater silence until the great Vigil of Easter is celebrated. Many Christians keep a fast from food, work, and entertainment on Good Friday and Holy Saturday. In the home, preparations can be made for the celebration of Easter: cleaning, coloring eggs, baking Easter breads, gathering greens or flowers to adorn crosses and sacred images. In those communities where baptisms will be celebrated, prayers may be offered for those to be received into the church.

Table Prayer for the Three Days

Blessed are you, O Lord our God.
With this food strengthen us on our journey from death to life.
We glory in the cross of Christ.
Raise us, with him, to the joy of the resurrection,
through Jesus Christ our Lord. Amen.

Thursday, April 1, 2021
Maundy Thursday

1 Corinthians 11:23-26
Proclaim the Lord's death

For I received from the Lord what I also handed on to you, that the Lord Jesus on the night when he was betrayed took a loaf of bread, and when he had given thanks, he broke it and said, "This is my body that is for you. Do this in remembrance of me." In the same way he took the cup also, after supper, saying, "This cup is the new covenant in my blood. Do this, as often as you drink it, in remembrance of me." For as often as you eat this bread and drink the cup, you proclaim the Lord's death until he comes. (1 Cor. 11:23-26)

Psalm
Psalm 116:1-2, 12-19
The cup of salvation

Additional Readings
Exodus 12:1-4 [5-10] 11-14
The passover of the Lord

John 13:1-17, 31b-35
The service of Christ: footwashing and meal

Hymn: Where Charity and Love Prevail, ELW 359

Eternal God, in the sharing of a meal your Son established a new covenant for all people, and in the washing of feet he showed us the dignity of service. Grant that by the power of your Holy Spirit these signs of our life in faith may speak again to our hearts, feed our spirits, and refresh our bodies, through Jesus Christ, our Savior and Lord, who lives and reigns with you and the Holy Spirit, one God, now and forever.

Friday, April 2, 2021
Good Friday

John 18:1—19:42
The passion and death of Jesus

Then Pilate entered the headquarters again, summoned Jesus, and asked him, "Are you the King of the Jews?" Jesus answered, "Do you ask this on your own, or did others tell you about me?" Pilate replied, "I am not a Jew, am I? Your own nation and the chief priests have handed you over to me. What have you done?" Jesus answered, "My kingdom is not from this world. If my kingdom were from this world, my followers would be fighting to keep me from being handed over to the Jews. But as it is, my kingdom is not from here." Pilate asked him, "So you are a king?" Jesus answered, "You say that I am a king. For this I was born, and for this I came into the world, to testify to the truth. Everyone who belongs to the truth listens to my voice." (John 18:33-37)

Psalm

Psalm 22
Why have you forsaken me?

Additional Readings

Isaiah 52:13—53:12
The suffering servant

Hebrews 10:16-25
The way to God is opened

Hymn: O Sacred Head, Now Wounded, ELW 351/352

Merciful God, your Son was lifted up on the cross to draw all people to himself. Grant that we who have been born out of his wounded side may at all times find mercy in him, Jesus Christ, our Savior and Lord, who lives and reigns with you and the Holy Spirit, one God, now and forever.

Saturday, April 3, 2021
Resurrection of Our Lord
Vigil of Easter

Romans 6:3-11
Dying and rising with Christ

Do you not know that all of us who have been baptized into Christ Jesus were baptized into his death? Therefore we have been buried with him by baptism into death, so that, just as Christ was raised from the dead by the glory of the Father, so we too might walk in newness of life.

For if we have been united with him in a death like his, we will certainly be united with him in a resurrection like his. We know that our old self was crucified with him so that the body of sin might be destroyed, and we might no longer be enslaved to sin. For whoever has died is freed from sin. (Rom. 6:3-7)

Psalm
Psalm 136:1-9, 23-26
God's mercy endures forever

Additional Readings
Genesis 1:1—2:4a
Creation

John 20:1-18
Seeing the risen Christ

Hymn: Come, You Faithful, Raise the Strain, ELW 363

O God, you are the creator of the world, the liberator of your people, and the wisdom of the earth. By the resurrection of your Son free us from our fears, restore us in your image, and ignite us with your light, through Jesus Christ, our Savior and Lord, who lives and reigns with you and the Holy Spirit, one God, now and forever.

Sunday, April 4, 2021
Resurrection of Our Lord
Easter Day

Benedict the African, confessor, died 1589

Mark 16:1-8
The resurrection is announced

As [Mary Magdalene, and Mary the mother of James, and Salome]
entered the tomb, they saw a young man, dressed in a white robe, sitting
on the right side; and they were alarmed. But he said to them, "Do not
be alarmed; you are looking for Jesus of Nazareth, who was crucified.
He has been raised; he is not here. Look, there is the place they laid
him. But go, tell his disciples and Peter that he is going ahead of you to
Galilee; there you will see him, just as he told you." So they went out and
fled from the tomb, for terror and amazement had seized them; and they
said nothing to anyone, for they were afraid. (Mark 16:5-8)

Psalm
Psalm 118:1-2, 14-24
On this day God has acted

Additional Readings
Acts 10:34-43
*God raised Jesus on the
third day*

1 Corinthians 15:1-11
Witnesses to the risen Christ

Hymn: At the Lamb's High Feast We Sing, ELW 362

*God of mercy, we no longer look for Jesus among the dead, for he is alive and
has become the Lord of life. Increase in our minds and hearts the risen life
we share with Christ, and help us to grow as your people toward the fullness
of eternal life with you, through Jesus Christ, our Savior and Lord, who
lives and reigns with you and the Holy Spirit, one God, now and forever.*

Easter

The Three Days flow into the rejoicing of the fifty days of Easter. During this "week of weeks," Christians explore the meaning of the central actions of baptism for daily life: the renouncing of evil and the professing of faith, washing in water, being marked with the cross, clothing in the white robe, receiving the light of the paschal/Easter candle, and eating and drinking the bread of life and the cup of salvation.

The fifty days were once called *Pentecost*, Greek for "fifty." On the fiftieth day of Easter, Christians celebrate the pentecostal mystery of the risen Christ breathing on the church the breath, the wind, and the fire of the Holy Spirit.

Table Prayer for the Season of Easter

O God of our risen Lord, we praise you, we bless you,
we worship you for the gifts of life you give us.
Always you offer us life, and for this we bless your holy name.
And we ask you,
give your life also to all who know only hunger and the pangs of death.
So may the whole world be raised to life,
through Jesus Christ, our Savior and Lord. Amen.

Monday, April 5, 2021
Week of Easter 1

Psalm 118:1-2, 14-24
On this day God has acted

I thank you that you have answered me
    and have become my salvation.
The stone that the builders rejected
    has become the chief cornerstone.
This is the Lord's doing;
    it is marvelous in our eyes.
This is the day that the Lord has made;
    let us rejoice and be glad in it. (Ps. 118:21-24)

Additional Readings

Genesis 1:1-19
God creates

1 Corinthians 15:35-49
The resurrected body

Hymn: By Gracious Powers, ELW 626

Creating God, you form new life from the chaos of suffering and sorrow. You hear our cries and respond with boundless grace. Open our hearts that we might see and rejoice in the salvation you have won for us.

Tuesday, April 6, 2021
Week of Easter 1

Albrecht Dürer, died 1528; Matthias Grünewald, died 1529; Lucas Cranach, died 1553; artists

1 Corinthians 15:50-58

The dead will be raised

What I am saying, brothers and sisters, is this: flesh and blood cannot inherit the kingdom of God, nor does the perishable inherit the imperishable. Listen, I will tell you a mystery! We will not all die, but we will all be changed, in a moment, in the twinkling of an eye, at the last trumpet. For the trumpet will sound, and the dead will be raised imperishable, and we will be changed. For this perishable body must put on imperishability, and this mortal body must put on immortality. (1 Cor. 15:50-53)

Psalm
Psalm 118:1-2, 14-24
On this day God has acted

Additional Reading
Genesis 1:20—2:4a
God creates

Hymn: This Joyful Eastertide, ELW 391

God of transformation, you promise us eternal life. As we wait for the day when we will be changed, clothed forever in your unending mercy, assure us of your steadfast love for us and for all creation.

Wednesday, April 7, 2021
Week of Easter 1

Mark 16:1-8
Mark's resurrection account

When the sabbath was over, Mary Magdalene, and Mary the mother of James, and Salome bought spices, so that they might go and anoint [Jesus]. And very early on the first day of the week, when the sun had risen, they went to the tomb. They had been saying to one another, "Who will roll away the stone for us from the entrance to the tomb?" When they looked up, they saw that the stone, which was very large, had already been rolled back. As they entered the tomb, they saw a young man, dressed in a white robe, sitting on the right side; and they were alarmed. But he said to them, "Do not be alarmed; you are looking for Jesus of Nazareth, who was crucified. He has been raised; he is not here. Look, there is the place they laid him. But go, tell his disciples and Peter that he is going ahead of you to Galilee; there you will see him, just as he told you." (Mark 16:1-7)

Psalm
Psalm 118:1-2, 14-24
On this day God has acted

Additional Reading
Song of Solomon 3:1-11
The song of the lover

Hymn: Christ Has Arisen, Alleluia, ELW 364

God, our strength and our salvation, in the midst of grief and confusion you surprise us with hope. Silence the fears that threaten to render us silent. Empower us to be witnesses to your undying love for the whole world.

Thursday, April 8, 2021
Week of Easter 1

Psalm 133
How good it is to live in unity

How very good and pleasant it is
   when kindred live together in unity!
It is like the precious oil on the head,
   running down upon the beard,
on the beard of Aaron,
   running down over the collar of his robes.
It is like the dew of Hermon,
   which falls on the mountains of Zion.
For there the LORD ordained his blessing,
   life forevermore. (Ps. 133:1-3)

Additional Readings
Daniel 1:1-21
Daniel in the court of Nebuchadnezzar

Acts 2:42-47
The believers' common life

Hymn: The Risen Christ, ELW 390

God, you desire for your people to be united in witness and vision. In the midst of division, give us glad and generous hearts filled with wisdom and insight. Inspire your people, day by day, to live together in unity.

Friday, April 9, 2021
Week of Easter 1

Dietrich Bonhoeffer, theologian, died 1945

Daniel 2:1-23

The king searches for wisdom

Daniel said:
"Blessed be the name of God from age to age,
   for wisdom and power are his.
He changes times and seasons,
   deposes kings and sets up kings;
he gives wisdom to the wise
   and knowledge to those who have understanding.
He reveals deep and hidden things;
   he knows what is in the darkness,
   and light dwells with him.
To you, O God of my ancestors,
   I give thanks and praise,
for you have given me wisdom and power,
   and have now revealed to me what we asked of you,
   for you have revealed to us what the king ordered." (Dan. 2:20-23)

Psalm

Psalm 133
How good it is to live in unity

Additional Reading

Acts 4:23-31
Prayer after Peter and John's release

Hymn: Christ Is Alive! Let Christians Sing, ELW 389

God of our ancestors, we thank and praise you for your persistent love through changing times and seasons. In the face of injustice and abuse of power, empower us to speak your healing word of justice and mercy with boldness.

Saturday, April 10, 2021
Week of Easter 1

Mikael Agricola, Bishop of Turku, died 1557

John 12:44-50

Believe in the one who sent me

Then Jesus cried aloud: "Whoever believes in me believes not in me but in him who sent me. And whoever sees me sees him who sent me. I have come as light into the world, so that everyone who believes in me should not remain in the darkness. I do not judge anyone who hears my words and does not keep them, for I came not to judge the world, but to save the world. The one who rejects me and does not receive my word has a judge; on the last day the word that I have spoken will serve as judge, for I have not spoken on my own, but the Father who sent me has himself given me a commandment about what to say and what to speak. And I know that his commandment is eternal life. What I speak, therefore, I speak just as the Father has told me." (John 12:44-50)

Psalm
Psalm 133
How good it is to live in unity

Additional Reading
Daniel 2:24-49
Daniel's rise to power

Hymn: Now All the Vault of Heaven Resounds, ELW 367

Gracious God, you've looked on us with love and your verdict is forgiveness, mercy, eternal life. Help us to see the world as you see it. Send us to speak your word of grace to a world in need.

Sunday, April 11, 2021
Second Sunday of Easter

John 20:19-31

Beholding the wounds of the risen Christ

A week later [Jesus'] disciples were again in the house, and Thomas was with them. Although the doors were shut, Jesus came and stood among them and said, "Peace be with you." Then he said to Thomas, "Put your finger here and see my hands. Reach out your hand and put it in my side. Do not doubt but believe." Thomas answered him, "My Lord and my God!" Jesus said to him, "Have you believed because you have seen me? Blessed are those who have not seen and yet have come to believe." (John 20:26-29)

Psalm

Psalm 133
How good it is to live in unity

Additional Readings

Acts 4:32-35
The believers' common life

1 John 1:1—2:2
Walking in the light

Hymn: We Walk by Faith, ELW 635

Almighty God, with joy we celebrate the day of our Lord's resurrection. By the grace of Christ among us, enable us to show the power of the resurrection in all that we say and do, through Jesus Christ, our Savior and Lord, who lives and reigns with you and the Holy Spirit, one God, now and forever.

Monday, April 12, 2021
Week of Easter 2

Psalm 135
Praise to God

Praise the LORD!
> Praise the name of the LORD;
> give praise, O servants of the LORD,
you that stand in the house of the LORD,
> in the courts of the house of our God.
Praise the LORD, for the LORD is good;
> sing to his name, for he is gracious.
For the LORD has chosen Jacob for himself,
> Israel as his own possession. (Ps. 135:1-4)

Additional Readings
Daniel 3:1-30
God saves the three men from the fire

1 John 2:3-11
A new commandment

Hymn: You Servants of God, ELW 825

We sing your praise, O God! We lift our voices in delight at the signs and wonders you work in our midst. Deliver us from fear. Empower and inspire us to trust in you alone, walking in your love.

Tuesday, April 13, 2021
Week of Easter 2

Daniel 6:1-28

God saves Daniel from the lions

Then King Darius wrote to all peoples and nations of every language throughout the whole world: "May you have abundant prosperity! I make a decree, that in all my royal dominion people should tremble and fear before the God of Daniel:

For he is the living God,
    enduring forever.
His kingdom shall never be destroyed,
    and his dominion has no end.
He delivers and rescues,
    he works signs and wonders in heaven and on earth;
for he has saved Daniel
    from the power of the lions." (Dan. 6:25-27)

Psalm

Psalm 135
Praise to God

Additional Reading

1 John 2:12-17
The world is passing away

Hymn: Thine the Amen, ELW 826

Living God, you deliver us from all that seeks to harm us. Shut the mouths of the lions that threaten to devour us—division, shame, and despair. Rescue us from apathy, pride, and isolation. Raise us up to praise you.

Wednesday, April 14, 2021
Week of Easter 2

Isaiah 26:1-15
Song of victory

O LORD, you will ordain peace for us,
    for indeed, all that we have done, you have done for us.
O LORD our God,
    other lords besides you have ruled over us,
    but we acknowledge your name alone.
The dead do not live;
    shades do not rise—
because you have punished and destroyed them,
    and wiped out all memory of them.
But you have increased the nation, O LORD,
    you have increased the nation; you are glorified;
    you have enlarged all the borders of the land. (Isa. 26:12-15)

Psalm
Psalm 135
Praise to God

Additional Reading
Mark 12:18-27
Jesus teaches about the resurrection

Hymn: Bring Peace to Earth Again, ELW 700

Just One, you are our souls' desire. We yearn for your peace to prevail and your justice to end all inequality and oppression. As we look toward the future with hope, help us to see the power of your love even now.

Thursday, April 15, 2021
Week of Easter 2

Psalm 4
God does wonders for the faithful

There are many who say, "O that we might see some good!
  Let the light of your face shine on us, O LORD!"
You have put gladness in my heart
  more than when their grain and wine abound.

I will both lie down and sleep in peace;
  for you alone, O LORD, make me lie down in safety. (Ps. 4:6-8)

Additional Readings
Daniel 9:1-19
Daniel pleads for the people in prayer

1 John 2:18-25
Remain in union with God

Hymn: Awake, My Heart, with Gladness, ELW 378

Answer us, O God, when we cry to you. We toss and turn, desperate for your peace to still our racing hearts and rest our burdened minds. Give us your gladness. Warm and fill all creation with your abiding love.

Friday, April 16, 2021
Week of Easter 2

1 John 2:26-28
Have confidence in the coming one

I write these things to you concerning those who would deceive you. As for you, the anointing that you received from him abides in you, and so you do not need anyone to teach you. But as his anointing teaches you about all things, and is true and is not a lie, and just as it has taught you, abide in him.

And now, little children, abide in him, so that when he is revealed we may have confidence and not be put to shame before him at his coming. (1 John 2:26-28)

Psalm
Psalm 4
God does wonders for the faithful

Additional Reading
Daniel 10:2-19
Daniel's vision strengthens him

Hymn: O God in Heaven, ELW 748

God, you give us courage to live with integrity in a world where lies and deception run rampant. Anoint us with your spirit that we might stand strong in the truth of your love and mercy for this weary world.

Saturday, April 17, 2021
Week of Easter 2

Luke 22:24-30
Eating and drinking at Christ's table

A dispute also arose among [the apostles] as to which one of them was to be regarded as the greatest. But [Jesus] said to them, "The kings of the Gentiles lord it over them; and those in authority over them are called benefactors. But not so with you; rather the greatest among you must become like the youngest, and the leader like one who serves. For who is greater, the one who is at the table or the one who serves? Is it not the one at the table? But I am among you as one who serves.

"You are those who have stood by me in my trials; and I confer on you, just as my Father has conferred on me, a kingdom, so that you may eat and drink at my table in my kingdom, and you will sit on thrones judging the twelve tribes of Israel." (Luke 22:24-30)

Psalm
Psalm 4
God does wonders for the faithful

Additional Reading
Acts 3:1-10
A man lame from birth is healed

Hymn: I Come with Joy, ELW 482

Servant God, you upend our notions of power and privilege and call your people to serve with humility. Turn us from vain words and notions of superiority to love our neighbors and bring your healing to a world pleading for good news.

Sunday, April 18, 2021
Third Sunday of Easter

Luke 24:36b-48

Eating with the risen Christ

Then [Jesus] said to [the disciples], "These are my words that I spoke to you while I was still with you—that everything written about me in the law of Moses, the prophets, and the psalms must be fulfilled." Then he opened their minds to understand the scriptures, and he said to them, "Thus it is written, that the Messiah is to suffer and to rise from the dead on the third day, and that repentance and forgiveness of sins is to be proclaimed in his name to all nations, beginning from Jerusalem. You are witnesses of these things." (Luke 24:44-48)

Psalm

Psalm 4
God does wonders for the faithful

Additional Readings

Acts 3:12-19
Health and forgiveness through Jesus

1 John 3:1-7
The revealing of the children of God

Hymn: With High Delight Let Us Unite, ELW 368

Holy and righteous God, you are the author of life, and you adopt us to be your children. Fill us with your words of life, that we may live as witnesses to the resurrection of your Son, Jesus Christ, our Savior and Lord, who lives and reigns with you and the Holy Spirit, one God, now and forever.

Monday, April 19, 2021
Week of Easter 3

Olavus Petri, priest, died 1552; Laurentius Petri, Bishop of Uppsala, died 1573;
renewers of the church

Psalm 150
Praise to God

Praise the LORD!
Praise God in his sanctuary;
    praise him in his mighty firmament!
Praise him for his mighty deeds;
    praise him according to his surpassing greatness!

Praise him with trumpet sound;
    praise him with lute and harp!
Praise him with tambourine and dance;
    praise him with strings and pipe!
Praise him with clanging cymbals;
    praise him with loud clashing cymbals!
Let everything that breathes praise the LORD!
    Praise the LORD! (Ps. 150:1-6)

Additional Readings
Jeremiah 30:1-11a　　　　　　**1 John 3:10-16**
God will save the people　　　　*Lay down life for one another*

Hymn: When in Our Music God Is Glorified, ELW 850/851

With every breath we praise you, God! You make warring people dance. You give anxious people quiet and ease. In the expanse of your gracious love we move from death to life. Inspire us to live the truth of your love.

Tuesday, April 20, 2021
Week of Easter 3

2 John 1-6

Love one another

The elder to the elect lady and her children, whom I love in the truth, and not only I but also all who know the truth, because of the truth that abides in us and will be with us forever:

Grace, mercy, and peace will be with us from God the Father and from Jesus Christ, the Father's Son, in truth and love.

I was overjoyed to find some of your children walking in the truth, just as we have been commanded by the Father. But now, dear lady, I ask you, not as though I were writing you a new commandment, but one we have had from the beginning, let us love one another. And this is love, that we walk according to his commandments; this is the commandment just as you have heard it from the beginning—you must walk in it. (2 John 1-6)

Psalm
Psalm 150
Praise to God

Additional Reading
Hosea 5:15—6:6
Salvation on the third day

Hymn: We Are Called, ELW 720

Gracious God, your command is to love one another as you have loved us. Heal us. Revive us. Come to us like the spring rains and refresh us with your grace. Give us the will to love wholeheartedly.

Wednesday, April 21, 2021
Week of Easter 3

Anselm, Bishop of Canterbury, died 1109

Proverbs 9:1-6

Wisdom invites to her feast

Wisdom has built her house,
>	she has hewn her seven pillars.
She has slaughtered her animals, she has mixed her wine,
>	she has also set her table.
She has sent out her servant girls, she calls
>	from the highest places in the town,
"You that are simple, turn in here!"
>	To those without sense she says,
"Come, eat of my bread
>	and drink of the wine I have mixed.
Lay aside immaturity, and live,
>	and walk in the way of insight." (Prov. 9:1-6)

Psalm
Psalm 150
Praise to God

Additional Reading
Mark 16:9-18
Jesus appears to the disciples

Hymn: We Eat the Bread of Teaching, ELW 518

God of radical hospitality, thank you for inviting us to your table. Feed us with your word. Strengthen us with your wisdom. Send us, fed and refreshed, to proclaim the good news of your love to all creation.

Thursday, April 22, 2021
Week of Easter 3

Psalm 23

God our shepherd

The Lord is my shepherd, I shall not want.
    He makes me lie down in green pastures;
he leads me beside still waters;
    he restores my soul.
He leads me in right paths
    for his name's sake.

Even though I walk through the darkest valley,
    I fear no evil;
for you are with me;
    your rod and your staff—
    they comfort me. (Ps. 23:1-4)

Additional Readings

Genesis 30:25-43
Jacob the shepherd

Acts 3:17-26
Peter preaches in Solomon's Portico

Hymn: My Shepherd, You Supply My Need, ELW 782

Shepherding God, with you beside us we live not in fear but in boundless hope. Open our ears to listen to your gentle voice. Turn us from exhaustion and resignation. Lead us to rest and refreshment.

Friday, April 23, 2021
Week of Easter 3

Toyohiko Kagawa, renewer of society, died 1960

Acts 4:1-4
Peter and John arrested

While Peter and John were speaking to the people, the priests, the captain of the temple, and the Sadducees came to them, much annoyed because they were teaching the people and proclaiming that in Jesus there is the resurrection of the dead. So they arrested them and put them in custody until the next day, for it was already evening. But many of those who heard the word believed; and they numbered about five thousand. (Acts 4:1-4)

Psalm
Psalm 23
God our shepherd

Additional Reading
Genesis 46:28—47:6
The shepherds of Israel sojourn in Egypt

Hymn: The Day of Resurrection! ELW 361

God of resurrection hope, strengthen us to proclaim your promise of new life for all creation. When our actions for the sake of the gospel are met with resistance, help us persist. We trust that your word cannot be chained.

Saturday, April 24, 2021
Week of Easter 3

Mark 6:30-34

Like sheep without a shepherd

The apostles gathered around Jesus, and told him all that they had done and taught. He said to them, "Come away to a deserted place all by yourselves and rest a while." For many were coming and going, and they had no leisure even to eat. And they went away in the boat to a deserted place by themselves. Now many saw them going and recognized them, and they hurried there on foot from all the towns and arrived ahead of them. As he went ashore, he saw a great crowd; and he had compassion for them, because they were like sheep without a shepherd; and he began to teach them many things. (Mark 6:30-34)

Psalm
Psalm 23
God our shepherd

Additional Reading
Genesis 48:8-19
God has been my shepherd

Hymn: Savior, like a Shepherd Lead Us, ELW 789

God, lead us to places where we can hear your voice apart from the din of constant need. Then, refreshed and renewed, send us to be your heart of compassion for all who yearn to be shepherded by your love.

Sunday, April 25, 2021
Fourth Sunday of Easter

Mark, Evangelist (transferred to April 26)

John 10:11-18
Christ the shepherd

[Jesus said,] "I am the good shepherd. The good shepherd lays down his life for the sheep. The hired hand, who is not the shepherd and does not own the sheep, sees the wolf coming and leaves the sheep and runs away—and the wolf snatches them and scatters them. The hired hand runs away because a hired hand does not care for the sheep. I am the good shepherd. I know my own and my own know me, just as the Father knows me and I know the Father. And I lay down my life for the sheep." (John 10:11-15)

Psalm
Psalm 23
God our shepherd

Additional Readings
Acts 4:5-12
Salvation in the name of Jesus

1 John 3:16-24
Love in truth and action

Hymn: Have No Fear, Little Flock, ELW 764

O Lord Christ, good shepherd of the sheep, you seek the lost and guide us into your fold. Feed us, and we shall be satisfied; heal us, and we shall be whole. Make us one with you, for you live and reign with the Father and the Holy Spirit, one God, now and forever.

Monday, April 26, 2021
Mark, Evangelist (transferred)

Mark 1:1-15
The beginning of the gospel of Jesus Christ

The beginning of the good news of Jesus Christ, the Son of God.
As it is written in the prophet Isaiah,
"See, I am sending my messenger ahead of you,
who will prepare your way;
the voice of one crying out in the wilderness:
'Prepare the way of the Lord,
make his paths straight,'"
John the baptizer appeared in the wilderness, proclaiming a baptism of repentance for the forgiveness of sins. And people from the whole Judean countryside and all the people of Jerusalem were going out to him, and were baptized by him in the river Jordan, confessing their sins. (Mark 1:1-5)

Psalm
Psalm 57
Be merciful to me, O God

Additional Readings
Isaiah 52:7-10
The messenger announces salvation

2 Timothy 4:6-11, 18
The good fight of faith

Hymn: By All Your Saints, st. 10, ELW 420

Almighty God, you have enriched your church with Mark's proclamation of the gospel. Give us grace to believe firmly in the good news of salvation and to walk daily in accord with it, through Jesus Christ, our Savior and Lord, who lives and reigns with you and the Holy Spirit, one God, now and forever.

Tuesday, April 27, 2021
Week of Easter 4

Revelation 7:13-17
The Lamb will be the shepherd

Then one of the elders addressed me, saying, "Who are these, robed in white, and where have they come from?" I said to him, "Sir, you are the one that knows." Then he said to me, "These are they who have come out of the great ordeal; they have washed their robes and made them white in the blood of the Lamb.

> For this reason they are before the throne of God,
>> and worship him day and night within his temple,
>> and the one who is seated on the throne will shelter them.
> They will hunger no more, and thirst no more;
>> the sun will not strike them,
>> nor any scorching heat;
> for the Lamb at the center of the throne will be their shepherd,
>> and he will guide them to springs of the water of life,
> and God will wipe away every tear from their eyes." (Rev. 7:13-17)

Psalm
Psalm 95
We are the sheep of God's hand

Additional Reading
1 Chronicles 11:1-9
The shepherd David made king

Hymn: Sing with All the Saints in Glory, ELW 426

God of heaven and earth, the day is coming when you will wipe every tear from our eyes. As we cling to future hope, claim us as your beloved ones and shelter us with your abiding love here and now.

Wednesday, April 28, 2021
Week of Easter 4

Mark 14:26-31
Christ the shepherd

When [Jesus and the Twelve] had sung the hymn, they went out to the Mount of Olives. And Jesus said to them, "You will all become deserters; for it is written,

> 'I will strike the shepherd,
>> and the sheep will be scattered.'

But after I am raised up, I will go before you to Galilee." Peter said to him, "Even though all become deserters, I will not." Jesus said to him, "Truly I tell you, this day, this very night, before the cock crows twice, you will deny me three times." But he said vehemently, "Even though I must die with you, I will not deny you." And all of them said the same. (Mark 14:26-31)

Psalm
Psalm 95
We are the sheep of God's hand

Additional Reading
Micah 7:8-20
God will shepherd the people

Hymn: The Lord's My Shepherd, ELW 778

God of new beginnings, our failures are never the end of our story. You do not leave us scattered and broken, but raise us up to wholeness of body, mind, and spirit. Shepherd us beyond shame to abundant life with you.

Thursday, April 29, 2021
Week of Easter 4

Catherine of Siena, theologian, died 1380

Psalm 22:25-31
All shall turn to the Lord

From you comes my praise in the great congregation;
    my vows I will pay before those who fear him.
The poor shall eat and be satisfied;
    those who seek him shall praise the LORD.
    May your hearts live forever!

All the ends of the earth shall remember
    and turn to the LORD;
and all the families of the nations
    shall worship before him.
For dominion belongs to the LORD,
    and he rules over the nations. (Ps. 22:25-28)

Additional Readings

Amos 8:1-7
Amos's vision of the basket of fruit

Acts 8:1b-8
Philip's ministry in Samaria

Hymn: Sing Praise to God, the Highest Good, ELW 871

God of every generation, throughout all times and places you stand on the side of the poor and afflicted. Your justice refuses to forget the suffering of your beloved ones. Work in us to bring joy to all creation.

Friday, April 30, 2021
Week of Easter 4

Amos 8:11-13

A famine of hearing the word of God

The time is surely coming, says the Lord GOD,
> when I will send a famine on the land;
not a famine of bread, or a thirst for water,
> but of hearing the words of the LORD.
They shall wander from sea to sea,
> and from north to east;
they shall run to and fro, seeking the word of the LORD,
> but they shall not find it.

In that day the beautiful young women and the young men
> shall faint for thirst. (Amos 8:11-13)

Psalm
Psalm 22:25-31
All shall turn to the Lord

Additional Reading
Acts 8:9-25
Philip and Simon the magician

Hymn: Word of God, Come Down on Earth, ELW 510

God of mercy, stir up in us a thirst for your life-changing word. Heal our hearts. Help us to see our complicity in systems that oppress the poor. Free us from our sin to work for economic justice for all.

Prayer List for May

_____

_____

_____

_____

_____

_____

_____

_____

_____

Saturday, May 1, 2021
Philip and James, Apostles

John 14:8-14
Jesus and the Father are one

Philip said to [Jesus], "Lord, show us the Father, and we will be satisfied." Jesus said to him, "Have I been with you all this time, Philip, and you still do not know me? Whoever has seen me has seen the Father. How can you say, 'Show us the Father'? Do you not believe that I am in the Father and the Father is in me? The words that I say to you I do not speak on my own; but the Father who dwells in me does his works." (John 14:8-10)

Psalm
Psalm 44:1-3, 20-26
Save us for the sake of your love

Additional Readings
Isaiah 30:18-21
God's mercy and justice

2 Corinthians 4:1-6
Proclaiming Jesus Christ as Lord

Hymn: You Are the Way, ELW 758

Almighty God, you gave to your apostles Philip and James grace and strength to bear witness to your Son. Grant that we, remembering their victory of faith, may glorify in life and death the name of our Lord Jesus Christ, who lives and reigns with you and the Holy Spirit, one God, now and forever.

Sunday, May 2, 2021
Fifth Sunday of Easter

Athanasius, Bishop of Alexandria, died 373

John 15:1-8
Christ the vine

[Jesus said,] "I am the true vine, and my Father is the vinegrower. He removes every branch in me that bears no fruit. Every branch that bears fruit he prunes to make it bear more fruit. You have already been cleansed by the word that I have spoken to you. Abide in me as I abide in you. Just as the branch cannot bear fruit by itself unless it abides in the vine, neither can you unless you abide in me. I am the vine, you are the branches. Those who abide in me and I in them bear much fruit, because apart from me you can do nothing." (John 15:1-5)

Psalm
Psalm 22:25-31
All shall turn to the Lord

Additional Readings
Acts 8:26-40
Philip teaches and baptizes an Ethiopian

1 John 4:7-21
Loving one another

Hymn: O Blessed Spring, ELW 447

O God, you give us your Son as the vine apart from whom we cannot live. Nourish our life in his resurrection, that we may bear the fruit of love and know the fullness of your joy, through Jesus Christ, our Savior and Lord, who lives and reigns with you and the Holy Spirit, one God, now and forever.

Monday, May 3, 2021
Week of Easter 5

Psalm 80
Israel, the vine

Turn again, O God of hosts;
>   look down from heaven, and see;
have regard for this vine,
>   the stock that your right hand planted.
They have burned it with fire, they have cut it down;
>   may they perish at the rebuke of your countenance.
But let your hand be upon the one at your right hand,
>   the one whom you made strong for yourself.
Then we will never turn back from you;
>   give us life, and we will call on your name. (Ps. 80:14-18)

Additional Readings
Isaiah 5:1-7
The unfaithful vineyard

Galatians 5:16-26
The fruits of the Spirit

Hymn: Alleluia! Jesus Is Risen! ELW 377

Life-giving God, you make creation burst forth with abundance. Strengthen all who support and care for your creation. Help us to be good stewards of your beautiful world. May our work share your fruitful bounty with others.

Tuesday, May 4, 2021
Week of Easter 5

Monica, mother of Augustine, died 387

James 3:17-18
Wisdom is full of good fruits

But the wisdom from above is first pure, then peaceable, gentle, willing to yield, full of mercy and good fruits, without a trace of partiality or hypocrisy. And a harvest of righteousness is sown in peace for those who make peace. (James 3:17-18)

Psalm
Psalm 80
Israel, the vine

Additional Reading
Isaiah 32:9-20
A fruitful field

Hymn: We Raise Our Hands to You, O Lord, ELW 690

Creating God, you not only created the whole world, but you created us. Help us, like the physical earth, to produce good fruit. Stir up within us wisdom, peace, mercy, and righteousness so others can be fed by them.

Wednesday, May 5, 2021
Week of Easter 5

John 14:18-31

Keeping God's word

[Jesus said,] "I will not leave you orphaned; I am coming to you. In a little while the world will no longer see me, but you will see me; because I live, you also will live. On that day you will know that I am in my Father, and you in me, and I in you. They who have my commandments and keep them are those who love me; and those who love me will be loved by my Father, and I will love them and reveal myself to them." (John 14:18-21)

Psalm
Psalm 80
Israel, the vine

Additional Reading
Isaiah 65:17-25
God's people like a tree

Hymn: Here, O Lord, Your Servants Gather, ELW 530

Ever-present God, you are with us no matter what comes. On the days when we feel alone and abandoned, remind us that you are here with us. In your love, reveal yourself to us and help us to see you.

Thursday, May 6, 2021
Week of Easter 5

Psalm 98
Shout with joy to God

Make a joyful noise to the LORD, all the earth;
> break forth into joyous song and sing praises.

Sing praises to the LORD with the lyre,
> with the lyre and the sound of melody.

With trumpets and the sound of the horn
> make a joyful noise before the King, the LORD. (Ps. 98:4-6)

Additional Readings

Isaiah 49:5-6
A light to the nations

Acts 10:1-34
Peter and Cornelius

Hymn: Oh, Sing to the Lord, ELW 822

God of all, you are worthy of our praise. Strengthen and inspire all musicians who use their talents to praise you and inspire others in worship. Help us all to lift our voices and songs to you.

Friday, May 7, 2021
Week of Easter 5

Acts 10:34-43

God shows no partiality

Then Peter began to speak to [the people with Cornelius]: "I truly understand that God shows no partiality, but in every nation anyone who fears him and does what is right is acceptable to him. You know the message he sent to the people of Israel, preaching peace by Jesus Christ—he is Lord of all. That message spread throughout Judea, beginning in Galilee after the baptism that John announced: how God anointed Jesus of Nazareth with the Holy Spirit and with power; how he went about doing good and healing all who were oppressed by the devil, for God was with him." (Acts 10:34-38)

Psalm
Psalm 98
Shout with joy to God

Additional Reading
Isaiah 42:5-9
God declares new things

Hymn: Earth and All Stars! ELW 731

Impartial God, you look upon all people with love and mercy. Stir our hearts to treat others in the same way. Help us put aside prejudice and stereotypes so that your abundant love can be shared with all people.

Saturday, May 8, 2021
Week of Easter 5

Julian of Norwich, renewer of the church, died around 1416

Deuteronomy 32:44-47

Take to heart the command of God

Moses came and recited all the words of this song in the hearing of the people, he and Joshua son of Nun. When Moses had finished reciting all these words to all Israel, he said to them: "Take to heart all the words that I am giving in witness against you today; give them as a command to your children, so that they may diligently observe all the words of this law. This is no trifling matter for you, but rather your very life; through it you may live long in the land that you are crossing over the Jordan to possess." (Deut. 32:44-47)

Psalm

Psalm 98
Shout with joy to God

Additional Reading

Mark 10:42-45
Jesus came to serve

Hymn: We Sing to You, O God, ELW 791

Parenting God, you love all of us as your children. Bless all parents and mentors who share your love and your commandments with children. Give them patience and strength, and give children open minds and loving hearts.

Sunday, May 9, 2021
Sixth Sunday of Easter

Nicolaus Ludwig von Zinzendorf, renewer of the church, hymnwriter, died 1760

John 15:9-17
Christ, the friend and lover

[Jesus said,] "As the Father has loved me, so I have loved you; abide in my love. If you keep my commandments, you will abide in my love, just as I have kept my Father's commandments and abide in his love. I have said these things to you so that my joy may be in you, and that your joy may be complete." (John 15:9-11)

Psalm
Psalm 98
Shout with joy to God

Additional Readings
Acts 10:44-48
The Spirit poured out on the Gentiles

1 John 5:1-6
The victory of faith

Hymn: Great God, Your Love Has Called Us, ELW 358

O God, you have prepared for those who love you joys beyond understanding. Pour into our hearts such love for you that, loving you above all things, we may obtain your promises, which exceed all we can desire; through Jesus Christ, your Son and our Lord, who lives and reigns with you and the Holy Spirit, one God, now and forever.

Monday, May 10, 2021
Week of Easter 6

Psalm 93
God reigns above the floods

The LORD is king, he is robed in majesty;
    the LORD is robed, he is girded with strength.
He has established the world; it shall never be moved;
    your throne is established from of old;
    you are from everlasting.

The floods have lifted up, O LORD,
    the floods have lifted up their voice;
    the floods lift up their roaring.
More majestic than the thunders of mighty waters,
    more majestic than the waves of the sea,
    majestic on high is the LORD!

Your decrees are very sure;
    holiness befits your house,
    O LORD, forevermore. (Ps. 93:1-5)

Additional Readings
Deuteronomy 7:1-11
Keeping God's commandments

1 Timothy 6:11-12
Pursue righteousness

Hymn: Come, Thou Almighty King, ELW 408

Majestic God, you are transcendent and yet come to us. You are king of the universe and yet you listen to us. You establish the earth and yet you care for us. We praise you, thank you, and adore you.

Tuesday, May 11, 2021
Week of Easter 6

1 Timothy 6:13-16
Keep the commandments until Christ comes

In the presence of God, who gives life to all things, and of Christ Jesus, who in his testimony before Pontius Pilate made the good confession, I charge you to keep the commandment without spot or blame until the manifestation of our Lord Jesus Christ, which he will bring about at the right time—he who is the blessed and only Sovereign, the King of kings and Lord of lords. It is he alone who has immortality and dwells in unapproachable light, whom no one has ever seen or can see; to him be honor and eternal dominion. Amen. (1 Tim. 6:13-16)

Psalm
Psalm 93
God reigns above the floods

Additional Reading
Deuteronomy 11:1-17
The rewards of obedience

Hymn: Come, Let Us Join Our Cheerful Songs, ELW 847

God of all, you gave the law as a gift for our lives. Give us the strength to follow your commands. Help our lives be faithful reflections of your love. May others see the light of Jesus in us.

Wednesday, May 12, 2021
Week of Easter 6

Deuteronomy 11:18-21
Teach God's words to your children

You shall put these words of mine in your heart and soul, and you shall bind them as a sign on your hand, and fix them as an emblem on your forehead. Teach them to your children, talking about them when you are at home and when you are away, when you lie down and when you rise. Write them on the doorposts of your house and on your gates, so that your days and the days of your children may be multiplied in the land that the LORD swore to your ancestors to give them, as long as the heavens are above the earth. (Deut. 11:18-21)

Psalm
Psalm 93
God reigns above the floods

Additional Reading
Mark 16:19-20
An account of Jesus' ascension

Hymn: O God of Mercy, God of Light, ELW 714

God of wisdom, throughout all generations you enable your word to be passed on to others. Bless all who share your word with the next generation. Bless parents, grandparents, teachers, pastors, volunteers, and others who share your good news with children.

Thursday, May 13, 2021
Ascension of Our Lord

Luke 24:44-53
Christ present in all times and places

Then [Jesus] led [his disciples] out as far as Bethany, and, lifting up his hands, he blessed them. While he was blessing them, he withdrew from them and was carried up into heaven. And they worshiped him, and returned to Jerusalem with great joy; and they were continually in the temple blessing God. (Luke 24:50-53)

Psalm
Psalm 47
God has gone up with a shout

Additional Readings
Acts 1:1-11
Jesus sends the apostles

Ephesians 1:15-23
Seeing the risen and ascended Christ

Hymn: Alleluia! Sing to Jesus, ELW 392

Almighty God, your blessed Son, our Savior Jesus Christ, ascended far above all heavens that he might fill all things. Mercifully give us faith to trust that, as he promised, he abides with us on earth to the end of time, who lives and reigns with you and the Holy Spirit, one God, now and forever.

Friday, May 14, 2021
Matthias, Apostle

Luke 6:12-16
Jesus calls the Twelve

Now during those days [Jesus] went out to the mountain to pray; and he spent the night in prayer to God. And when day came, he called his disciples and chose twelve of them, whom he also named apostles: Simon, whom he named Peter, and his brother Andrew, and James, and John, and Philip, and Bartholomew, and Matthew, and Thomas, and James son of Alphaeus, and Simon, who was called the Zealot, and Judas son of James, and Judas Iscariot, who became a traitor. (Luke 6:12-16)

Psalm

Psalm 56
I am bound by the vow I made to you

Additional Readings

Isaiah 66:1-2
Heaven is God's throne, earth is God's footstool

Acts 1:15-26
The apostles cast lots for Matthias

Hymn: Give Thanks for Saints, ELW 428

Almighty God, you chose your faithful servant Matthias to be numbered among the twelve. Grant that your church may always be taught and guided by faithful and true pastors, through Jesus Christ our shepherd, who lives and reigns with you and the Holy Spirit, one God, now and forever.

Saturday, May 15, 2021
Week of Easter 6

John 16:4-11
Jesus will send the Advocate

[Jesus said,] "I did not say these things to you from the beginning, because I was with you. But now I am going to him who sent me; yet none of you asks me, 'Where are you going?' But because I have said these things to you, sorrow has filled your hearts. Nevertheless I tell you the truth: it is to your advantage that I go away, for if I do not go away, the Advocate will not come to you; but if I go, I will send him to you." (John 16:4b-7)

Psalm
Psalm 47
God has gone up with a shout

Additional Reading
Deuteronomy 34:1-7
Moses goes up to see the promised land

Hymn: Love Divine, All Loves Excelling, ELW 631

Abiding God, you have promised to be with us. In times of anxiety, stress, worry, fear, and doubt remind us of your promise. Open our hearts to know the presence of your Spirit among us.

Sunday, May 16, 2021
Seventh Sunday of Easter

John 17:6-19

Christ's prayer for his disciples

[While looking up to heaven Jesus said,] "But now I am coming to you, and I speak these things in the world so that they may have my joy made complete in themselves. I have given them your word, and the world has hated them because they do not belong to the world, just as I do not belong to the world. I am not asking you to take them out of the world, but I ask you to protect them from the evil one. They do not belong to the world, just as I do not belong to the world." (John 17:13-16)

Psalm

Psalm 1
The way of the righteous

Additional Readings

Acts 1:15-17, 21-26
Matthias added to the apostles

1 John 5:9-13
Life in the Son of God

Hymn: Lord, Who the Night You Were Betrayed, ELW 463

Gracious and glorious God, you have chosen us as your own, and by the powerful name of Christ you protect us from evil. By your Spirit transform us and your beloved world, that we may find our joy in your Son, Jesus Christ, our Savior and Lord, who lives and reigns with you and the Holy Spirit, one God, now and forever.

Monday, May 17, 2021
Week of Easter 7

Psalm 115
God's blessings on the chosen ones

The LORD has been mindful of us; he will bless us;
>he will bless the house of Israel;
>he will bless the house of Aaron;
he will bless those who fear the LORD,
>both small and great.

May the LORD give you increase,
>both you and your children.
May you be blessed by the LORD,
>who made heaven and earth. (Ps. 115:12-15)

Additional Readings
Exodus 28:29-38
Aaron prays for the people

Philippians 1:3-11
Paul prays for the church at Philippi

Hymn: Go, My Children, with My Blessing, ELW 543

Almighty God, you shower your people with blessing. You remember us. We are not worthy of your care or your abundance and yet you give them to us anyway. Help our lives to reflect that generous care to others.

Tuesday, May 18, 2021
Week of Easter 7

Erik, King of Sweden, martyr, died 1160

Titus 1:1-9

The ministry entrusted to Titus by Paul

[Paul wrote to Titus:] I left you behind in Crete for this reason, so that you should put in order what remained to be done, and should appoint elders in every town, as I directed you: someone who is blameless, married only once, whose children are believers, not accused of debauchery and not rebellious. For a bishop, as God's steward, must be blameless; he must not be arrogant or quick-tempered or addicted to wine or violent or greedy for gain; but he must be hospitable, a lover of goodness, prudent, upright, devout, and self-controlled. He must have a firm grasp of the word that is trustworthy in accordance with the teaching, so that he may be able both to preach with sound doctrine and to refute those who contradict it. (Titus 1:5-9)

Psalm

Psalm 115
God's blessings on the chosen ones

Additional Reading

Numbers 8:5-22
The Levites consecrated for service

Hymn: O Christ, Your Heart, Compassionate, ELW 722

Leading God, you have called people of all ages in your church to share your gospel. Give them courage and strength to be the people you want them to be. Give them the words you want them to share.

Wednesday, May 19, 2021
Week of Easter 7

John 16:16-24
Sorrow turned to joy

[Jesus said,] "Very truly, I tell you, you will weep and mourn, but the world will rejoice; you will have pain, but your pain will turn into joy. When a woman is in labor, she has pain, because her hour has come. But when her child is born, she no longer remembers the anguish because of the joy of having brought a human being into the world. So you have pain now; but I will see you again, and your hearts will rejoice, and no one will take your joy from you. On that day you will ask nothing of me. Very truly, I tell you, if you ask anything of the Father in my name, he will give it to you. Until now you have not asked for anything in my name. Ask and you will receive, so that your joy may be complete." (John 16:20-24)

Psalm
Psalm 115
God's blessings on the chosen ones

Additional Reading
Ezra 9:5-15
Ezra prays for the people

Hymn: Jerusalem, My Happy Home, ELW 628

God of love, you have promised us life in the midst of sorrow. During our times of pain and labor, remind us of your promises. Keep us steadfast in your word. Remind us of the joy that awaits us.

Thursday, May 20, 2021
Week of Easter 7

Psalm 33:12-22
Our help and our shield

Our soul waits for the Lord;
>	he is our help and shield.
Our heart is glad in him,
>	because we trust in his holy name.
Let your steadfast love, O Lord, be upon us,
>	even as we hope in you. (Ps. 33:20-22)

Additional Readings
Genesis 2:4b-7
God breathes life into humankind

1 Corinthians 15:42b-49
We bear Christ's image

Hymn: O God, Our Help in Ages Past, ELW 632

Protecting God, you are our refuge and shield, our hope in the midst of trouble. When tragedy is all around us and when our hearts are broken, give us your peace. Help our hearts to be glad in you.

Friday, May 21, 2021
Week of Easter 7

Helena, mother of Constantine, died around 330

1 Corinthians 15:50-57

The dead will be raised

When this perishable body puts on imperishability, and this mortal body puts on immortality, then the saying that is written will be fulfilled:

> "Death has been swallowed up in victory."
> "Where, O death, is your victory?
> Where, O death, is your sting?"

The sting of death is sin, and the power of sin is the law. But thanks be to God, who gives us the victory through our Lord Jesus Christ. (1 Cor. 15:54-57)

Psalm
Psalm 33:12-22
Our help and our shield

Additional Reading
Job 37:1-13
The powerful breath of God

Hymn: Praise and Thanks and Adoration, ELW 783

God of new life, you promise us resurrection. When our hearts are aching with grief, bring us your peace. When we mourn, hold us in your loving care. When death stings, comfort us with the hope of life in Christ.

Saturday, May 22, 2021
Vigil of Pentecost

Romans 8:14-17, 22-27
Praying with the Spirit

We know that the whole creation has been groaning in labor pains until now; and not only the creation, but we ourselves, who have the first fruits of the Spirit, groan inwardly while we wait for adoption, the redemption of our bodies. For in hope we were saved. Now hope that is seen is not hope. For who hopes for what is seen? But if we hope for what we do not see, we wait for it with patience. (Rom. 8:22-25)

Psalm
Psalm 33:12-22
Our help and our shield

Additional Readings
Exodus 19:1-9
The covenant at Sinai

John 7:37-39
The living water of the Spirit

Hymn: Like the Murmur of the Dove's Song, ELW 403

Almighty and ever-living God, you fulfilled the promise of Easter by sending the gift of your Holy Spirit. Look upon your people gathered in prayer, open to receive the Spirit's flame. May it come to rest in our hearts and heal the divisions of word and tongue, that with one voice and one song we may praise your name in joy and thanksgiving; through Jesus Christ, our Savior and Lord, who lives and reigns with you and the Holy Spirit, one God, now and forever.

Pentecost

Christians pray to God "in the power of the Spirit." The gifts of the Spirit are faith, hope, and love. Whenever two or more gather in Jesus' name, the Spirit is present. At every baptism and communion, we pray for the Spirit's presence to forgive and strengthen, inspire and refresh. In the household, we pray for the Spirit's guidance, for the deepening of faith, hope, and love, for the patience and wisdom to live in peace with each other and our neighbors.

Table Prayer for Pentecost

Blessed are you, O Lord our God,
who gathers the whole world into the Spirit of your Son.
You have given us food for another day:
blessed be God forever!
We beg you to pour out food for the needy,
that all peoples and languages may praise your name,
through Jesus Christ our Lord. Amen.

Thanksgiving for the Holy Spirit

Use this prayer during the week following Pentecost Sunday.

O Spirit of God, seek us;
Good Spirit, pray with us;
Spirit of counsel, inform us;
Spirit of might, free us;
Spirit of truth, enlighten us;
Spirit of Christ, raise us;
O Holy Spirit, dwell in us. Amen.

Sunday, May 23, 2021
Day of Pentecost

John 15:26-27; 16:4b-15

Christ sends the Spirit of truth

[Jesus said,] "I still have many things to say to you, but you cannot bear them now. When the Spirit of truth comes, he will guide you into all the truth; for he will not speak on his own, but will speak whatever he hears, and he will declare to you the things that are to come. He will glorify me, because he will take what is mine and declare it to you. All that the Father has is mine. For this reason I said that he will take what is mine and declare it to you." (John 16:12-15)

Psalm

Psalm 104:24-34, 35b
Renewing the face of the earth

Additional Readings

Acts 2:1-21
Filled with the Spirit

Romans 8:22-27
Praying with the Spirit

Hymn: Come, Holy Ghost, God and Lord, ELW 395

Mighty God, you breathe life into our bones, and your Spirit brings truth to the world. Send us this Spirit, transform us by your truth, and give us language to proclaim your gospel, through Jesus Christ, our Savior and Lord, who lives and reigns with you and the Holy Spirit, one God, now and forever.

Monday, May 24, 2021
Time after Pentecost

Nicolaus Copernicus, died 1543; Leonhard Euler, died 1783; scientists

Psalm 104:24-34, 35b
Renewing the face of the earth

May the glory of the LORD endure forever;
    may the LORD rejoice in his works—
who looks on the earth and it trembles,
    who touches the mountains and they smoke.
I will sing to the LORD as long as I live;
    I will sing praise to my God while I have being. (Ps. 104:31-33)

Additional Readings
Joel 2:18-29   1 Corinthians 12:4-11
God's spirit poured out   *Various gifts, the same Spirit*

Hymn: Oh, Worship the King, ELW 842

God of creation, you create, save, and sustain the world. Open us to the wonder of where we live. Help us to be awestruck by the daily beauty you give us. May our lives show gratitude for all of your creation.

Tuesday, May 25, 2021
Time after Pentecost

1 Corinthians 12:12-27
Many members, one body of Christ

For just as the body is one and has many members, and all the members of the body, though many, are one body, so it is with Christ. For in the one Spirit we were all baptized into one body—Jews or Greeks, slaves or free—and we were all made to drink of one Spirit. . . .

Now you are the body of Christ and individually members of it. (1 Cor. 12:12-13, 27)

Psalm
Psalm 104:24-34, 35b
Renewing the face of the earth

Additional Reading
Genesis 11:1-9
The fragmenting of human tongues

Hymn: All Creatures, Worship God Most High! ELW 835

God of life and health, you give us wonderful bodies. Bless all medical professionals who help individuals stay healthy. Bless leaders in the church who help the body of Christ stay healthy too.

Wednesday, May 26, 2021
Time after Pentecost

Ezekiel 37:1-14
Life to dry bones

So I prophesied as I had been commanded; and as I prophesied, suddenly there was a noise, a rattling, and the bones came together, bone to its bone. I looked, and there were sinews on them, and flesh had come upon them, and skin had covered them; but there was no breath in them. Then he said to me, "Prophesy to the breath, prophesy, mortal, and say to the breath: Thus says the Lord GOD: Come from the four winds, O breath, and breathe upon these slain, that they may live." I prophesied as he commanded me, and the breath came into them, and they lived, and stood on their feet, a vast multitude. (Ezek. 37:7-10)

Psalm
Psalm 104:24-34, 35b
Renewing the face of the earth

Additional Reading
John 20:19-23
Jesus breathes the Spirit

Hymn: The Word of God Is Source and Seed, ELW 506

Life-giving God, your spirit brings us all to life. Stir up that spirit in all who proclaim your word to others. Help that word to bring comfort to the troubled, hope to the sorrowful, and life to the dead.

Thursday, May 27, 2021
Time after Pentecost

John Calvin, renewer of the church, died 1564

Psalm 29
Worship God in holiness

Ascribe to the LORD, O heavenly beings,
    ascribe to the LORD glory and strength.
Ascribe to the LORD the glory of his name;
    worship the LORD in holy splendor.

The voice of the LORD is over the waters;
    the God of glory thunders,
    the LORD, over mighty waters.
The voice of the LORD is powerful;
    the voice of the LORD is full of majesty. (Ps. 29:1-4)

Additional Readings

Isaiah 1:1-4, 16-20
A vision concerning God's people

Romans 8:1-8
The Spirit is life and peace

Hymn: All Glory Be to God on High, ELW 410

God of all, you are worthy of our praise and worship. Move us to praise you with both our words and our actions. Make us bold to proclaim your name. Help us worship you in all times and places.

Friday, May 28, 2021
Time after Pentecost

Romans 8:9-11

The Spirit dwells in you

But you are not in the flesh; you are in the Spirit, since the Spirit of God dwells in you. Anyone who does not have the Spirit of Christ does not belong to him. But if Christ is in you, though the body is dead because of sin, the Spirit is life because of righteousness. If the Spirit of him who raised Jesus from the dead dwells in you, he who raised Christ from the dead will give life to your mortal bodies also through his Spirit that dwells in you. (Rom. 8:9-11)

Psalm

Psalm 29
Worship God in holiness

Additional Reading

Isaiah 2:1-5
A vision concerning God's people

Hymn: Awake, O Sleeper, Rise from Death, ELW 452

God of hope, your spirit strengthens us and stirs up faith within us. As we die to sin, raise us to new life in Christ. Guide our lives so that others may see your spirit at work in us.

Saturday, May 29, 2021
Time after Pentecost

Jiří Třanovský, hymnwriter, died 1637

John 15:18-20, 26-27

Testify in the face of persecution

[Jesus said,] "When the Advocate comes, whom I will send to you from the Father, the Spirit of truth who comes from the Father, he will testify on my behalf. You also are to testify because you have been with me from the beginning." (John 15:26-27)

Psalm

Psalm 29
Worship God in holiness

Additional Reading

Isaiah 5:15-24
A vision concerning God's people

Hymn: Gracious Spirit, Heed Our Pleading, ELW 401

Empowering God, you strengthen the weak and give courage to the faint-hearted. When we are scared to proclaim your name, make us bold by your spirit. Give us the energy and confidence we need to share your message with others.

Time after Pentecost
Summer

The weeks and months following the Day of Pentecost coincide with the natural seasons of summer, autumn, and late autumn/November. Christian communities refer to this time in different ways. Whatever name is used to describe the many weeks between Pentecost and Christ the King (the last Sunday of the church year), the seasons and calendars of North America offer some distinctive periods through which we may shape prayer in the household.

The Day of Pentecost is celebrated close to the end of the school year. A connection exists between graduations/new beginnings and our prayer for the Spirit's guidance in new endeavors. For many people, the months of June, July, and August signal a slightly altered schedule attuned to the weather, harvests, and vacations. Summer months offer their unique grace to those who spend time in discerning the many images which link the scriptures and the patient growth of the seed in the soil.

Table Prayer for Summer

The earth is the LORD's and all that is in it,
the world, and those who live in it. (Ps. 24:1)

All here gathered, food from the land,
all is gift from your gracious hand.
Feed us today; feed all those who hunger;
teach us to feed one another.
We ask this in the name of the one who is our bread, Jesus Christ.
Amen.

Sunday, May 30, 2021
The Holy Trinity

John 3:1-17

Entering the reign of God

Nicodemus said to [Jesus], "How can anyone be born after having grown old? Can one enter a second time into the mother's womb and be born?" Jesus answered, "Very truly, I tell you, no one can enter the kingdom of God without being born of water and Spirit. What is born of the flesh is flesh, and what is born of the Spirit is spirit. Do not be astonished that I said to you, 'You must be born from above.' The wind blows where it chooses, and you hear the sound of it, but you do not know where it comes from or where it goes. So it is with everyone who is born of the Spirit." (John 3:4-8)

Psalm

Psalm 29
Worship God in holiness

Additional Readings

Isaiah 6:1-8
Isaiah's vision and call

Romans 8:12-17
Living by the Spirit

Hymn: Holy, Holy, Holy, Lord God Almighty! ELW 413

God of heaven and earth, before the foundation of the universe and the beginning of time you are the triune God: Author of creation, eternal Word of salvation, life-giving Spirit of wisdom. Guide us to all truth by your Spirit, that we may proclaim all that Christ has revealed and rejoice in the glory he shares with us. Glory and praise to you, Father, Son, and Holy Spirit, now and forever.

Monday, May 31, 2021
Visit of Mary to Elizabeth

Luke 1:39-57

Mary greets Elizabeth

In those days Mary set out and went with haste to a Judean town in the hill country, where she entered the house of Zechariah and greeted Elizabeth. When Elizabeth heard Mary's greeting, the child leaped in her womb. And Elizabeth was filled with the Holy Spirit and exclaimed with a loud cry, "Blessed are you among women, and blessed is the fruit of your womb." (Luke 1:39-42)

Psalm

Psalm 113
God, the helper of the needy

Additional Readings

1 Samuel 2:1-10
Hannah's thanksgiving

Romans 12:9-16b
Rejoice with those who rejoice

Hymn: Unexpected and Mysterious, ELW 258

Mighty God, by whose grace Elizabeth rejoiced with Mary and greeted her as the mother of the Lord: look with favor on your lowly servants that, with Mary, we may magnify your holy name and rejoice to acclaim her Son as our Savior, who lives and reigns with you and the Holy Spirit, one God, now and forever.

Prayer List for June

_____

_____

_____

_____

_____

_____

_____

_____

Tuesday, June 1, 2021
Time after Pentecost

Justin, martyr at Rome, died around 165

1 Corinthians 2:1-10
God's wisdom revealed through the Spirit

When I came to you, brothers and sisters, I did not come proclaiming the mystery of God to you in lofty words or wisdom. For I decided to know nothing among you except Jesus Christ, and him crucified. And I came to you in weakness and in fear and in much trembling. My speech and my proclamation were not with plausible words of wisdom, but with a demonstration of the Spirit and of power, so that your faith might rest not on human wisdom but on the power of God. (1 Cor. 2:1-5)

Psalm
Psalm 20
The name of God

Additional Reading
Exodus 25:1-22
God in the ark and its mercy seat

Hymn: Holy Spirit, Ever Dwelling, ELW 582

Almighty God, you spoke and the world came to be. Your words move hearts and minds. Inspire us with your eternal word that we may live lives of power focusing on your son, Jesus Christ.

Wednesday, June 2, 2021
Time after Pentecost

Numbers 6:22-27
Aaronic blessing

The Lord spoke to Moses, saying: Speak to Aaron and his sons, saying,
Thus you shall bless the Israelites: You shall say to them,

> The Lord bless you and keep you;
> the Lord make his face to shine upon you, and be gracious to you;
> the Lord lift up his countenance upon you, and give you peace.

So they shall put my name on the Israelites, and I will bless them.
(Num. 6:22-27)

Psalm
Psalm 20
The name of God

Additional Reading
Mark 4:21-25
Secrets come to light

Hymn: Lord, Dismiss Us with Your Blessing, ELW 545

O Lord, you delivered Israel out of slavery and led them to the promised land. What you bless stays blessed. Keep us close and shine upon the way. Show us your face and be our peace.

Thursday, June 3, 2021
Time after Pentecost

The Martyrs of Uganda, died 1886
John XXIII, Bishop of Rome, died 1963

Psalm 130
With you there is forgiveness

Out of the depths I cry to you, O LORD.
    LORD, hear my voice!
Let your ears be attentive
    to the voice of my supplications!

If you, O LORD, should mark iniquities,
    LORD, who could stand?
But there is forgiveness with you,
    so that you may be revered. (Ps. 130:1-4)

Additional Readings
Isaiah 28:9-13
The people of God refuse to hear

1 Peter 4:7-19
Entrusting ourselves to a faithful Creator

Hymn: Listen, God Is Calling, ELW 513

O God, the summit of our existence. We look to you in hope from the valleys of our lives. Come join us where we are. Turn our cries to you into heartfelt comfort and knowledge of your grace and love.

Friday, June 4, 2021
Time after Pentecost

2 Corinthians 5:1-5

What is mortal is swallowed up in life

For we know that if the earthly tent we live in is destroyed, we have a building from God, a house not made with hands, eternal in the heavens. For in this tent we groan, longing to be clothed with our heavenly dwelling—if indeed, when we have taken it off we will not be found naked. For while we are still in this tent, we groan under our burden, because we wish not to be unclothed but to be further clothed, so that what is mortal may be swallowed up by life. He who has prepared us for this very thing is God, who has given us the Spirit as a guarantee. (2 Cor. 5:1-5)

Psalm

Psalm 130
With you there is forgiveness

Additional Reading

Deuteronomy 1:34-40
The innocent enter the good land

Hymn: Built on a Rock, ELW 652

God of grace, in holy baptism you clothed us entirely with the everlasting love of Christ. We have not only been united with him in death but in resurrection and new life. Turn our groans of longing into joyful praise.

Saturday, June 5, 2021
Time after Pentecost

Boniface, Bishop of Mainz, missionary to Germany, martyr, died 754

Genesis 2:4b-14
The tree of knowledge

In the day that the LORD God made the earth and the heavens, when no plant of the field was yet in the earth and no herb of the field had yet sprung up—for the LORD God had not caused it to rain upon the earth, and there was no one to till the ground; but a stream would rise from the earth, and water the whole face of the ground—then the LORD God formed man from the dust of the ground, and breathed into his nostrils the breath of life; and the man became a living being. And the LORD God planted a garden in Eden, in the east; and there he put the man whom he had formed. Out of the ground the LORD God made to grow every tree that is pleasant to the sight and good for food, the tree of life also in the midst of the garden, and the tree of the knowledge of good and evil. (Gen. 2:4b-9)

Psalm
Psalm 130
With you there is forgiveness

Additional Reading
Luke 8:4-15
Hearing and living the word of God

Hymn: Lord, Let My Heart Be Good Soil, ELW 512

Lord of all creation, your holy breath is the air we breathe to live. You brought forth the life of growing things to sustain us. Just like your first garden may we too bear fruit that brings life to the world.

Sunday, June 6, 2021
Time after Pentecost

Mark 3:20-35

Doing the work of God

Then [Jesus'] mother and his brothers came; and standing outside, they sent to him and called him. A crowd was sitting around him; and they said to him, "Your mother and your brothers and sisters are outside, asking for you." And he replied, "Who are my mother and my brothers?" And looking at those who sat around him, he said, "Here are my mother and my brothers! Whoever does the will of God is my brother and sister and mother." (Mark 3:31-35)

Psalm

Psalm 130
With you there is forgiveness

Additional Readings

Genesis 3:8-15
God confronts Adam and Eve

2 Corinthians 4:13—5:1
Renewed in the inner nature

Hymn: Joyful, Joyful We Adore Thee, ELW 836

All-powerful God, in Jesus Christ you turned death into life and defeat into victory. Increase our faith and trust in him, that we may triumph over all evil in the strength of the same Jesus Christ, our Savior and Lord.

Monday, June 7, 2021
Time after Pentecost

Seattle, chief of the Duwamish Confederacy, died 1866

Psalm 74
God will save us from the enemy

O God, why do you cast us off forever?
>   Why does your anger smoke against the sheep of your pasture?
Remember your congregation, which you acquired long ago,
>   which you redeemed to be the tribe of your heritage.
>   Remember Mount Zion, where you came to dwell.
Direct your steps to the perpetual ruins;
>   the enemy has destroyed everything in the sanctuary. (Ps. 74:1-3)

Additional Readings
1 Samuel 16:14-23
David calms Saul's evil spirit

Revelation 20:1-6
The first resurrection

Hymn: O God of Love, O King of Peace, ELW 749

God of righteousness and justice, we often fear your absence in difficult times. This we know: you do not forget the children of your hands and the apples of your eye. Keep us ever mindful of your saving love for us.

Tuesday, June 8, 2021
Time after Pentecost

Revelation 20:7-15
Satan's doom

When the thousand years are ended, Satan will be released from his prison and will come out to deceive the nations at the four corners of the earth, Gog and Magog, in order to gather them for battle; they are as numerous as the sands of the sea. They marched up over the breadth of the earth and surrounded the camp of the saints and the beloved city. And fire came down from heaven and consumed them. And the devil who had deceived them was thrown into the lake of fire and sulfur, where the beast and the false prophet were, and they will be tormented day and night forever and ever. (Rev. 20:7-10)

Psalm
Psalm 74
God will save us from the enemy

Additional Reading
1 Kings 18:17-40
Elijah destroys the evil prophets

Hymn: If You But Trust in God to Guide You, ELW 769

Victorious God, your word promises that you will win the day at the end of the ages. Give us comfort in your strength and help us trust in you when we too feel under attack by all that life brings.

Wednesday, June 9, 2021
Time after Pentecost

Columba, died 597; Aidan, died 651; Bede, died 735; renewers of the church

Luke 11:14-28
Jesus and Beelzebul

Now [Jesus] was casting out a demon that was mute; when the demon had gone out, the one who had been mute spoke, and the crowds were amazed. But some of them said, "He casts out demons by Beelzebul, the ruler of the demons." Others, to test him, kept demanding from him a sign from heaven. But he knew what they were thinking and said to them, "Every kingdom divided against itself becomes a desert, and house falls on house. If Satan also is divided against himself, how will his kingdom stand?—for you say that I cast out the demons by Beelzebul. Now if I cast out the demons by Beelzebul, by whom do your exorcists cast them out? Therefore they will be your judges." (Luke 11:14-19)

Psalm
Psalm 74
God will save us from the enemy

Additional Reading
Isaiah 26:16—27:1
God destroys Leviathan

Hymn: Abide, O Dearest Jesus, ELW 539

O Ruler of heavens and the earth, we have so often been caught up in division. Unite us in our service to you. Drive out our own personal demons and lead us on the path of healing in your name.

Thursday, June 10, 2021
Time after Pentecost

Psalm 92:1-4, 12-15
The righteous are like a cedar of Lebanon

The righteous flourish like the palm tree,
> and grow like a cedar in Lebanon.
They are planted in the house of the Lord;
> they flourish in the courts of our God.
In old age they still produce fruit;
> they are always green and full of sap,
showing that the Lord is upright;
> he is my rock, and there is no unrighteousness in him.
(Ps. 92:12-15)

Additional Readings
Genesis 3:14-24
Deprived of the tree of life

Hebrews 2:5-9
Christ tastes death for everyone

Hymn: Be Thou My Vision, ELW 793

Divine foundation of our lives, may we find our place in your house and in your courts. Feed us with your love that we may grow in you and produce fruits of righteousness. May those fruits be blessings to the world.

Friday, June 11, 2021
Barnabas, Apostle

Acts 11:19-30; 13:1-3
Barnabas and Saul are set apart

Now in the church at Antioch there were prophets and teachers: Barnabas, Simeon who was called Niger, Lucius of Cyrene, Manaen a member of the court of Herod the ruler, and Saul. While they were worshiping the Lord and fasting, the Holy Spirit said, "Set apart for me Barnabas and Saul for the work to which I have called them." Then after fasting and praying they laid their hands on them and sent them off. (Acts 13:1-3)

Psalm

Psalm 112
Happy are the God-fearing

Additional Readings

Isaiah 42:5-12
The Lord calls us in righteousness

Matthew 10:7-16
Jesus sends out the Twelve

Hymn: O Zion, Haste, ELW 668

We praise you, O God, for the life of your faithful servant Barnabas, who, seeking not his own renown but the well-being of your church, gave generously of his life and possessions for the relief of the poor and the spread of the gospel. Grant that we may follow his example and by our actions give glory to you, Father, Son, and Holy Spirit, now and forever.

Saturday, June 12, 2021
Time after Pentecost

Mark 4:1-20
The parable of the sower

[Jesus said,] "Listen! A sower went out to sow. And as he sowed, some seed fell on the path, and the birds came and ate it up. Other seed fell on rocky ground, where it did not have much soil, and it sprang up quickly, since it had no depth of soil. And when the sun rose, it was scorched; and since it had no root, it withered away. Other seed fell among thorns, and the thorns grew up and choked it, and it yielded no grain. Other seed fell into good soil and brought forth grain, growing up and increasing and yielding thirty and sixty and a hundredfold." And he said, "Let anyone with ears to hear listen!" (Mark 4:3-9)

Psalm
Psalm 92:1-4, 12-15
The righteous are like a cedar of Lebanon

Additional Reading
2 Kings 14:1-14
A thornbush confronts a cedar of Lebanon

Hymn: Almighty God, Your Word Is Cast, ELW 516

Great sower of faith, you shower us again and again with the seeds of your love. Enable us to be fertile soil for your word. Give us shade and cut back the thorns of life. Nurture our growth in you.

.

Sunday, June 13, 2021
Time after Pentecost

Mark 4:26-34
The parable of the mustard seed

[Jesus] also said, "With what can we compare the kingdom of God, or what parable will we use for it? It is like a mustard seed, which, when sown upon the ground, is the smallest of all the seeds on earth; yet when it is sown it grows up and becomes the greatest of all shrubs, and puts forth large branches, so that the birds of the air can make nests in its shade." (Mark 4:30-32)

Psalm
Psalm 92:1-4, 12-15
The righteous are like a cedar of Lebanon

Additional Readings
Ezekiel 17:22-24
The sign of the cedar

2 Corinthians 5:6-10 [11-13] 14-17
In Christ, a new creation

Hymn: Lord, Your Hands Have Formed, ELW 554

O God, you are the tree of life, offering shelter to all the world. Graft us into yourself and nurture our growth, that we may bear your truth and love to those in need, through Jesus Christ, our Savior and Lord.

Monday, June 14, 2021
Time after Pentecost

Basil the Great, Bishop of Caesarea, died 379; Gregory, Bishop of Nyssa, died around 385; Gregory of Nazianzus, Bishop of Constantinople, died around 389; Macrina, teacher, died around 379

Psalm 52
Like an olive tree in God's house

Why do you boast, O mighty one,
>	of mischief done against the godly?
>	All day long you are plotting destruction.
Your tongue is like a sharp razor,
>	you worker of treachery.
You love evil more than good,
>	and lying more than speaking the truth.
You love all words that devour,
>	O deceitful tongue.

But God will break you down forever;
>	he will snatch and tear you from your tent;
>	he will uproot you from the land of the living. (Ps. 52:1-5)

Additional Readings
Ezekiel 31:1-12
Evil can be a towering cedar

Galatians 6:11-18
A new creation is everything

Hymn: When I Survey the Wondrous Cross, ELW 803

Loving God, there are times in our lives when we are so self-destructive. Sometimes we cannot even admit that to ourselves. Hold us close and love us back into the relationship we seek to have with you.

Tuesday, June 15, 2021
Time after Pentecost

Revelation 21:22—22:5
The tree of life

Then the angel showed me the river of the water of life, bright as crystal, flowing from the throne of God and of the Lamb through the middle of the street of the city. On either side of the river is the tree of life with its twelve kinds of fruit, producing its fruit each month; and the leaves of the tree are for the healing of the nations. Nothing accursed will be found there any more. But the throne of God and of the Lamb will be in it, and his servants will worship him; they will see his face, and his name will be on their foreheads. And there will be no more night; they need no light of lamp or sun, for the Lord God will be their light, and they will reign forever and ever. (Rev. 22:1-5)

Psalm
Psalm 52
Like an olive tree in God's house

Additional Reading
Jeremiah 21:11-14
A fire in Judah's forest

Hymn: O Day Full of Grace, ELW 627

God our light, you are not content to leave us hungry and cut off from you. Lead us to your gifts of love and grace. Feed us all with good things and help us bring your healing to the nations.

Wednesday, June 16, 2021
Time after Pentecost

Luke 6:43-45

A tree and its fruit

[Jesus said,] "No good tree bears bad fruit, nor again does a bad tree bear good fruit; for each tree is known by its own fruit. Figs are not gathered from thorns, nor are grapes picked from a bramble bush. The good person out of the good treasure of the heart produces good, and the evil person out of evil treasure produces evil; for it is out of the abundance of the heart that the mouth speaks." (Luke 6:43-45)

Psalm
Psalm 52
Like an olive tree in God's house

Additional Reading
Jeremiah 22:1-9
The evil will be cut down

Hymn: Lord of Glory, You Have Bought Us, ELW 707

God of the harvest, you have planted in us knowledge of your teachings and your love. Prune away the parts of us that get in the way so that we may bear good fruit in your name.

Thursday, June 17, 2021
Time after Pentecost

Emanuel Nine, martyrs, died 2015

Psalm 107:1-3, 23-32
God stilled the storm

Then they cried to the LORD in their trouble,
    and he brought them out from their distress;
he made the storm be still,
    and the waves of the sea were hushed.
Then they were glad because they had quiet,
    and he brought them to their desired haven.
Let them thank the LORD for his steadfast love,
    for his wonderful works to humankind.
Let them extol him in the congregation of the people,
    and praise him in the assembly of the elders. (Ps. 107:28-32)

Additional Readings
Job 29:1-20
Job makes his defense

Acts 20:1-16
Paul's travels

Hymn: Jesus, Savior, Pilot Me, ELW 755

Lord God, you are worthy of our praise. You have brought us out of many times of trouble. Strengthen our voices when we would be silent. Lift our hearts in thankfulness for all you've done.

Friday, June 18, 2021
Time after Pentecost

Acts 21:1-16
Paul is warned about future persecution

While we were staying [in Caesarea] for several days, a prophet named Agabus came down from Judea. He came to us and took Paul's belt, bound his own feet and hands with it, and said, "Thus says the Holy Spirit, 'This is the way the Jews in Jerusalem will bind the man who owns this belt and will hand him over to the Gentiles.'" When we heard this, we and the people there urged him not to go up to Jerusalem. Then Paul answered, "What are you doing, weeping and breaking my heart? For I am ready not only to be bound but even to die in Jerusalem for the name of the Lord Jesus." Since he would not be persuaded, we remained silent except to say, "The Lord's will be done." (Acts 21:10-14)

Psalm
Psalm 107:1-3, 23-32
God stilled the storm

Additional Reading
Job 29:21—30:15
Job laments his losses

Hymn: Our Father, God in Heaven Above, ELW 746/747

God of freedom, you have bound yourself to us in Jesus your son. May we see signs of you in the times when we are in bondage of any kind. Break those bonds and lead us into a new freedom in you.

Saturday, June 19, 2021
Time after Pentecost

Luke 21:25-28
The roaring of the sea and the waves

[Jesus said,] "There will be signs in the sun, the moon, and the stars, and on the earth distress among nations confused by the roaring of the sea and the waves. People will faint from fear and foreboding of what is coming upon the world, for the powers of the heavens will be shaken. Then they will see 'the Son of Man coming in a cloud' with power and great glory. Now when these things begin to take place, stand up and raise your heads, because your redemption is drawing near." (Luke 21:25-28)

Psalm
Psalm 107:1-3, 23-32
God stilled the storm

Additional Reading
Job 37:1-13
Elihu extols God's power

Hymn: Lo! He Comes with Clouds Descending, ELW 435

God of calm within the storm, we see signs all around us that cause fear. Draw us away from our worries so that in all we do we may see Jesus coming ever closer to us.

Sunday, June 20, 2021
Time after Pentecost

Mark 4:35-41
Christ calming the sea

On that day, when evening had come, [Jesus] said to [his disciples], "Let us go across to the other side." And leaving the crowd behind, they took him with them in the boat, just as he was. Other boats were with him. A great windstorm arose, and the waves beat into the boat, so that the boat was already being swamped. But he was in the stern, asleep on the cushion; and they woke him up and said to him, "Teacher, do you not care that we are perishing?" He woke up and rebuked the wind, and said to the sea, "Peace! Be still!" Then the wind ceased, and there was a dead calm. He said to them, "Why are you afraid? Have you still no faith?" And they were filled with great awe and said to one another, "Who then is this, that even the wind and the sea obey him?" (Mark 4:35-41)

Psalm
Psalm 107:1-3, 23-32
God stilled the storm

Additional Readings
Job 38:1-11
The Creator of earth and sea

2 Corinthians 6:1-13
Paul's defense of his ministry

Hymn: Eternal Father, Strong to Save, ELW 756

O God of creation, eternal majesty, you preside over land and sea, sunshine and storm. By your strength pilot us, by your power preserve us, by your wisdom instruct us, and by your hand protect us, through Jesus Christ, our Savior and Lord.

Monday, June 21, 2021
Time after Pentecost

Onesimos Nesib, translator, evangelist, died 1931

Psalm 65
God silences the seas

By awesome deeds you answer us with deliverance,
    O God of our salvation;
you are the hope of all the ends of the earth
    and of the farthest seas.
By your strength you established the mountains;
    you are girded with might.
You silence the roaring of the seas,
    the roaring of their waves,
    the tumult of the peoples.
Those who live at earth's farthest bounds are awed by your signs;
you make the gateways of the morning and the evening shout for joy.
(Ps. 65:5-8)

Additional Readings
Exodus 7:14-24
God turns the Nile into blood

Acts 27:13-38
Paul and the storm at sea

Hymn: Praise and Thanksgiving, ELW 689

God, our hope and our strength, you have delivered us in the past and you shine like the sun today. Show us the way to you and bring your children together from all the ends of the earth.

Tuesday, June 22, 2021
Time after Pentecost

Exodus 9:13-35
God sends hail

The LORD said to Moses, "Stretch out your hand toward heaven so that hail may fall on the whole land of Egypt, on humans and animals and all the plants of the field in the land of Egypt." Then Moses stretched out his staff toward heaven, and the LORD sent thunder and hail, and fire came down on the earth. And the LORD rained hail on the land of Egypt; there was hail with fire flashing continually in the midst of it, such heavy hail as had never fallen in all the land of Egypt since it became a nation. The hail struck down everything that was in the open field throughout all the land of Egypt, both human and animal; the hail also struck down all the plants of the field, and shattered every tree in the field. Only in the land of Goshen, where the Israelites were, there was no hail. (Exod. 9:22-26)

Psalm
Psalm 65
God silences the seas

Additional Reading
Acts 27:39-44
Safe arrival on land

Hymn: On Our Way Rejoicing, ELW 537

Eternal Creator, we know you can control the elements of the world you made. We have also experienced the awesome power of nature in our lives. Protect us in stormy times and guide us to keep our eyes focused on you.

Wednesday, June 23, 2021
Time after Pentecost

Mark 6:45-52

Jesus walks on the water

When evening came, the boat was out on the sea, and [Jesus] was alone on the land. When he saw that [the disciples] were straining at the oars against an adverse wind, he came towards them early in the morning, walking on the sea. He intended to pass them by. But when they saw him walking on the sea, they thought it was a ghost and cried out; for they all saw him and were terrified. But immediately he spoke to them and said, "Take heart, it is I; do not be afraid." Then he got into the boat with them and the wind ceased. And they were utterly astounded, for they did not understand about the loaves, but their hearts were hardened. (Mark 6:47-52)

Psalm
Psalm 65
God silences the seas

Additional Reading
Joshua 10:1-14
God makes the sun stand still

Hymn: God of the Sparrow, ELW 740

God of our heart, Jesus and your angels proclaim your message over and over for us not to be afraid. When the chaos and uncertainties of life paralyze us in fear, don't pass us by. Stop and give us strength to take heart.

Thursday, June 24, 2021
John the Baptist

Luke 1:57-67 [68-80]
The birth and naming of John

On the eighth day [Elizabeth and her neighbors and relatives] came to circumcise the child, and they were going to name him Zechariah after his father. But his mother said, "No; he is to be called John." They said to her, "None of your relatives has this name." Then they began motioning to his father to find out what name he wanted to give him. He asked for a writing tablet and wrote, "His name is John." And all of them were amazed. Immediately his mouth was opened and his tongue freed, and he began to speak, praising God. (Luke 1:59-64)

Psalm
Psalm 141
My eyes are turned to God

Additional Readings
Malachi 3:1-4
My messenger, a refiner and purifier

Acts 13:13-26
The gospel for the descendants of Abraham

Hymn: Blessed Be the God of Israel, ELW 552

Almighty God, by your gracious providence your servant John the Baptist was born to Elizabeth and Zechariah. Grant to your people the wisdom to see your purpose and the openness to hear your will, that the light of Christ may increase in us, through Jesus Christ, our Savior and Lord, who lives and reigns with you and the Holy Spirit, one God, now and forever.

Friday, June 25, 2021
Time after Pentecost

Presentation of the Augsburg Confession, 1530
Philipp Melanchthon, renewer of the church, died 1560

2 Corinthians 8:1-7
Encouragement to be generous

We want you to know, brothers and sisters, about the grace of God that has been granted to the churches of Macedonia; for during a severe ordeal of affliction, their abundant joy and their extreme poverty have overflowed in a wealth of generosity on their part. For, as I can testify, they voluntarily gave according to their means, and even beyond their means, begging us earnestly for the privilege of sharing in this ministry to the saints—and this, not merely as we expected; they gave themselves first to the Lord and, by the will of God, to us, so that we might urge Titus that, as he had already made a beginning, so he should also complete this generous undertaking among you. Now as you excel in everything—in faith, in speech, in knowledge, in utmost eagerness, and in our love for you—so we want you to excel also in this generous undertaking. (2 Cor. 8:1-7)

Psalm
Psalm 30
You have lifted me up

Additional Reading
Lamentations 2:1-12
God's warnings fulfilled

Hymn: God, Whose Giving Knows No Ending, ELW 678

God, in you we find true abundance. We often take your gifts for granted and enjoy them only for ourselves. Inspire us to trust that your gifts are limitless and encourage us to share with others the wealth we have from you.

Saturday, June 26, 2021
Time after Pentecost

Lamentations 2:18-22
Pour out your heart before God

Cry aloud to the Lord!
    O wall of daughter Zion!
Let tears stream down like a torrent
    day and night!
Give yourself no rest,
    your eyes no respite!

Arise, cry out in the night,
    at the beginning of the watches!
Pour out your heart like water
    before the presence of the Lord!
Lift your hands to him for the lives of your children,
    who faint for hunger at the head of every street. (Lam. 2:18-19)

Psalm
Psalm 30
You have lifted me up

Additional Reading
Luke 4:31-37
The man with an unclean spirit

Hymn: Lost in the Night, ELW 243

God of laughter, God of tears, you are with us in the ups and downs of life. Help us to find strength in crying out and to trust that you hear us and listen to us. Help us to let go and embrace you.

Sunday, June 27, 2021
Time after Pentecost

Cyril, Bishop of Alexandria, died 444

Mark 5:21-43
Christ heals a woman and Jairus's daughter

While [Jesus] was still speaking, some people came from the leader's house to say, "Your daughter is dead. Why trouble the teacher any further?" But overhearing what they said, Jesus said to the leader of the synagogue, "Do not fear, only believe." He allowed no one to follow him except Peter, James, and John, the brother of James. When they came to the house of the leader of the synagogue, he saw a commotion, people weeping and wailing loudly. When he had entered, he said to them, "Why do you make a commotion and weep? The child is not dead but sleeping." (Mark 5:35-39)

Psalm
Psalm 30
You have lifted me up

Additional Readings
Lamentations 3:22-33
Great is God's faithfulness

2 Corinthians 8:7-15
Excel in generosity, following Jesus

Hymn: We Come to You for Healing, Lord, ELW 617

Almighty and merciful God, we implore you to hear the prayers of your people. Be our strong defense against all harm and danger, that we may live and grow in faith and hope, through Jesus Christ, our Savior and Lord.

Monday, June 28, 2021
Time after Pentecost

Irenaeus, Bishop of Lyons, died around 202

Psalm 88
Prayer for restoration

O LORD, why do you cast me off?
    Why do you hide your face from me?
Wretched and close to death from my youth up,
    I suffer your terrors; I am desperate.
Your wrath has swept over me;
    your dread assaults destroy me.
They surround me like a flood all day long;
    from all sides they close in on me.
You have caused friend and neighbor to shun me;
    my companions are in darkness. (Ps. 88:14-18)

Additional Readings
Leviticus 21:1-15   **2 Corinthians 8:16-24**
Dead bodies are unclean   *The administration of generous gifts*

Hymn: My Faith Looks Up to Thee, ELW 759

*Hidden God, life with trauma and stress so often keeps us from seeing
your face. Break through all that would keep us apart and shine your
countenance upon us. Be the light we so desperately need.*

Tuesday, June 29, 2021
Peter and Paul, Apostles

John 21:15-19

Jesus says to Peter: Tend my sheep

When they had finished breakfast, Jesus said to Simon Peter, "Simon son of John, do you love me more than these?" He said to him, "Yes, Lord; you know that I love you." Jesus said to him, "Feed my lambs." A second time he said to him, "Simon son of John, do you love me?" He said to him, "Yes, Lord; you know that I love you." Jesus said to him, "Tend my sheep." He said to him the third time, "Simon son of John, do you love me?" Peter felt hurt because he said to him the third time, "Do you love me?" And he said to him, "Lord, you know everything; you know that I love you." Jesus said to him, "Feed my sheep. Very truly, I tell you, when you were younger, you used to fasten your own belt and to go wherever you wished. But when you grow old, you will stretch out your hands, and someone else will fasten a belt around you and take you where you do not wish to go." (John 21:15-18)

Psalm

Psalm 87:1-3, 5-7
Glorious things are spoken of you

Additional Readings

Acts 12:1-11
Peter released from prison

2 Timothy 4:6-8, 17-18
The good fight of faith

Hymn: Faith of Our Fathers, ELW 812

Almighty God, we praise you that your blessed apostles Peter and Paul glorified you by their martyrdoms. Grant that your church throughout the world may always be instructed by their teaching and example, be knit together in unity by your Spirit, and ever stand firm upon the one foundation who is Jesus Christ our Lord, for he lives and reigns with you and the Holy Spirit, one God, now and forever.

Wednesday, June 30, 2021
Time after Pentecost

2 Kings 20:1-11
God heals Hezekiah

Hezekiah said to Isaiah, "What shall be the sign that the LORD will heal me, and that I shall go up to the house of the LORD on the third day?" Isaiah said, "This is the sign to you from the LORD, that the LORD will do the thing that he has promised: the shadow has now advanced ten intervals; shall it retreat ten intervals?" Hezekiah answered, "It is normal for the shadow to lengthen ten intervals; rather let the shadow retreat ten intervals." The prophet Isaiah cried to the LORD; and he brought the shadow back the ten intervals, by which the sun had declined on the dial of Ahaz. (2 Kings 20:8-11)

Psalm
Psalm 88
Prayer for restoration

Additional Reading
Mark 9:14-29
Jesus heals a child

Hymn: Where Cross the Crowded Ways of Life, ELW 719

God, the time is now for you to bring your healing power to bear in our lives. We are impatient because we trust in you to make us whole. Give us patience to be ready as you hurry to our aid.

Prayer List for July

_____

_____

_____

_____

_____

_____

_____

_____

_____

Thursday, July 1, 2021
Time after Pentecost

Catherine Winkworth, died 1878; John Mason Neale, died 1866; hymn translators

Psalm 123
Our eyes look to you, O God

To you I lift up my eyes,
> O you who are enthroned in the heavens!
As the eyes of servants
> look to the hand of their master,
as the eyes of a maid
> to the hand of her mistress,
so our eyes look to the LORD our God,
> until he has mercy upon us.

Have mercy upon us, O LORD, have mercy upon us,
> for we have had more than enough of contempt.
Our soul has had more than its fill
> of the scorn of those who are at ease,
> of the contempt of the proud. (Ps. 123:1-4)

Additional Readings
Jeremiah 7:1-15
Do not trust deceptive words

1 Corinthians 4:8-13
We are weak, but you are strong

Hymn: Rise, O Sun of Righteousness, ELW 657

Life-giving God, you provide everything that we have. When we are selfish and cling to possessions, time, or influence, kindle gratitude in us. Reveal to us the many ways that you are calling us to serve our neighbors and your world.

Friday, July 2, 2021
Time after Pentecost

2 Corinthians 10:7-11
Paul's bodily presence is weak

Look at what is before your eyes. If you are confident that you belong to Christ, remind yourself of this, that just as you belong to Christ, so also do we. Now, even if I boast a little too much of our authority, which the Lord gave for building you up and not for tearing you down, I will not be ashamed of it. I do not want to seem as though I am trying to frighten you with my letters. For they say, "His letters are weighty and strong, but his bodily presence is weak, and his speech contemptible." Let such people understand that what we say by letter when absent, we will also do when present. (2 Cor. 10:7-11)

Psalm
Psalm 123
Our eyes look to you, O God

Additional Reading
Jeremiah 7:16-26
Walk in the way God commands

Hymn: Just a Closer Walk with Thee, ELW 697

Dear God, your word indicts and reveals our weakness, but at times we get stuck in shame. Free us with your promise to boldly proclaim the freedom of your gospel, so that our lives may bear witness to your transforming presence in our lives and the world.

Saturday, July 3, 2021
Thomas, Apostle

John 14:1-7

Jesus, the way, the truth, the life

Thomas said to [Jesus], "Lord, we do not know where you are going. How can we know the way?" Jesus said to him, "I am the way, and the truth, and the life. No one comes to the Father except through me. If you know me, you will know my Father also. From now on you do know him and have seen him." (John 14:5-7)

Psalm

Psalm 136:1-4, 23-26
God's mercy endures forever

Additional Readings

Judges 6:36-40
God affirms Gideon's calling

Ephesians 4:11-16
The body of Christ has various gifts

Hymn: O Sons and Daughters, Let Us Sing, ELW 386

Ever-living God, you strengthened your apostle Thomas with firm and certain faith in the resurrection of your Son. Grant that we too may confess our faith in Jesus Christ, our Lord and our God, who lives and reigns with you and the Holy Spirit, one God, now and forever.

Sunday, July 4, 2021
Time after Pentecost

Mark 6:1-13
The Twelve sent to preach and heal

[Jesus] called the twelve and began to send them out two by two, and gave them authority over the unclean spirits. He ordered them to take nothing for their journey except a staff; no bread, no bag, no money in their belts; but to wear sandals and not to put on two tunics. He said to them, "Wherever you enter a house, stay there until you leave the place. If any place will not welcome you and they refuse to hear you, as you leave, shake off the dust that is on your feet as a testimony against them." So they went out and proclaimed that all should repent. They cast out many demons, and anointed with oil many who were sick and cured them. (Mark 6:7-13)

Psalm

Psalm 123
Our eyes look to you, O God

Additional Readings

Ezekiel 2:1-5
The call of Ezekiel

2 Corinthians 12:2-10
God's power made perfect in weakness

Hymn: Healer of Our Every Ill, ELW 612

God of the covenant, in our baptism you call us to proclaim the coming of your kingdom. Give us the courage you gave the apostles, that we may faithfully witness to your love and peace in every circumstance of life, in the name of Jesus Christ, our Savior and Lord.

Monday, July 5, 2021
Time after Pentecost

Psalm 119:81-88
The faithful persecuted

How long must your servant endure?
> When will you judge those who persecute me?
The arrogant have dug pitfalls for me;
> they flout your law.
All your commandments are enduring;
> I am persecuted without cause; help me!
They have almost made an end of me on earth;
> but I have not forsaken your precepts.
In your steadfast love spare my life,
> so that I may keep the decrees of your mouth. (Ps. 119:84-88)

Additional Readings
Ezekiel 2:8—3:11
Ezekiel to eat the scroll

2 Corinthians 11:16-33
Paul's sufferings

Hymn: How Long, O God, ELW 698

God, your gospel is freedom. We pray for people who are persecuted for their witness to the good news. Where economies oppress, inspire generosity. Where politics prey on the weak, lift up the lowly, so that all creation may hear the witness of your children.

Tuesday, July 6, 2021
Time after Pentecost

Jan Hus, martyr, died 1415

James 5:7-12
Suffering and patience

Be patient, therefore, beloved, until the coming of the Lord. The farmer waits for the precious crop from the earth, being patient with it until it receives the early and the late rains. You also must be patient. Strengthen your hearts, for the coming of the Lord is near. Beloved, do not grumble against one another, so that you may not be judged. See, the Judge is standing at the doors! As an example of suffering and patience, beloved, take the prophets who spoke in the name of the Lord. Indeed we call blessed those who showed endurance. You have heard of the endurance of Job, and you have seen the purpose of the Lord, how the Lord is compassionate and merciful. (James 5:7-11)

Psalm
Psalm 119:81-88
The faithful persecuted

Additional Reading
Jeremiah 16:1-13
Jeremiah's celibacy and message

Hymn: When Memory Fades, ELW 792

Living breath of God, we often seek quick answers or instant gratification. Return us to our breath, the source of life, to give us patience in every moment, so that we may wait for your kingdom on earth as it is in heaven.

Wednesday, July 7, 2021
Time after Pentecost

John 7:1-9
Unbelief of Jesus' brothers

After this Jesus went about in Galilee. He did not wish to go about in Judea because the Jews were looking for an opportunity to kill him. Now the Jewish festival of Booths was near. So his brothers said to him, "Leave here and go to Judea so that your disciples also may see the works you are doing; for no one who wants to be widely known acts in secret. If you do these things, show yourself to the world." (For not even his brothers believed in him.) Jesus said to them, "My time has not yet come, but your time is always here. The world cannot hate you, but it hates me because I testify against it that its works are evil. Go to the festival yourselves. I am not going to this festival, for my time has not yet fully come." After saying this, he remained in Galilee. (John 7:1-9)

Psalm
Psalm 119:81-88
The faithful persecuted

Additional Reading
Jeremiah 16:14-21
God will forgive Israel

Hymn: God of Tempest, God of Whirlwind, ELW 400

God of love, at times your work is in secret, while we long for audacious displays of your presence and power. Inspire us by your vulnerability to see your acts of love around every corner.

Thursday, July 8, 2021
Time after Pentecost

Psalm 85:8-13
Listen to what God is saying

Steadfast love and faithfulness will meet;
>   righteousness and peace will kiss each other.
Faithfulness will spring up from the ground,
>   and righteousness will look down from the sky.
The Lord will give what is good,
>   and our land will yield its increase.
Righteousness will go before him,
>   and will make a path for his steps. (Ps. 85:10-13)

Additional Readings

Amos 2:6-16
God's condemnation of Israel

Colossians 2:1-5
Christ, the mystery of God

Hymn: Christ, Whose Glory Fills the Skies, ELW 553

God, you give what is good. Show us your love and embrace us with your peace, so that we might encounter your transforming presence even in the rustling leaves and flowing breeze.

Friday, July 9, 2021
Time after Pentecost

Colossians 4:2-18
Declaring the mystery of Christ

Devote yourselves to prayer, keeping alert in it with thanksgiving. At the same time pray for us as well that God will open to us a door for the word, that we may declare the mystery of Christ, for which I am in prison, so that I may reveal it clearly, as I should.

Conduct yourselves wisely toward outsiders, making the most of the time. Let your speech always be gracious, seasoned with salt, so that you may know how you ought to answer everyone. (Col. 4:2-6)

Psalm
Psalm 85:8-13
Listen to what God is saying

Additional Reading
Amos 3:1-12
Who can but prophesy?

Hymn: Lord, Teach Us How to Pray Aright, ELW 745

God we long for clarity even when faith is veiled in mystery. Ground our being with your word of promise, that our freedom may be revealed in love for our neighbor and care for your creation.

Saturday, July 10, 2021
Time after Pentecost

Luke 1:57-80
The birth of John the Baptist

On the eighth day [Elizabeth and her neighbors and relatives] came to circumcise the child, and they were going to name him Zechariah after his father. But his mother said, "No; he is to be called John." They said to her, "None of your relatives has this name." Then they began motioning to his father to find out what name he wanted to give him. He asked for a writing tablet and wrote, "His name is John." And all of them were amazed. (Luke 1:59-63)

Psalm
Psalm 85:8-13
Listen to what God is saying

Additional Reading
Amos 4:6-13
Prepare to meet your God

Hymn: Blessed Be the God of Israel, ELW 250

God, prophets and preachers prepare the way for your coming. Prepare our hearts for your transforming presence with prayer. Equip our bodies for service with gratitude. Embolden our witness to your way of peace.

Sunday, July 11, 2021
Time after Pentecost

Benedict of Nursia, Abbot of Monte Cassino, died around 540

Mark 6:14-29
The death of John the Baptist

King Herod heard of [the disciples' preaching], for Jesus' name had become known. Some were saying, "John the baptizer has been raised from the dead; and for this reason these powers are at work in him." But others said, "It is Elijah." And others said, "It is a prophet, like one of the prophets of old." But when Herod heard of it, he said, "John, whom I beheaded, has been raised." (Mark 6:14-16)

Psalm

Psalm 85:8-13
Listen to what God is saying

Additional Readings

Amos 7:7-15
The sign of the plumb line

Ephesians 1:3-14
Chosen to live in praise of God

Hymn: Lead On, O King Eternal! ELW 805

O God, from you come all holy desires, all good counsels, and all just works. Give to us, your servants, that peace which the world cannot give, that our hearts may be set to obey your commandments; and also that we, being defended from the fear of our enemies, may live in peace and quietness, through Jesus Christ, our Savior and Lord.

Monday, July 12, 2021
Time after Pentecost

Nathan Söderblom, Bishop of Uppsala, died 1931

Psalm 142
Prayer for deliverance

I cry to you, O LORD;
> I say, "You are my refuge,
> my portion in the land of the living."
Give heed to my cry,
> for I am brought very low.

Save me from my persecutors,
> for they are too strong for me.
Bring me out of prison,
> so that I may give thanks to your name.
The righteous will surround me,
> for you will deal bountifully with me. (Ps. 142:5-7)

Additional Readings
Amos 5:1-9
Seek me and live

Acts 21:27-39
Paul arrested

Hymn: Out of the Depths I Cry to You, ELW 600

Hear our cries, O God. Give us words to name our deepest longings. Give us patience to hear your persistent voice in every breath we take. Sustain our lives with your living word, in Jesus' name.

Tuesday, July 13, 2021
Time after Pentecost

Amos 9:1-4

God searches out rebellious Israel

I saw the LORD standing beside the altar, and he said:
Strike the capitals until the thresholds shake,
    and shatter them on the heads of all the people;
and those who are left I will kill with the sword;
    not one of them shall flee away,
    not one of them shall escape.

Though they dig into Sheol,
    from there shall my hand take them;
though they climb up to heaven,
    from there I will bring them down. (Amos 9:1-2)

Psalm
Psalm 142
Prayer for deliverance

Additional Reading
Acts 23:12-35
Plot to kill Paul

Hymn: O God of Every Nation, ELW 713

Dear God, uproot corruption and uplift integrity. Shake the houses of power to inspire policies of justice and practices of peace. Forgive our apathy and embolden our witness so that our voices may resonate with your call for justice.

Wednesday, July 14, 2021
Time after Pentecost

Luke 7:31-35

Refusing the witness of John the Baptist and Jesus

[Jesus said,] "To what then will I compare the people of this generation, and what are they like? They are like children sitting in the marketplace and calling to one another,

> 'We played the flute for you, and you did not dance;
>> we wailed, and you did not weep.'

For John the Baptist has come eating no bread and drinking no wine, and you say, 'He has a demon'; the Son of Man has come eating and drinking, and you say, 'Look, a glutton and a drunkard, a friend of tax collectors and sinners!' Nevertheless, wisdom is vindicated by all her children." (Luke 7:31-35)

Psalm

Psalm 142
Prayer for deliverance

Additional Reading

Amos 9:11-15
God will restore the fortunes of Israel

Hymn: O Christ the Same, ELW 760

God, we ignore the witness of your messengers with quick excuses. When our imagination is limited, ignite our curiosity to dream the dreams of your prophets and to work for the wellbeing of all creation.

Thursday, July 15, 2021
Time after Pentecost

Psalm 23
The Lord is my shepherd

The LORD is my shepherd, I shall not want.
    He makes me lie down in green pastures;
he leads me beside still waters;
    he restores my soul.
He leads me in right paths
    for his name's sake.

Even though I walk through the darkest valley,
    I fear no evil;
for you are with me;
    your rod and your staff—
    they comfort me. (Ps. 23:1-4)

Additional Readings
Jeremiah 10:1-16
Following scarecrows

Colossians 1:15-23
God reconciles all things through Christ

Hymn: Shepherd Me, O God, ELW 780

Good Shepherd, you still our wandering minds. You feed our longing spirits.
You provide every good thing. Accompany our journeying in this world, so
that we may share your abundance with our neighbors in need.

Friday, July 16, 2021
Time after Pentecost

Jeremiah 10:17-25
Stupid shepherds scatter the flock

Woe is me because of my hurt!
>   My wound is severe.
But I said, "Truly this is my punishment,
>   and I must bear it."
My tent is destroyed,
>   and all my cords are broken;
my children have gone from me,
>   and they are no more;
there is no one to spread my tent again,
>   and to set up my curtains.
For the shepherds are stupid,
>   and do not inquire of the LORD;
therefore they have not prospered,
>   and all their flock is scattered. (Jer. 10:19-21)

Psalm
Psalm 23
The Lord is my shepherd

Additional Reading
Acts 17:16-31
Assurance for all through Christ

Hymn: Have No Fear, Little Flock, ELW 764

Faithful God, at times we fail to heed your word, yet your promise is persistent. Have mercy on us. Forgive our ignorance and gather your flock, so that we might all hear the call of our loving shepherd.

Saturday, July 17, 2021
Time after Pentecost

Bartolomé de Las Casas, missionary to the Indies, died 1566

Luke 18:35-43

Jesus heals a blind beggar

As [Jesus] approached Jericho, a blind man was sitting by the roadside begging. When he heard a crowd going by, he asked what was happening. They told him, "Jesus of Nazareth is passing by." Then he shouted, "Jesus, Son of David, have mercy on me!" Those who were in front sternly ordered him to be quiet; but he shouted even more loudly, "Son of David, have mercy on me!" Jesus stood still and ordered the man to be brought to him; and when he came near, he asked him, "What do you want me to do for you?" He said, "Lord, let me see again." Jesus said to him, "Receive your sight; your faith has saved you." Immediately he regained his sight and followed him, glorifying God; and all the people, when they saw it, praised God. (Luke 18:35-43)

Psalm

Psalm 23
The Lord is my shepherd

Additional Reading

Jeremiah 12:1-13
Shepherds who destroy God's vineyard

Hymn: God, Whose Almighty Word, ELW 673

Lord God, pretentious voices quiet the witness of the faithful, but your mercy is for all. Create faith in us and free us to amplify the voices of all who cry out for your love.

Sunday, July 18, 2021
Time after Pentecost

Mark 6:30-34, 53-56
Christ healing the multitudes

The apostles gathered around Jesus, and told him all that they had done and taught. He said to them, "Come away to a deserted place all by yourselves and rest a while." For many were coming and going, and they had no leisure even to eat. And they went away in the boat to a deserted place by themselves. Now many saw them going and recognized them, and they hurried there on foot from all the towns and arrived ahead of them. As he went ashore, he saw a great crowd; and he had compassion for them, because they were like sheep without a shepherd; and he began to teach them many things. (Mark 6:30-34)

Psalm
Psalm 23
The Lord is my shepherd

Additional Readings
Jeremiah 23:1-6
A righteous shepherd for Israel

Ephesians 2:11-22
Reconciled to God through Christ

Hymn: I Heard the Voice of Jesus Say, ELW 611

O God, powerful and compassionate, you shepherd your people, faithfully feeding and protecting us. Heal each of us, and make us a whole people, that we may embody the justice and peace of your Son, Jesus Christ, our Savior and Lord.

Monday, July 19, 2021
Time after Pentecost

Psalm 100
We are God's sheep

Make a joyful noise to the LORD, all the earth.
>Worship the LORD with gladness;
>come into his presence with singing.

Know that the LORD is God.
>It is he that made us, and we are his;
>we are his people, and the sheep of his pasture.

Enter his gates with thanksgiving,
>and his courts with praise.
>Give thanks to him, bless his name.

For the LORD is good;
>his steadfast love endures forever,
>and his faithfulness to all generations. (Ps. 100:1-5)

Additional Readings
Jeremiah 50:1-7
God the true pasture

Hebrews 13:17-25
Jesus, the great shepherd of the sheep

Hymn: Open Now Thy Gates of Beauty, ELW 533

God, we lift our prayers in the perfectly tuned harmonies of song, the noisy chatter of children, and the spirited discussion of the faithful. Receive all of our noise in gratitude for your abundant blessings.

Tuesday, July 20, 2021
Time after Pentecost

Zechariah 9:14—10:2
God will save the flock

On that day the LORD their God will save them
>   for they are the flock of his people;
for like the jewels of a crown
>   they shall shine on his land.
For what goodness and beauty are his!
>   Grain shall make the young men flourish,
>   and new wine the young women. (Zech. 9:16-17)

Psalm
Psalm 100
We are God's sheep

Additional Reading
Acts 20:17-38
The elders are shepherds

Hymn: Savior, like a Shepherd Lead Us, ELW 789

God of creation, you choose a broken people to bless all of creation. Enrich us with your call to tend your flock, to care for creation, and to rejoice in the countless ways that you preserve all that lives.

Wednesday, July 21, 2021
Time after Pentecost

Luke 15:1-7
Parable of the lost sheep

So [Jesus] told them this parable: "Which one of you, having a hundred sheep and losing one of them, does not leave the ninety-nine in the wilderness and go after the one that is lost until he finds it? When he has found it, he lays it on his shoulders and rejoices. And when he comes home, he calls together his friends and neighbors, saying to them, 'Rejoice with me, for I have found my sheep that was lost.' Just so, I tell you, there will be more joy in heaven over one sinner who repents than over ninety-nine righteous persons who need no repentance." (Luke 15:3-7)

Psalm
Psalm 100
We are God's sheep

Additional Reading
2 Samuel 5:1-12
David is to shepherd Israel

Hymn: Softly and Tenderly Jesus Is Calling, ELW 608

Good Shepherd, we are a people who wander. We are easily distracted by the newest fad and are constantly drawn away from your good gifts. Find us in our apathy and gather us into your community so that we may be refreshed and reminded of our call to feed your sheep.

Thursday, July 22, 2021
Mary Magdalene, Apostle

John 20:1-2, 11-18
Mary Magdalene meets Jesus in the garden

Jesus said to [Mary Magdalene], "Woman, why are you weeping? Whom are you looking for?" Supposing him to be the gardener, she said to him, "Sir, if you have carried him away, tell me where you have laid him, and I will take him away." Jesus said to her, "Mary!" She turned and said to him in Hebrew, "Rabbouni!" (which means Teacher). Jesus said to her, "Do not hold on to me, because I have not yet ascended to the Father. But go to my brothers and say to them, 'I am ascending to my Father and your Father, to my God and your God.'" Mary Magdalene went and announced to the disciples, "I have seen the Lord"; and she told them that he had said these things to her. (John 20:15-18)

Psalm
Psalm 73:23-28
I will speak of all God's works

Additional Readings
Ruth 1:6-18
Ruth stays with Naomi

Acts 13:26-33a
The raising of Jesus fulfills God's promise

Hymn: For All the Faithful Women, st. 9, ELW 419

Almighty God, your Son first entrusted the apostle Mary Magdalene with the joyful news of his resurrection. Following the example of her witness, may we proclaim Christ as our living Lord and one day see him in glory, for he lives and reigns with you and the Holy Spirit, one God, now and forever.

Friday, July 23, 2021
Time after Pentecost

Birgitta of Sweden, renewer of the church, died 1373

Colossians 3:12-17
Let the peace of Christ rule in your hearts

As God's chosen ones, holy and beloved, clothe yourselves with compassion, kindness, humility, meekness, and patience. Bear with one another and, if anyone has a complaint against another, forgive each other; just as the Lord has forgiven you, so you also must forgive. Above all, clothe yourselves with love, which binds everything together in perfect harmony. And let the peace of Christ rule in your hearts, to which indeed you were called in the one body. And be thankful. Let the word of Christ dwell in you richly; teach and admonish one another in all wisdom; and with gratitude in your hearts sing psalms, hymns, and spiritual songs to God. And whatever you do, in word or deed, do everything in the name of the Lord Jesus, giving thanks to God the Father through him. (Col. 3:12-17)

Psalm
Psalm 145:10-18
You open wide your hand

Additional Reading
2 Kings 3:4-20
Elisha and the miracle of water

Hymn: Oh, for a Thousand Tongues to Sing, ELW 886

God, your love is the substance that makes human relationships possible. Rule in our hearts with your compassion and peace, and call us to love your people with the love that fills our spirits.

Saturday, July 24, 2021
Time after Pentecost

2 Kings 4:38-41

Elisha purifies the pot of stew

When Elisha returned to Gilgal, there was a famine in the land. As the company of prophets was sitting before him, he said to his servant, "Put the large pot on, and make some stew for the company of prophets." One of them went out into the field to gather herbs; he found a wild vine and gathered from it a lapful of wild gourds, and came and cut them up into the pot of stew, not knowing what they were. They served some for the men to eat. But while they were eating the stew, they cried out, "O man of God, there is death in the pot!" They could not eat it. He said, "Then bring some flour." He threw it into the pot, and said, "Serve the people and let them eat." And there was nothing harmful in the pot. (2 Kings 4:38-41)

Psalm
Psalm 145:10-18
You open wide your hand

Additional Reading
John 4:31-38
Food that you do not know about

Hymn: Guide Me Ever, Great Redeemer, ELW 618

God, your people are a bunch of wild gourds, poisoning our communities with disdain. Purify our language, transform our gestures, and make of us a people that responds to our neighbors in need through acts of justice and mercy.

Sunday, July 25, 2021
Time after Pentecost

James, Apostle (transferred to July 26)

John 6:1-21
Jesus feeds 5000

One of [Jesus'] disciples, Andrew, Simon Peter's brother, said to him, "There is a boy here who has five barley loaves and two fish. But what are they among so many people?" Jesus said, "Make the people sit down." Now there was a great deal of grass in the place; so they sat down, about five thousand in all. Then Jesus took the loaves, and when he had given thanks, he distributed them to those who were seated; so also the fish, as much as they wanted. (John 6:8-11)

Psalm

Psalm 145:10-18
You open wide your hand

Additional Readings

2 Kings 4:42-44
Elisha feeds a hundred people

Ephesians 3:14-21
Prayer to Christ

Hymn: All Who Hunger, Gather Gladly, ELW 461

Gracious God, you have placed within the hearts of all your children a longing for your word and a hunger for your truth. Grant that we may know your Son to be the true bread of heaven and share this bread with all the world, through Jesus Christ, our Savior and Lord.

Monday, July 26, 2021
James, Apostle (transferred)

Mark 10:35-45

Whoever wishes to be great must serve

James and John, the sons of Zebedee, came forward to [Jesus] and said to him, "Teacher, we want you to do for us whatever we ask of you." And he said to them, "What is it you want me to do for you?" And they said to him, "Grant us to sit, one at your right hand and one at your left, in your glory." But Jesus said to them, "You do not know what you are asking. Are you able to drink the cup that I drink, or be baptized with the baptism that I am baptized with?" They replied, "We are able." Then Jesus said to them, "The cup that I drink you will drink; and with the baptism with which I am baptized, you will be baptized; but to sit at my right hand or at my left is not mine to grant, but it is for those for whom it has been prepared." (Mark 10:35-40)

Psalm
Psalm 7:1-10
God, my shield and defense

Additional Readings
1 Kings 19:9-18
Elijah hears God in the midst of silence

Acts 11:27—12:3a
James is killed by Herod

Hymn: In Our Day of Thanksgiving, ELW 429

Gracious God, we remember before you today your servant and apostle James, the first among the twelve to be martyred for the name of Jesus Christ. Pour out on the leaders of your church that spirit of self-denying service which is the true mark of authority among your people, through Jesus Christ our servant, who lives and reigns with you and the Holy Spirit, one God, now and forever.

Tuesday, July 27, 2021
Time after Pentecost

Romans 15:22-33

Gentiles share their material blessings

This is the reason that I have so often been hindered from coming to you. But now, with no further place for me in these regions, I desire, as I have for many years, to come to you when I go to Spain. For I do hope to see you on my journey and to be sent on by you, once I have enjoyed your company for a little while. At present, however, I am going to Jerusalem in a ministry to the saints; for Macedonia and Achaia have been pleased to share their resources with the poor among the saints at Jerusalem. (Rom. 15:22-26)

Psalm

Psalm 111
God gives food

Additional Reading

Exodus 24:1-11
The elders eat with God

Hymn: O Bread of Life from Heaven, ELW 480

Gracious God, the needs of your church throughout the world are great. Embolden us to share our wealth with the many who are in great need. Transform us by these relationships across your church catholic and send us to witness to your love.

Wednesday, July 28, 2021
Time after Pentecost

Johann Sebastian Bach, died 1750; Heinrich Schütz, died 1672;
George Frederick Handel, died 1759; musicians

Isaiah 25:6-10a

A feast on the mountain

On this mountain the LORD of hosts will make for all peoples
    a feast of rich food, a feast of well-aged wines,
    of rich food filled with marrow, of well-aged wines strained clear.
And he will destroy on this mountain
    the shroud that is cast over all peoples,
    the sheet that is spread over all nations;
    he will swallow up death forever.
Then the Lord GOD will wipe away the tears from all faces,
    and the disgrace of his people he will take away from all the earth,
    for the LORD has spoken. (Isa. 25:6-8)

Psalm

Psalm 111
God gives food

Additional Reading

Mark 6:35-44
Jesus feeds 5000

Hymn: Arise, My Soul, Arise! ELW 827

Eternal God, we long for your abundant blessing in our daily lives. While we await in the here-and-not-yet moments, ground us in your promise, so that we might live out of your excessive love rather than hoard what you so freely give.

Thursday, July 29, 2021
Time after Pentecost

Mary, Martha, and Lazarus of Bethany
Olaf, King of Norway, martyr, died 1030

Psalm 78:23-29
Manna rains down

Yet he commanded the skies above,
  and opened the doors of heaven;
he rained down on them manna to eat,
  and gave them the grain of heaven.
Mortals ate of the bread of angels;
  he sent them food in abundance. (Ps. 78:23-25)

Additional Readings
Exodus 12:33-42
Unleavened bread for the exodus

1 Corinthians 11:17-22
Abuses at the Lord's Supper

Hymn: Praise, Praise! You Are My Rock, ELW 862

Creator God, you rain down gifts from above. Yet, like your people Israel, when we attempt to gather too much the prospect vanishes in our hands. Remind us that we have enough and help us to share from our abundance.

Friday, July 30, 2021
Time after Pentecost

1 Corinthians 11:27-34

Discerning the body of Christ

Whoever, therefore, eats the bread or drinks the cup of the Lord in an unworthy manner will be answerable for the body and blood of the Lord. Examine yourselves, and only then eat of the bread and drink of the cup. For all who eat and drink without discerning the body, eat and drink judgment against themselves. . . . So then, my brothers and sisters, when you come together to eat, wait for one another. If you are hungry, eat at home, so that when you come together, it will not be for your condemnation. (1 Cor. 11:27-29; 33-34a)

Psalm
Psalm 78:23-29
Manna rains down

Additional Reading
Exodus 12:43—13:2
Directions for the Passover

Hymn: I Come with Joy, ELW 482

God of welcome, many barriers stand between your people and the promise at your table. Tear them down and equip us to welcome all to your table. Just as Jesus dined with the sinner and the tax-collector, embolden us to share meals across division.

Saturday, July 31, 2021
Time after Pentecost

Exodus 13:3-10
The festival of unleavened bread

Moses said to the people, "Remember this day on which you came out of Egypt, out of the house of slavery, because the LORD brought you out from there by strength of hand; no leavened bread shall be eaten. Today, in the month of Abib, you are going out. When the LORD brings you into the land of the Canaanites, the Hittites, the Amorites, the Hivites, and the Jebusites, which he swore to your ancestors to give you, a land flowing with milk and honey, you shall keep this observance in this month. Seven days you shall eat unleavened bread, and on the seventh day there shall be a festival to the LORD." (Exod. 13:3-6)

Psalm
Psalm 78:23-29
Manna rains down

Additional Reading
Matthew 16:5-12
Bread as a sign of other things

Hymn: Bless Now, O God, the Journey, ELW 326

Holy God, the Jewish people, who first shared your promise, keep your festivals and honor your commands. Inspire in us an admiration for our siblings of other traditions and grant us understanding and hope that we can work together for all of your creation.

Prayer List for August

_____

_____

_____

_____

_____

_____

_____

_____

_____

Sunday, August 1, 2021
Time after Pentecost

John 6:24-35
Christ, the bread of life

So when the crowd saw that neither Jesus nor his disciples were there, they themselves got into the boats and went to Capernaum looking for Jesus.

When they found him on the other side of the sea, they said to him, "Rabbi, when did you come here?" Jesus answered them, "Very truly, I tell you, you are looking for me, not because you saw signs, but because you ate your fill of the loaves. Do not work for the food that perishes, but for the food that endures for eternal life, which the Son of Man will give you. For it is on him that God the Father has set his seal." (John 6:24-27)

Psalm
Psalm 78:23-29
Manna rains down

Additional Readings
Exodus 16:2-4, 9-15
Manna in the wilderness

Ephesians 4:1-16
Maintain the unity of the faith

Hymn: What Feast of Love, ELW 487

O God, eternal goodness, immeasurable love, you place your gifts before us; we eat and are satisfied. Fill us and this world in all its need with the life that comes only from you, through Jesus Christ, our Savior and Lord.

Monday, August 2, 2021
Time after Pentecost

Psalm 107:1-3, 33-43
God feeds the hungry

He turns rivers into a desert,
>   springs of water into thirsty ground,
a fruitful land into a salty waste,
>   because of the wickedness of its inhabitants.
He turns a desert into pools of water,
>   a parched land into springs of water.
And there he lets the hungry live,
>   and they establish a town to live in;
they sow fields, and plant vineyards,
>   and get a fruitful yield.
By his blessing they multiply greatly,
>   and he does not let their cattle decrease. (Ps. 107:33-38)

Additional Readings
Numbers 11:16-23, 31-32
God sends quail

Ephesians 4:17-24
The new life

Hymn: We Come to the Hungry Feast, ELW 479

God of blessings, you have made your creation thrive with resources to create and sustain life. Lead us into conscientious care of all that you have made and fill us with the water of life.

Tuesday, August 3, 2021
Time after Pentecost

1 Corinthians 12:27-31
You are the body of Christ

Now you are the body of Christ and individually members of it. And God has appointed in the church first apostles, second prophets, third teachers; then deeds of power, then gifts of healing, forms of assistance, forms of leadership, various kinds of tongues. Are all apostles? Are all prophets? Are all teachers? Do all work miracles? Do all possess gifts of healing? Do all speak in tongues? Do all interpret? But strive for the greater gifts. And I will show you a still more excellent way. (1 Cor. 12:27-31)

Psalm
Psalm 107:1-3, 33-43
God feeds the hungry

Additional Reading
Deuteronomy 8:1-20
You will eat your fill

Hymn: Come to Us, Creative Spirit, ELW 687

Holy and blessed Trinity, you have knit your people together into a diverse and beautiful body. Keep us united in faith and help us find common ground, that we might serve you with our unique and varied gifts.

Wednesday, August 4, 2021
Time after Pentecost

Mark 8:1-10
Jesus feeds 4000

In those days when there was again a great crowd without anything to eat, Jesus called his disciples and said to them, "I have compassion for the crowd, because they have been with me now for three days and have nothing to eat. If I send them away hungry to their homes, they will faint on the way—and some of them have come from a great distance." His disciples replied, "How can one feed these people with bread here in the desert?" He asked them, "How many loaves do you have?" They said, "Seven." Then he ordered the crowd to sit down on the ground; and he took the seven loaves, and after giving thanks he broke them and gave them to his disciples to distribute; and they distributed them to the crowd. (Mark 8:1-6)

Psalm
Psalm 107:1-3, 33-43
God feeds the hungry

Additional Reading
Isaiah 55:1-9
Come and eat

Hymn: Bread of Life from Heaven, ELW 474

Compassionate God, you know our needs and find ways to meet them. Give us eyes to see and ears to hear the needs of our neighbors. Inspire us to generosity and creativity in our gospel-led actions.

Thursday, August 5, 2021
Time after Pentecost

Psalm 34:1-8
Taste and see

I sought the LORD, and he answered me,
>and delivered me from all my fears.
Look to him, and be radiant;
>so your faces shall never be ashamed.
This poor soul cried, and was heard by the LORD,
>and was saved from every trouble.
The angel of the LORD encamps
>around those who fear him, and delivers them.
O taste and see that the LORD is good;
>happy are those who take refuge in him. (Ps. 34:4-8)

Additional Readings
1 Samuel 28:20-25
Food for Saul's journey

Romans 15:1-6
Living in harmony

Hymn: Taste and See, ELW 493

God of deliverance, you stand on the side of the oppressed, hurting, and fearful. Give freedom, healing, and strength to all who call upon you. Protect the vulnerable and empower us to join in this holy work.

Friday, August 6, 2021
Time after Pentecost

Galatians 6:1-10
Bear one another's burdens

My friends, if anyone is detected in a transgression, you who have received the Spirit should restore such a one in a spirit of gentleness. Take care that you yourselves are not tempted. Bear one another's burdens, and in this way you will fulfill the law of Christ. For if those who are nothing think they are something, they deceive themselves. All must test their own work; then that work, rather than their neighbor's work, will become a cause for pride. For all must carry their own loads. (Gal. 6:1-5)

Psalm
Psalm 34:1-8
Taste and see

Additional Reading
2 Samuel 17:15-29
Food in the wilderness

Hymn: Will You Let Me Be Your Servant, ELW 659

Gracious God, in you we find forgiveness and restoration. When we are wronged or faced with the sins of others, remind us that your love is irrepressible. Allow us to proclaim your mercy and grace as we seek a new way forward.

Saturday, August 7, 2021
Time after Pentecost

Matthew 7:7-11
Bread and stones

[Jesus said,] "Ask, and it will be given you; search, and you will find; knock, and the door will be opened for you. For everyone who asks receives, and everyone who searches finds, and for everyone who knocks, the door will be opened. Is there anyone among you who, if your child asks for bread, will give a stone? Or if the child asks for a fish, will give a snake? If you then, who are evil, know how to give good gifts to your children, how much more will your Father in heaven give good things to those who ask him!" (Matt. 7:7-11)

Psalm
Psalm 34:1-8
Taste and see

Additional Reading
1 Kings 2:1-9
David's instructions to Solomon

Hymn: Eternal Spirit of the Living Christ, ELW 402

O Divine Parent, you provide every good thing, even before we ask. Encourage us to seek you out in prayer, trusting that your blessings will abound in our lives and every prayer will be heard.

Sunday, August 8, 2021
Time after Pentecost

Dominic, founder of the Order of Preachers (Dominicans), died 1221

John 6:35, 41-51

Christ, the bread of life

[Jesus said,] "Very truly, I tell you, whoever believes has eternal life. I am the bread of life. Your ancestors ate the manna in the wilderness, and they died. This is the bread that comes down from heaven, so that one may eat of it and not die. I am the living bread that came down from heaven. Whoever eats of this bread will live forever; and the bread that I will give for the life of the world is my flesh." (John 6:47-51)

Psalm

Psalm 34:1-8
Taste and see

Additional Readings

1 Kings 19:4-8
Elijah given bread for his journey

Ephesians 4:25—5:2
Put away evil, live in love

Hymn: O Living Bread from Heaven, ELW 542

Gracious God, your blessed Son came down from heaven to be the true bread that gives life to the world. Give us this bread always, that he may live in us and we in him, and that, strengthened by this food, we may live as his body in the world, through Jesus Christ, our Savior and Lord.

Monday, August 9, 2021
Time after Pentecost

Psalm 81
God will feed us

"But my people did not listen to my voice;
  Israel would not submit to me.
So I gave them over to their stubborn hearts,
  to follow their own counsels.
O that my people would listen to me,
  that Israel would walk in my ways!
Then I would quickly subdue their enemies,
  and turn my hand against their foes.
Those who hate the LORD would cringe before him,
  and their doom would last forever.
I would feed you with the finest of the wheat,
  and with honey from the rock I would satisfy you." (Ps. 81:11-16)

Additional Readings

1 Kings 17:1-16
God feeds the widow of Zarephath

Ephesians 5:1-14
Fruits of the light

Hymn: You Satisfy the Hungry Heart, ELW 484

Loving God, your voice calls out to the nations. Expand our hearts to receive your word. Deepen our commitment to walk in the paths you have laid for us and feed us for the journey.

Tuesday, August 10, 2021
Time after Pentecost

Lawrence, deacon, martyr, died 258

2 Peter 3:14-18
Grow in grace and knowledge

Therefore, beloved, while you are waiting for these things, strive to be found by him at peace, without spot or blemish; and regard the patience of our Lord as salvation. So also our beloved brother Paul wrote to you according to the wisdom given him, speaking of this as he does in all his letters. There are some things in them hard to understand, which the ignorant and unstable twist to their own destruction, as they do the other scriptures. You therefore, beloved, since you are forewarned, beware that you are not carried away with the error of the lawless and lose your own stability. But grow in the grace and knowledge of our Lord and Savior Jesus Christ. To him be the glory both now and to the day of eternity. Amen. (2 Peter 3:14-18)

Psalm
Psalm 81
God will feed us

Additional Reading
Ruth 2:1-23
Ruth gleans in Boaz's field

Hymn: O Master, Let Me Walk with You, ELW 818

Almighty God, you have given us wisdom and truth in the words of holy scripture. Create in us a hunger to explore and embrace your word and give us discerning hearts to seek your will.

Wednesday, August 11, 2021
Time after Pentecost

Clare, Abbess of San Damiano, died 1253

Jeremiah 31:1-6
God promises fruitful vineyards

At that time, says the LORD, I will be the God of all the families of Israel,
and they shall be my people.
Thus says the LORD:
The people who survived the sword
found grace in the wilderness;
when Israel sought for rest,
the LORD appeared to him from far away.
I have loved you with an everlasting love;
therefore I have continued my faithfulness to you.
Again I will build you, and you shall be built,
O virgin Israel!
Again you shall take your tambourines,
and go forth in the dance of the merrymakers.
Again you shall plant vineyards
on the mountains of Samaria;
the planters shall plant,
and shall enjoy the fruit. (Jer. 31:1-5)

Psalm
Psalm 81
God will feed us

Additional Reading
John 6:35-40
Doing God's will

Hymn: God the Sculptor of the Mountains, ELW 736

*Loyal God, you have never left those who love you or the world you created.
Continue to guide your people in faithful and holy living, so we might reflect
your good intention for everything that exists.*

Thursday, August 12, 2021
Time after Pentecost

Psalm 34:9-14
Seeking God

Come, O children, listen to me;
    I will teach you the fear of the LORD.
Which of you desires life,
    and covets many days to enjoy good?
Keep your tongue from evil,
    and your lips from speaking deceit.
Depart from evil, and do good;
    seek peace, and pursue it. (Ps. 34:11-14)

Additional Readings
Job 11:1-20
Zophar counsels Job about wisdom

Acts 6:8-15
Stephen's compelling wisdom

Hymn: There's a Wideness in God's Mercy, ELW 587/588

God of peace, you desire for all humanity to seek life and to do good. Incline our wandering hearts to your saving word and holy wisdom, and teach us the ways you would have us go.

Friday, August 13, 2021
Time after Pentecost

Florence Nightingale, died 1910; Clara Maass, died 1901; renewers of society

Romans 16:17-20

Being wise in what is good

I urge you, brothers and sisters, to keep an eye on those who cause dissensions and offenses, in opposition to the teaching that you have learned; avoid them. For such people do not serve our Lord Christ, but their own appetites, and by smooth talk and flattery they deceive the hearts of the simple-minded. For while your obedience is known to all, so that I rejoice over you, I want you to be wise in what is good and guileless in what is evil. The God of peace will shortly crush Satan under your feet. The grace of our Lord Jesus Christ be with you. (Rom. 16:17-20)

Psalm
Psalm 34:9-14
Seeking God

Additional Reading
Job 12:1-25
Job sees wisdom and strength in God

Hymn: O Day of Peace, ELW 711

God of wisdom, you rejoice when your people are united in faith and support one another in life. Keep our focus on your will and teaching, and help us to tune out voices that would lead us astray.

Saturday, August 14, 2021
Time after Pentecost

Maximilian Kolbe, died 1941; Kaj Munk, died 1944; martyrs

John 4:7-26

Christ, the living water

The woman said to [Jesus], "Sir, you have no bucket, and the well is deep. Where do you get that living water? Are you greater than our ancestor Jacob, who gave us the well, and with his sons and his flocks drank from it?" Jesus said to her, "Everyone who drinks of this water will be thirsty again, but those who drink of the water that I will give them will never be thirsty. The water that I will give will become in them a spring of water gushing up to eternal life." The woman said to him, "Sir, give me this water, so that I may never be thirsty or have to keep coming here to draw water." (John 4:11-15)

Psalm
Psalm 34:9-14
Seeking God

Additional Reading
Job 13:1-19
When silence is wisdom

Hymn: Come to Me, All Pilgrims Thirsty, ELW 777

Holy One, you understand us inside and out and know what we are thirsting for. Give us your living water, that we might be sustained in our lives of faith and restored in hope.

Sunday, August 15, 2021
Time after Pentecost

Mary, Mother of Our Lord (transferred to August 16)

John 6:51-58
Christ, the true food and drink

The Jews then disputed among themselves, saying, "How can this man give us his flesh to eat?" So Jesus said to them, "Very truly, I tell you, unless you eat the flesh of the Son of Man and drink his blood, you have no life in you. Those who eat my flesh and drink my blood have eternal life, and I will raise them up on the last day; for my flesh is true food and my blood is true drink." (John 6:52-55)

Psalm

Psalm 34:9-14
Seeking God

Additional Readings

Proverbs 9:1-6
Invited to dine at wisdom's feast

Ephesians 5:15-20
Filled with the Spirit

Hymn: We Eat the Bread of Teaching, ELW 518

Ever-loving God, your Son gives himself as living bread for the life of the world. Fill us with such a knowledge of his presence that we may be strengthened and sustained by his risen life to serve you continually, through Jesus Christ, our Savior and Lord.

Monday, August 16, 2021
Mary, Mother of Our Lord (transferred)

Luke 1:46-55

Mary's thanksgiving

And Mary said,
"My soul magnifies the Lord,
    and my spirit rejoices in God my Savior,
for he has looked with favor on the lowliness of his servant.
    Surely, from now on all generations will call me blessed;
for the Mighty One has done great things for me,
    and holy is his name." (Luke 1:46-49)

Psalm

Psalm 34:1-9
O magnify the Lord with me

Additional Readings

Isaiah 61:7-11
God will cause righteousness to spring up

Galatians 4:4-7
We are no longer slaves, but children

Hymn: Canticle of the Turning, ELW 723

Almighty God, in choosing the virgin Mary to be the mother of your Son, you made known your gracious regard for the poor, the lowly, and the despised. Grant us grace to receive your word in humility, and so to be made one with your Son, Jesus Christ our Savior and Lord, who lives and reigns with you and the Holy Spirit, one God, now and forever.

Tuesday, August 17, 2021
Time after Pentecost

Acts 7:9-16
Joseph's family is fed in Egypt

[Stephen said,] "The patriarchs, jealous of Joseph, sold him into Egypt; but God was with him, and rescued him from all his afflictions, and enabled him to win favor and to show wisdom when he stood before Pharaoh, king of Egypt, who appointed him ruler over Egypt and over all his household. Now there came a famine throughout Egypt and Canaan, and great suffering, and our ancestors could find no food. But when Jacob heard that there was grain in Egypt, he sent our ancestors there on their first visit. On the second visit Joseph made himself known to his brothers, and Joseph's family became known to Pharaoh. Then Joseph sent and invited his father Jacob and all his relatives to come to him, seventy-five in all; so Jacob went down to Egypt." (Acts 7:9-15)

Psalm
Psalm 36
God saves humans and animals

Additional Reading
Genesis 45:1-15
Joseph provides food

Hymn: As Rain from the Clouds, ELW 508

God our maker, you filled this world with remarkable beauty and abundance. Abide with us always and support us in times of trouble or turmoil. Encourage us to share your bounty with others.

Wednesday, August 18, 2021
Time after Pentecost

Genesis 47:13-26
Famine even in Egypt

So Joseph bought all the land of Egypt for Pharaoh. All the Egyptians sold their fields, because the famine was severe upon them; and the land became Pharaoh's. As for the people, he made slaves of them from one end of Egypt to the other. Only the land of the priests he did not buy; for the priests had a fixed allowance from Pharaoh, and lived on the allowance that Pharaoh gave them; therefore they did not sell their land. Then Joseph said to the people, "Now that I have this day bought you and your land for Pharaoh, here is seed for you; sow the land. And at the harvests you shall give one-fifth to Pharaoh, and four-fifths shall be your own, as seed for the field and as food for yourselves and your households, and as food for your little ones." They said, "You have saved our lives; may it please my lord, we will be slaves to Pharaoh." So Joseph made it a statute concerning the land of Egypt, and it stands to this day, that Pharaoh should have the fifth. (Gen. 47:20-26)

Psalm
Psalm 36
God saves humans and animals

Additional Reading
Mark 8:14-21
Jesus teaches about bread

Hymn: We Plow the Fields and Scatter, ELW 680/681

God of discernment, you have called great and courageous leaders to guide your people in the past. Inspire us to follow their example and to elect just and merciful leaders in our local communities and across our nation.

Thursday, August 19, 2021
Time after Pentecost

Psalm 34:15-22
God's eyes are upon the righteous

The eyes of the LORD are on the righteous,
　　and his ears are open to their cry.
The face of the LORD is against evildoers,
　　to cut off the remembrance of them from the earth.
When the righteous cry for help, the LORD hears,
　　and rescues them from all their troubles.
The LORD is near to the brokenhearted,
　　and saves the crushed in spirit. (Ps. 34:15-18)

Additional Readings
Joshua 22:1-9
Joshua blesses eastern tribes

1 Thessalonians 5:1-11
The breastplate of faith and love

Hymn: O Jesus, Joy of Loving Hearts, ELW 658

Ever-listening God, you know what is in our hearts when we cry out to you. Help us, guide us, and rescue us when we are in any need, that we might be beacons of your love for others to witness.

Friday, August 20, 2021
Time after Pentecost

Bernard, Abbot of Clairvaux, died 1153

Romans 13:11-14

Put on the armor of light

Besides this, you know what time it is, how it is now the moment for you to wake from sleep. For salvation is nearer to us now than when we became believers; the night is far gone, the day is near. Let us then lay aside the works of darkness and put on the armor of light; let us live honorably as in the day, not in reveling and drunkenness, not in debauchery and licentiousness, not in quarreling and jealousy. Instead, put on the Lord Jesus Christ, and make no provision for the flesh, to gratify its desires. (Rom. 13:11-14)

Psalm

Psalm 34:15-22
God's eyes are upon the righteous

Additional Reading

Joshua 22:10-20
Concern about loyalty to God

Hymn: Goodness Is Stronger than Evil, ELW 721

Illuminating God, you reveal the truth and keep the shadows of sin at bay. Brighten our lives with your light and cast out those things that should remain hidden, clothing us with the grace of Christ.

Saturday, August 21, 2021
Time after Pentecost

Luke 11:5-13

Ask, and it will be given

[Jesus said,] "So I say to you, Ask, and it will be given you; search, and you will find; knock, and the door will be opened for you. For everyone who asks receives, and everyone who searches finds, and for everyone who knocks, the door will be opened. Is there anyone among you who, if your child asks for a fish, will give a snake instead of a fish? Or if the child asks for an egg, will give a scorpion? If you then, who are evil, know how to give good gifts to your children, how much more will the heavenly Father give the Holy Spirit to those who ask him!" (Luke 11:9-13)

Psalm

Psalm 34:15-22
God's eyes are upon the righteous

Additional Reading

Joshua 22:21-34
An altar to the one Lord

Hymn: Our Father, God in Heaven Above, ELW 746/747

God of compassion, you care for your people as a loving parent cares for a child. Keep us in your warm embrace, that we might be encouraged to show the same care and love to others.

Sunday, August 22, 2021
Time after Pentecost

John 6:56-69

The bread of eternal life

[Jesus said,] "Those who eat my flesh and drink my blood abide in me, and I in them. Just as the living Father sent me, and I live because of the Father, so whoever eats me will live because of me. This is the bread that came down from heaven, not like that which your ancestors ate, and they died. But the one who eats this bread will live forever." [Jesus] said these things while he was teaching in the synagogue at Capernaum. (John 6:56-59)

Psalm

Psalm 34:15-22
God's eyes are upon the righteous

Additional Readings

Joshua 24:1-2a, 14-18
Serve the Lord

Ephesians 6:10-20
Put on the armor of God

Hymn: Come, Gracious Spirit, Heavenly Dove, ELW 404

Holy God, your word feeds your people with life that is eternal. Direct our choices and preserve us in your truth, that, renouncing what is false and evil, we may live in you, through your Son, Jesus Christ, our Savior and Lord.

Monday, August 23, 2021
Time after Pentecost

Psalm 119:97-104
God's word is sweet

Oh, how I love your law!
    It is my meditation all day long.
Your commandment makes me wiser than my enemies,
    for it is always with me....
How sweet are your words to my taste,
    sweeter than honey to my mouth!
Through your precepts I get understanding;
    therefore I hate every false way. (Ps. 119:97-98, 103-104)

Additional Readings
Nehemiah 9:1-15   **Ephesians 5:21—6:9**
God's care of the people   *A household code*

Hymn: Spirit of Gentleness, ELW 396

Eternal God, your law is a gift of love to help us live in community with you and with one another. Help us dwell in your word and receive your wisdom, that we might follow in the path you desire.

Tuesday, August 24, 2021
Bartholomew, Apostle

John 1:43-51

Jesus says: Follow me

When Jesus saw Nathanael coming toward him, he said of him, "Here is truly an Israelite in whom there is no deceit!" Nathanael asked him, "Where did you get to know me?" Jesus answered, "I saw you under the fig tree before Philip called you." Nathanael replied, "Rabbi, you are the Son of God! You are the King of Israel!" Jesus answered, "Do you believe because I told you that I saw you under the fig tree? You will see greater things than these." And he said to him, "Very truly, I tell you, you will see heaven opened and the angels of God ascending and descending upon the Son of Man." (John 1:47-51)

Psalm

Psalm 12
A plea for help in evil times

Additional Readings

Exodus 19:1-6
Israel is God's priestly kingdom

1 Corinthians 12:27-31a
The body of Christ

Hymn: We All Are One in Mission, ELW 576

Almighty and everlasting God, you gave to your apostle Bartholomew grace truly to believe and courageously to preach your word. Grant that your church may proclaim the good news to the ends of the earth, through Jesus Christ, our Savior and Lord, who lives and reigns with you and the Holy Spirit, one God, now and forever.

Wednesday, August 25, 2021
Time after Pentecost

Isaiah 33:10-16
The righteous will eat

Hear, you who are far away, what I have done;
and you who are near, acknowledge my might.
The sinners in Zion are afraid;
trembling has seized the godless:
"Who among us can live with the devouring fire?
Who among us can live with everlasting flames?"
Those who walk righteously and speak uprightly,
who despise the gain of oppression,
who wave away a bribe instead of accepting it,
who stop their ears from hearing of bloodshed
and shut their eyes from looking on evil,
they will live on the heights;
their refuge will be the fortresses of rocks;
their food will be supplied, their water assured. (Isa. 33:13-16)

Psalm
Psalm 119:97-104
God's word is sweet

Additional Reading
John 15:16-25
I chose you

Hymn: Around You, O Lord Jesus, ELW 468

Almighty God, you see all the ways we fall short and still find us worthy of righteousness before you. Forgive our sins, help us move past our failures, and create in us clean and renewed hearts.

Thursday, August 26, 2021
Time after Pentecost

Psalm 15
Dwelling in God's tabernacle

O Lord, who may abide in your tent?
>   Who may dwell on your holy hill?

Those who walk blamelessly, and do what is right,
>   and speak the truth from their heart;
who do not slander with their tongue,
>   and do no evil to their friends,
>   nor take up a reproach against their neighbors;
in whose eyes the wicked are despised,
>   but who honor those who fear the Lord;
who stand by their oath even to their hurt;
who do not lend money at interest,
>   and do not take a bribe against the innocent.

Those who do these things shall never be moved. (Ps. 15:1-5)

Additional Readings
Exodus 32:1-14
The Israelites make themselves a god

James 1:1-8
One who doubts is like a wave of the sea

Hymn: Oh, That the Lord Would Guide My Ways, ELW 772

Holy One, you seek to gather all creation to you and you dwell among us. In the midst of a broken world, kindle passion in us to walk in your ways and lead upright and blameless lives.

Friday, August 27, 2021
Time after Pentecost

James 1:9-16
Blessed are those who endure temptation

Blessed is anyone who endures temptation. Such a one has stood the test and will receive the crown of life that the Lord has promised to those who love him. No one, when tempted, should say, "I am being tempted by God"; for God cannot be tempted by evil and he himself tempts no one. But one is tempted by one's own desire, being lured and enticed by it; then, when that desire has conceived, it gives birth to sin, and that sin, when it is fully grown, gives birth to death. Do not be deceived, my beloved. (James 1:12-16)

Psalm
Psalm 15
Dwelling in God's tabernacle

Additional Reading
Exodus 32:15-35
Moses punishes the Israelites' evil

Hymn: Holy Spirit, Truth Divine, ELW 398

Faithful God, your people have faced temptations from the beginning of our existence and you have never abandoned us. Keep us steadfast in faith and increase our trust in you, that we might remain examples of discipleship.

Saturday, August 28, 2021
Time after Pentecost

Augustine, Bishop of Hippo, died 430

Moses the Black, monk, martyr, died around 400

John 18:28-32

Ritual defilement and the Passover

Then [the police] took Jesus from Caiaphas to Pilate's headquarters. It was early in the morning. They themselves did not enter the headquarters, so as to avoid ritual defilement and to be able to eat the Passover. So Pilate went out to them and said, "What accusation do you bring against this man?" They answered, "If this man were not a criminal, we would not have handed him over to you." Pilate said to them, "Take him yourselves and judge him according to your law." The Jews replied, "We are not permitted to put anyone to death." (This was to fulfill what Jesus had said when he indicated the kind of death he was to die.) (John 18:28-32)

Psalm
Psalm 15
Dwelling in God's tabernacle

Additional Reading
Exodus 34:8-28
The covenant renewed

Hymn: My Lord of Light, ELW 832

Mighty One, you stand with all who are oppressed or unjustly accused. Enable us to call for justice in our world, that no one may have their humanity stripped away in the name of unbalanced due process.

Sunday, August 29, 2021
Time after Pentecost

Mark 7:1-8, 14-15, 21-23

Authentic religion

So the Pharisees and the scribes asked [Jesus], "Why do your disciples not live according to the tradition of the elders, but eat with defiled hands?" He said to them, "Isaiah prophesied rightly about you hypocrites, as it is written,

> 'This people honors me with their lips,
>> but their hearts are far from me;
> in vain do they worship me,
>> teaching human precepts as doctrines.'

You abandon the commandment of God and hold to human tradition." (Mark 7:5-8)

Psalm

Psalm 15
Dwelling in God's tabernacle

Additional Readings

Deuteronomy 4:1-2, 6-9
God's law: sign of a great nation

James 1:17-27
Be doers of the word

Hymn: O God, My Faithful God, ELW 806

O God our strength, without you we are weak and wayward creatures. Protect us from all dangers that attack us from the outside, and cleanse us from all evil that arises from within ourselves, that we may be preserved through your Son, Jesus Christ, our Savior and Lord.

Monday, August 30, 2021
Time after Pentecost

Psalm 106:1-6, 13-23, 47-48
God will remember the people

Praise the LORD!
>O give thanks to the LORD, for he is good;
>>for his steadfast love endures forever.

Who can utter the mighty doings of the LORD,
>>or declare all his praise?

Happy are those who observe justice,
>>who do righteousness at all times.

Remember me, O LORD, when you show favor to your people;
>>help me when you deliver them;

that I may see the prosperity of your chosen ones,
>>that I may rejoice in the gladness of your nation,
>>that I may glory in your heritage. (Ps. 106:1-5)

Additional Readings
Deuteronomy 4:9-14
Teach your children

1 Timothy 4:6-16
Set the believers an example

Hymn: Voices Raised to You, ELW 845

God of deliverance, you bring your people forth into freedom from everything that would bind us. Increase our joy and let our ceaseless praise sound forth in deep gratitude for all that you have done.

Tuesday, August 31, 2021
Time after Pentecost

Deuteronomy 4:15-20
Do not be led astray

Since you saw no form when the LORD spoke to you at Horeb out of the fire, take care and watch yourselves closely, so that you do not act corruptly by making an idol for yourselves, in the form of any figure—the likeness of male or female, the likeness of any animal that is on the earth, the likeness of any winged bird that flies in the air, the likeness of anything that creeps on the ground, the likeness of any fish that is in the water under the earth. And when you look up to the heavens and see the sun, the moon, and the stars, all the host of heaven, do not be led astray and bow down to them and serve them, things that the LORD your God has allotted to all the peoples everywhere under heaven. But the LORD has taken you and brought you out of the iron-smelter, out of Egypt, to become a people of his very own possession, as you are now. (Deut. 4:15-20)

Psalm
Psalm 106:1-6, 13-23, 47-48
God will remember the people

Additional Reading
1 Peter 2:19-25
Christ leaves an example

Hymn: Praise the Lord! O Heavens, ELW 823

Creator of the universe, you are unlike anything in our world, and yet we find your presence in every atom. Keep our hearts fixed on you and fill us with your love, that we might continue to worship you alone.

Prayer List for September

_____

_____

_____

_____

_____

_____

_____

_____

_____

Time after Pentecost
Autumn

The days of early autumn (September and October) herald the resumption of a more regular schedule: school begins, church education programs commence, and the steady rhythms of work are accompanied by cooling breezes and the changing colors of the landscape. During these months, various crops are harvested and appear on roadside stands and in grocery stores. In many countries the harvest days of September and October are marked with prayer, feasting, and special care for the poor and hungry.

Table Prayer for Autumn

We praise you and bless you, O God,
for autumn days,
and for the gifts of this table.
Grant us grace to share your goodness,
until all people are fed by the harvest of the earth.
We ask this through Christ our Lord. Amen.

Wednesday, September 1, 2021
Time after Pentecost

Mark 7:9-23
Jesus teaches about tradition

Then [Jesus] said to [the Pharisees and scribes], "You have a fine way of rejecting the commandment of God in order to keep your tradition! For Moses said, 'Honor your father and your mother'; and, 'Whoever speaks evil of father or mother must surely die.' But you say that if anyone tells father or mother, 'Whatever support you might have had from me is Corban' (that is, an offering to God)—then you no longer permit doing anything for a father or mother, thus making void the word of God through your tradition that you have handed on. And you do many things like this." (Mark 7:9-13)

Psalm
Psalm 106:1-6, 13-23, 47-48
God will remember the people

Additional Reading
Deuteronomy 4:21-40
Moses urges faithfulness

Hymn: God's Word Is Our Great Heritage, ELW 509

O God, we are often self-absorbed, yet you call us to follow you and to care for others as we would care for ourselves. Empower us to be compassionate and gracious to all your people.

Thursday, September 2, 2021
Time after Pentecost

Nikolai Frederik Severin Grundtvig, bishop, renewer of the church, died 1872

Psalm 146
Help and hope come from God

The LORD sets the prisoners free;
    the LORD opens the eyes of the blind.
The LORD lifts up those who are bowed down;
    the LORD loves the righteous.
The LORD watches over the strangers;
    he upholds the orphan and the widow,
    but the way of the wicked he brings to ruin.

The LORD will reign forever,
    your God, O Zion, for all generations.
Praise the LORD! (Ps. 146:7c-10)

Additional Readings
Isaiah 30:27-33
God sifts the nations

Romans 2:1-11
Divine judgment applies to all

Hymn: Praise the One Who Breaks the Darkness, ELW 843

Merciful God of might, you break the darkness of our hearts and you promise to remove the sin that shrouds the world. Give us strength to be charitable and merciful to prisoners, orphans, strangers, widows, and others on the margins of life.

Friday, September 3, 2021
Time after Pentecost

Romans 2:12-16

Gentiles obey the law instinctively

All who have sinned apart from the law will also perish apart from the law, and all who have sinned under the law will be judged by the law. For it is not the hearers of the law who are righteous in God's sight, but the doers of the law who will be justified. When Gentiles, who do not possess the law, do instinctively what the law requires, these, though not having the law, are a law to themselves. They show that what the law requires is written on their hearts, to which their own conscience also bears witness; and their conflicting thoughts will accuse or perhaps excuse them on the day when, according to my gospel, God, through Jesus Christ, will judge the secret thoughts of all. (Rom. 2:12-16)

Psalm

Psalm 146
Help and hope come from God

Additional Reading

Isaiah 32:1-8
The noble stand by noble things

Hymn: Salvation unto Us Has Come, ELW 590

Lord God, you desire that we follow your laws and trust in your promises. Let your grace kindle in us an impulse to follow your ways so that our thoughts and actions might reflect your generous mercy and love.

Saturday, September 4, 2021
Time after Pentecost

Isaiah 33:1-9

The fear of God is Zion's treasure

O LORD, be gracious to us; we wait for you.
>   Be our arm every morning,
>   our salvation in the time of trouble.
At the sound of tumult, peoples fled;
>   before your majesty, nations scattered.
Spoil was gathered as the caterpillar gathers;
>   as locusts leap, they leaped upon it.
The LORD is exalted, he dwells on high;
>   he filled Zion with justice and righteousness;
he will be the stability of your times,
>   abundance of salvation, wisdom, and knowledge;
>   the fear of the LORD is Zion's treasure. (Isa. 33:2-6)

Psalm
Psalm 146
Help and hope come from God

Additional Reading
Matthew 15:21-31
Jesus heals

Hymn: O Savior, Precious Savior, ELW 820

O Lord, you promise to be stable when our lives are unstable. When we are overwhelmed, afraid, at our wits' end, or feeling troubled, remind us that you are not far away. Be gracious to us because we wait for you.

Sunday, September 5, 2021
Time after Pentecost

Mark 7:24-37

Christ heals a little girl and a deaf man

Then [Jesus] returned from the region of Tyre, and went by way of Sidon towards the Sea of Galilee, in the region of the Decapolis. [The disciples] brought to him a deaf man who had an impediment in his speech; and they begged him to lay his hand on him. He took him aside in private, away from the crowd, and put his fingers into his ears, and he spat and touched his tongue. Then looking up to heaven, he sighed and said to him, "Ephphatha," that is, "Be opened." And immediately his ears were opened, his tongue was released, and he spoke plainly. (Mark 7:31-35)

Psalm

Psalm 146
Help and hope come from God

Additional Readings

Isaiah 35:4-7a
God comes with healing

James 2:1-10 [11-13] 14-17
Faith without works is dead

Hymn: Lord of All Nations, Grant Me Grace, ELW 716

Gracious God, throughout the ages you transform sickness into health and death into life. Open us to the power of your presence, and make us a people ready to proclaim your promises to the whole world, through Jesus Christ, our healer and Lord.

Monday, September 6, 2021
Time after Pentecost

Isaiah 38:10-20

Prayer for health

O Lord, by these things people live,
>   and in all these is the life of my spirit.
>   Oh, restore me to health and make me live!
Surely it was for my welfare
>   that I had great bitterness;
but you have held back my life
>   from the pit of destruction,
for you have cast all my sins
>   behind your back. . . .

The living, the living, they thank you,
>   as I do this day;
fathers make known to children
>   your faithfulness. (Isa. 38:16-17, 19)

Additional Readings

Joshua 6:1-21
The Israelites conquer Jericho

Hebrews 11:29—12:2
The heroes of faith

Hymn: Great Is Thy Faithfulness, ELW 733

Generous God, we thank you for your faithfulness throughout our lives and we ask for your generous goodness to be with those who are in need of better health. Grant to all of us a real sense of your presence and never-ending care.

Tuesday, September 7, 2021
Time after Pentecost

Hebrews 12:3-13
Trials for the sake of discipline

Endure trials for the sake of discipline. God is treating you as children; for what child is there whom a parent does not discipline? If you do not have that discipline in which all children share, then you are illegitimate and not his children. Moreover, we had human parents to discipline us, and we respected them. Should we not be even more willing to be subject to the Father of spirits and live? For they disciplined us for a short time as seemed best to them, but he disciplines us for our good, in order that we may share his holiness. Now, discipline always seems painful rather than pleasant at the time, but later it yields the peaceful fruit of righteousness to those who have been trained by it. (Heb. 12:7-11)

Psalm
Isaiah 38:10-20
Prayer for health

Additional Reading
Joshua 8:1-23
The Israelites conquer Ai

Hymn: How Clear Is Our Vocation, Lord, ELW 580

Lord God, we often struggle to see your grace-filled presence when bad things happen. Guide us as a gentle parent guides a child, so that we bear the peaceful fruit of righteousness in the midst of tough situations.

Wednesday, September 8, 2021
Time after Pentecost

Matthew 17:14-21

Healing by faith

When [Jesus and the disciples] came to the crowd, a man came to [Jesus], knelt before him, and said, "Lord, have mercy on my son, for he is an epileptic and he suffers terribly; he often falls into the fire and often into the water. And I brought him to your disciples, but they could not cure him." Jesus answered, "You faithless and perverse generation, how much longer must I be with you? How much longer must I put up with you? Bring him here to me." And Jesus rebuked the demon, and it came out of him, and the boy was cured instantly. Then the disciples came to Jesus privately and said, "Why could we not cast it out?" He said to them, "Because of your little faith. For truly I tell you, if you have faith the size of a mustard seed, you will say to this mountain, 'Move from here to there,' and it will move; and nothing will be impossible for you." (Matt. 17:14-20)

Psalm
Isaiah 38:10-20
Prayer for health

Additional Reading
Judges 15:9-20
Samson slays the Philistines

Hymn: Now to the Holy Spirit Let Us Pray, ELW 743

Comforting God, you offer healing that is beyond our knowledge. As the father who asked for mercy on behalf of his son, may your grace incite us to ask for mercy and compassion for others.

Thursday, September 9, 2021
Time after Pentecost

Peter Claver, priest, missionary to Colombia, died 1654

Psalm 116:1-9
I will walk in God's presence

Gracious is the LORD, and righteous;
> our God is merciful.
The LORD protects the simple;
> when I was brought low, he saved me.
Return, O my soul, to your rest,
> for the LORD has dealt bountifully with you.

For you have delivered my soul from death,
> my eyes from tears,
> my feet from stumbling.
I walk before the LORD
> in the land of the living. (Ps. 116:5-9)

Additional Readings

Joshua 2:1-14
Rahab shelters Joshua's spies

Hebrews 11:17-22
Abraham, Isaac, and Jacob act on faith

Hymn: All Depends on Our Possessing, ELW 589

Lord God, in you we find our rest and our help. Ever since we were born you have offered limitless protection, generosity, and mercy. Help us to walk in your presence with gratitude.

Friday, September 10, 2021
Time after Pentecost

James 2:17-26
Abraham and Rahab's faith

. . . So faith by itself, if it has no works, is dead.

But someone will say, "You have faith and I have works." Show me your faith apart from your works, and I by my works will show you my faith. You believe that God is one; you do well. Even the demons believe—and shudder. Do you want to be shown, you senseless person, that faith apart from works is barren? Was not our ancestor Abraham justified by works when he offered his son Isaac on the altar? You see that faith was active along with his works, and faith was brought to completion by the works. (James 2:17-22)

Psalm
Psalm 116:1-9
I will walk in God's presence

Additional Reading
Joshua 2:15-24
An oath to save Rahab and her family

Hymn: For by Grace You Have Been Saved, ELW 598

Good Shepherd, in your divine mercy you lead us and provide for us. Guide us to walk in your presence always and keep us active in faith, so that our good works glorify you and bring praise to your name.

Saturday, September 11, 2021
Time after Pentecost

Matthew 21:23-32

The faith of tax collectors and prostitutes

[Jesus said,] "What do you think? A man had two sons; he went to the first and said, 'Son, go and work in the vineyard today.' He answered, 'I will not'; but later he changed his mind and went. The father went to the second and said the same; and he answered, 'I go, sir'; but he did not go. Which of the two did the will of his father?" They said, "The first." Jesus said to them, "Truly I tell you, the tax collectors and the prostitutes are going into the kingdom of God ahead of you. For John came to you in the way of righteousness and you did not believe him, but the tax collectors and the prostitutes believed him; and even after you saw it, you did not change your minds and believe him." (Matt. 21:28-32)

Psalm
Psalm 116:1-9
I will walk in God's presence

Additional Reading
Joshua 6:22-27
Rahab and her family are spared

Hymn: Let Us Ever Walk with Jesus, ELW 802

Gracious Father, your grace extends to all people and it knows no end. Remind us of your unending love for us and inspire us to see other people as worthy of the same love.

Sunday, September 12, 2021
Time after Pentecost

Mark 8:27-38

Peter's confession of faith

Jesus went on with his disciples to the villages of Caesarea Philippi; and on the way he asked his disciples, "Who do people say that I am?" And they answered him, "John the Baptist; and others, Elijah; and still others, one of the prophets." He asked them, "But who do you say that I am?" Peter answered him, "You are the Messiah." And he sternly ordered them not to tell anyone about him. (Mark 8:27-30)

Psalm

Psalm 116:1-9
I will walk in God's presence

Additional Readings

Isaiah 50:4-9a
The servant is vindicated by God

James 3:1-12
Dangers of the unbridled tongue

Hymn: O Jesus, I Have Promised, ELW 810

O God, through suffering and rejection you bring forth our salvation, and by the glory of the cross you transform our lives. Grant that for the sake of the gospel we may turn from the lure of evil, take up our cross, and follow your Son, Jesus Christ, our Savior and Lord.

Monday, September 13, 2021
Time after Pentecost

John Chrysostom, Bishop of Constantinople, died 407

Psalm 119:169-176
God's law my delight

Let your hand be ready to help me,
>for I have chosen your precepts.
I long for your salvation, O LORD,
>and your law is my delight.
Let me live that I may praise you,
>and let your ordinances help me.
I have gone astray like a lost sheep; seek out your servant,
>for I do not forget your commandments. (Ps. 119:173-176)

Additional Readings
1 Kings 13:1-10
Obeying the word of God

Romans 3:9-20
The unrighteous tongue deceives

Hymn: O Holy Spirit, Root of Life, ELW 399

O Lord, when we feel like lost sheep, seek us out. When we are in need of your help, grant to us a sense of your presence. When we have forgotten your mercy, remind us of your love.

Tuesday, September 14, 2021
Holy Cross Day

John 3:13-17

The Son of Man will be lifted up

[Jesus said to Nicodemus,] "No one has ascended into heaven except the one who descended from heaven, the Son of Man. And just as Moses lifted up the serpent in the wilderness, so must the Son of Man be lifted up, that whoever believes in him may have eternal life.

"For God so loved the world that he gave his only Son, so that everyone who believes in him may not perish but may have eternal life.

"Indeed, God did not send the Son into the world to condemn the world, but in order that the world might be saved through him." (John 3:13-17)

Psalm

Psalm 98:1-4
God has done marvelous things

Additional Readings

Numbers 21:4b-9
A bronze serpent in the wilderness

1 Corinthians 1:18-24
The cross is the power of God

Hymn: Lift High the Cross, ELW 660

Almighty God, your Son, Jesus Christ, was lifted high upon the cross so that he might draw the whole world to himself. To those who look upon the cross, grant your wisdom, healing, and eternal life, through Jesus Christ, our Savior and Lord, who lives and reigns with you and the Holy Spirit, one God, now and forever.

Wednesday, September 15, 2021
Time after Pentecost

John 7:25-36
Jesus the Messiah

Now some of the people of Jerusalem were saying, "Is not this the man whom they are trying to kill? And here he is, speaking openly, but they say nothing to him! Can it be that the authorities really know that this is the Messiah? Yet we know where this man is from; but when the Messiah comes, no one will know where he is from." Then Jesus cried out as he was teaching in the temple, "You know me, and you know where I am from. I have not come on my own. But the one who sent me is true, and you do not know him. I know him, because I am from him, and he sent me." (John 7:25-29)

Psalm
Psalm 119:169-176
God's law my delight

Additional Reading
Isaiah 10:12-20
Evil will be destroyed

Hymn: He Comes to Us as One Unknown, ELW 737

Lord God, there are so many different voices telling us how to be your followers that it is easy to be discouraged and overwhelmed. Grant to us a clear trust in your promises so that when we stumble we are not swayed from following you.

Thursday, September 16, 2021
Time after Pentecost

Cyprian, Bishop of Carthage, martyr, died around 258

Psalm 54
God is my helper

Save me, O God, by your name,
>and vindicate me by your might.
Hear my prayer, O God;
>give ear to the words of my mouth.

For the insolent have risen against me,
>the ruthless seek my life;
>they do not set God before them.

But surely, God is my helper;
>the Lord is the upholder of my life.
He will repay my enemies for their evil.
>In your faithfulness, put an end to them. (Ps. 54:1-5)

Additional Readings

Judges 6:1-10
Israel ignores a prophet of God

1 Corinthians 2:1-5
Beyond human wisdom

Hymn: Lord of Our Life, ELW 766

You, O Lord, are our helper and the upholder of our lives. When we feel threatened and afraid of things happening or things to come, help us so that we might trust in you no matter what comes our way.

Friday, September 17, 2021
Time after Pentecost

Hildegard, Abbess of Bingen, died 1179

Romans 11:25-32
Do not claim to be wiser than you are

So that you may not claim to be wiser than you are, brothers and sisters, I want you to understand this mystery: a hardening has come upon part of Israel, until the full number of the Gentiles has come in. And so all Israel will be saved; as it is written,

> "Out of Zion will come the Deliverer;
>> he will banish ungodliness from Jacob."

> "And this is my covenant with them,
>> when I take away their sins."

As regards the gospel they are enemies of God for your sake; but as regards election they are beloved, for the sake of their ancestors; for the gifts and the calling of God are irrevocable. (Rom. 11:25-29)

Psalm	Additional Reading
Psalm 54	1 Kings 22:24-40
God is my helper	*A prophet imprisoned*

Hymn: Blessed Be the God of Israel, ELW 552

Lord God, teach us humility so that we do not claim to be wiser than we actually are. Help us to treat people of other faiths with respect, even in the midst of our confidence that your love is shown to us most fully in Christ Jesus.

Saturday, September 18, 2021
Time after Pentecost

Dag Hammarskjöld, renewer of society, died 1961

2 Kings 17:5-18
Israel refuses to listen to the prophets

Yet the LORD warned Israel and Judah by every prophet and every seer, saying, "Turn from your evil ways and keep my commandments and my statutes, in accordance with all the law that I commanded your ancestors and that I sent to you by my servants the prophets." They would not listen but were stubborn, as their ancestors had been, who did not believe in the LORD their God. (2 Kings 17:13-14)

Psalm
Psalm 54
God is my helper

Additional Reading
Matthew 23:29-39
Woe to those who kill and crucify the prophets

Hymn: Open Your Ears, O Faithful People, ELW 519

God of grace, you have given to us prophets and seers who call us to live with mercy, compassion, and justice. When we refuse to listen to their witness, redirect us back to your ways.

Sunday, September 19, 2021
Time after Pentecost

Mark 9:30-37

Prediction of the passion

[Jesus and the disciples] went on from there and passed through Galilee. He did not want anyone to know it; for he was teaching his disciples, saying to them, "The Son of Man is to be betrayed into human hands, and they will kill him, and three days after being killed, he will rise again." But they did not understand what he was saying and were afraid to ask him. (Mark 9:30-32)

Psalm

Psalm 54
God is my helper

Additional Readings

Jeremiah 11:18-20
The prophet is like a lamb

James 3:13—4:3, 7-8a
The wisdom from above

Hymn: Children of the Heavenly Father, ELW 781

O God, our teacher and guide, you draw us to yourself and welcome us as beloved children. Help us to lay aside all envy and selfish ambition, that we may walk in your ways of wisdom and understanding as servants of your Son, Jesus Christ, our Savior and Lord.

Monday, September 20, 2021
Time after Pentecost

Psalm 139:1-18

Formed in my mother's womb

For it was you who formed my inward parts;
>you knit me together in my mother's womb.

I praise you, for I am fearfully and wonderfully made.
>Wonderful are your works;

that I know very well.
>My frame was not hidden from you,

when I was being made in secret,
>intricately woven in the depths of the earth. (Ps. 139:13-15)

Additional Readings

2 Kings 5:1-14
The girl servant saves her master

James 4:8-17
Draw near to God

Hymn: Borning Cry, ELW 732

*Creating God, the whole world sings the wonders of your grace-filled work.
Help us to trust that you know us better than ourselves so that, when we are
filled with doubt, we can rely on your faith in us.*

Tuesday, September 21, 2021
Matthew, Apostle and Evangelist

Matthew 9:9-13
Jesus calls to Matthew: Follow me

As Jesus was walking along, he saw a man called Matthew sitting at the tax booth; and he said to him, "Follow me." And he got up and followed him.

And as he sat at dinner in the house, many tax collectors and sinners came and were sitting with him and his disciples. When the Pharisees saw this, they said to his disciples, "Why does your teacher eat with tax collectors and sinners?" But when he heard this, he said, "Those who are well have no need of a physician, but those who are sick. Go and learn what this means, 'I desire mercy, not sacrifice.' For I have come to call not the righteous but sinners." (Matt. 9:9-13)

Psalm
Psalm 119:33-40
Give me understanding

Additional Readings
Ezekiel 2:8—3:11
A prophet to the house of Israel

Ephesians 2:4-10
By grace you have been saved

Hymn: Gracious Spirit, Heed Our Pleading, ELW 401

Almighty God, your Son our Savior called a despised tax collector to become one of his apostles. Help us, like Matthew, to respond to the transforming call of Jesus Christ, who lives and reigns with you and the Holy Spirit, one God, now and forever.

Wednesday, September 22, 2021
Time after Pentecost

Jeremiah 1:4-10
God calls Jeremiah

Now the word of the LORD came to me saying,

"Before I formed you in the womb I knew you,
  and before you were born I consecrated you;
  I appointed you a prophet to the nations."

Then I said, "Ah, LORD GOD! Truly I do not know how to speak, for I am only a boy." But the LORD said to me,

  "Do not say, 'I am only a boy';
  for you shall go to all to whom I send you,
  and you shall speak whatever I command you,
  Do not be afraid of them,
  for I am with you to deliver you,
    says the LORD." (Jer. 1:4-8)

Psalm
Psalm 139:1-18
Formed in my mother's womb

Additional Reading
John 8:21-38
Being disciples of Jesus

Hymn: Lord, Take My Hand and Lead Me, ELW 767

Lord God, you have been a blessing in our lives even before we were born. Remind us daily that you have known us and loved us. When we feel incapable of serving you, help us to remember that you are leading us.

Thursday, September 23, 2021
Time after Pentecost

Psalm 19:7-14

The law gives light

The law of the LORD is perfect,
  reviving the soul;
the decrees of the LORD are sure,
  making wise the simple;
the precepts of the LORD are right,
  rejoicing the heart;
the commandment of the LORD is clear,
  enlightening the eyes;
the fear of the LORD is pure,
  enduring forever;
the ordinances of the LORD are true
  and righteous altogether. (Ps. 19:7-9)

Additional Readings

Exodus 18:13-27
Moses appoints judges to keep peace

Acts 4:13-31
The believers pray for boldness

Hymn: O Spirit of Life, ELW 405

O Lord, your words revive our souls and enlighten us so that we can act with mercy, justice, and compassion in a world that so often lacks those very things. Enable us by your spirit to do your will and follow your ways of love for all creation.

Friday, September 24, 2021
Time after Pentecost

Acts 12:20-25

A leader fails to give glory to God

Now Herod was angry with the people of Tyre and Sidon. So they came to him in a body; and after winning over Blastus, the king's chamberlain, they asked for a reconciliation, because their country depended on the king's country for food. On an appointed day Herod put on his royal robes, took his seat on the platform, and delivered a public address to them. The people kept shouting, "The voice of a god, and not of a mortal!" And immediately, because he had not given the glory to God, an angel of the Lord struck him down, and he was eaten by worms and died.

But the word of God continued to advance and gain adherents. Then after completing their mission Barnabas and Saul returned to Jerusalem and brought with them John, whose other name was Mark. (Acts 12:20-25)

Psalm
Psalm 19:7-14
The law gives light

Additional Reading
Deuteronomy 1:1-18
Moses charges the judges

Hymn: O Word of God Incarnate, ELW 514

O God, your word and grace are always advancing even when leaders do not follow your ways. Kindle in our hearts a desire to trust in you instead of leaders who offer only false hopes.

Saturday, September 25, 2021
Time after Pentecost

Matthew 5:13-20

You are salt and light

[Jesus said to his disciples,] "You are the salt of the earth; but if salt has lost its taste, how can its saltiness be restored? It is no longer good for anything, but is thrown out and trampled under foot.

"You are the light of the world. A city built on a hill cannot be hid. No one after lighting a lamp puts it under the bushel basket, but on the lampstand, and it gives light to all in the house. In the same way, let your light shine before others, so that they may see your good works and give glory to your Father in heaven." (Matt. 5:13-16)

Psalm

Psalm 19:7-14
The law gives light

Additional Reading

Deuteronomy 27:1-10
Moses and the elders charge Israel

Hymn: Go, Make Disciples, ELW 540

Lord God, you consecrate us to live empowered by your love and grace. Grant to us the patience and humility to trust that your love blesses us to be salt and light in the world.

Sunday, September 26, 2021
Time after Pentecost

Mark 9:38-50

Warnings to those who obstruct faith

[Jesus said,] "If any of you put a stumbling block before one of these little ones who believe in me, it would be better for you if a great millstone were hung around your neck and you were thrown into the sea. If your hand causes you to stumble, cut it off; it is better for you to enter life maimed than to have two hands and to go to hell, to the unquenchable fire. And if your foot causes you to stumble, cut it off; it is better for you to enter life lame than to have two feet and to be thrown into hell. And if your eye causes you to stumble, tear it out; it is better for you to enter the kingdom of God with one eye than to have two eyes and to be thrown into hell, where their worm never dies, and the fire is never quenched." (Mark 9:42-48)

Psalm

Psalm 19:7-14
The law gives light

Additional Readings

Numbers 11:4-6, 10-16, 24-29
The spirit is upon seventy elders

James 5:13-20
Prayer and anointing in the community

Hymn: Where Cross the Crowded Ways of Life, ELW 719

Generous God, your Son gave his life that we might come to peace with you. Give us a share of your Spirit, and in all we do empower us to bear the name of Jesus Christ, our Savior and Lord.

Monday, September 27, 2021
Time after Pentecost

Psalm 5
Lead me in righteousness

Lead me, O LORD, in your righteousness
    because of my enemies;
    make your way straight before me.

For there is no truth in their mouths;
    their hearts are destruction;
their throats are open graves;
    they flatter with their tongues.
Make them bear their guilt, O God;
    let them fall by their own counsels;
because of their many transgressions cast them out,
    for they have rebelled against you. (Ps. 5:8-10)

Additional Readings
Zechariah 6:9-15
Far and near led to build the temple

1 Peter 1:3-9
The outcome of faith is salvation

Hymn: Precious Lord, Take My Hand, ELW 773

O Lord, when we feel overwhelmed and hopeless and see no end in sight, lead us in your righteousness. Help us to trust in your promises and faithfulness when our belief is shallow and our faithfulness wanes.

Tuesday, September 28, 2021
Time after Pentecost

Zechariah 8:18-23
The nations seek God in Jerusalem

Thus says the LORD of hosts: Peoples shall yet come, the inhabitants of many cities; the inhabitants of one city shall go to another, saying, "Come, let us go to entreat the favor of the LORD, and to seek the LORD of hosts; I myself am going." Many peoples and strong nations shall come to seek the LORD of hosts in Jerusalem, and to entreat the favor of the LORD. Thus says the LORD of hosts: In those days ten men from nations of every language shall take hold of a Jew, grasping his garment and saying, "Let us go with you, for we have heard that God is with you." (Zech. 8:20-23)

Psalm
Psalm 5
Lead me in righteousness

Additional Reading
1 John 2:18-25
Anointed by the Holy One

Hymn: Come, We That Love the Lord, ELW 625

Lord of hosts, remind us daily of your faithfulness to your people so that when we are burdened by life we may come to you and trust that you are with us.

Wednesday, September 29, 2021
Michael and All Angels

Luke 10:17-20
Jesus gives his followers authority

The seventy returned with joy, saying, "Lord, in your name even the demons submit to us!" Jesus said to them, "I watched Satan fall from heaven like a flash of lightning. See, I have given you authority to tread on snakes and scorpions, and over all the power of the enemy; and nothing will hurt you. Nevertheless, do not rejoice at this, that the spirits submit to you, but rejoice that your names are written in heaven." (Luke 10:17-20)

Psalm
Psalm 103:1-5, 20-22
Bless the Lord, you angels

Additional Readings
Daniel 10:10-14; 12:1-3
Michael shall arise

Revelation 12:7-12
Michael defeats Satan in a cosmic battle

Hymn: Ye Watchers and Ye Holy Ones, ELW 424

Everlasting God, you have wonderfully established the ministries of angels and mortals. Mercifully grant that as Michael and the angels contend against the cosmic forces of evil, so by your direction they may help and defend us here on earth, through your Son, Jesus Christ our Lord, who lives and reigns with you and the Holy Spirit, one God whom we worship and praise with angels and archangels and all the company of heaven, now and forever.

Thursday, September 30, 2021
Time after Pentecost

Jerome, translator, teacher, died 420

Psalm 8
You adorn us with glory and honor

When I look at your heavens, the work of your fingers,
    the moon and the stars that you have established;
what are human beings that you are mindful of them,
    mortals that you care for them?

Yet you have made them a little lower than God,
    and crowned them with glory and honor.
You have given them dominion over the works of your hands;
    you have put all things under their feet,
all sheep and oxen,
    and also the beasts of the field,
the birds of the air, and the fish of the sea,
    whatever passes along the paths of the seas. (Ps. 8:3-8)

Additional Readings
Genesis 20:1-18
Abraham pretends Sarah is his sister

Galatians 3:23-29
Children of God in Christ

Hymn: Many and Great, O God, ELW 837

Creator God, you adorn humanity with glory and honor and all of creation shows the majesty of your work. Grant to us the humility to care for the creation over which you have given us charge.

Prayer List for October

_____

_____

_____

_____

_____

_____

_____

_____

_____

Friday, October 1, 2021
Time after Pentecost

Romans 8:1-11
Life in the Spirit

There is therefore now no condemnation for those who are in Christ Jesus. For the law of the Spirit of life in Christ Jesus has set you free from the law of sin and of death. For God has done what the law, weakened by the flesh, could not do: by sending his own Son in the likeness of sinful flesh, and to deal with sin, he condemned sin in the flesh, so that the just requirement of the law might be fulfilled in us, who walk not according to the flesh but according to the Spirit. For those who live according to the flesh set their minds on the things of the flesh, but those who live according to the Spirit set their minds on the things of the Spirit. (Rom. 8:1-5)

Psalm
Psalm 8
You adorn us with glory and honor

Additional Reading
Genesis 21:22-34
Abraham reconciles with Abimelech

Hymn: O Holy Spirit, Enter In, ELW 786

Freed by your grace, loving God, we live without condemnation. Call us today, in the spirit of freedom, to love and serve those who are crying, yearning, and searching for life in you.

Saturday, October 2, 2021
Time after Pentecost

Luke 16:14-18

The law endures

The Pharisees, who were lovers of money, heard all this, and they ridiculed [Jesus]. So he said to them, "You are those who justify yourselves in the sight of others; but God knows your hearts; for what is prized by human beings is an abomination in the sight of God.

"The law and the prophets were in effect until John came; since then the good news of the kingdom of God is proclaimed, and everyone tries to enter it by force. But it is easier for heaven and earth to pass away, than for one stroke of a letter in the law to be dropped.

"Anyone who divorces his wife and marries another commits adultery, and whoever marries a woman divorced from her husband commits adultery." (Luke 16:14-18)

Psalm
Psalm 8
You adorn us with glory and honor

Additional Reading
Genesis 23:1-20
Abraham buries Sarah

Hymn: Spirit of Gentleness, ELW 396

Spirit of gentleness, it's so tempting to make more rules that build walls between us. You tear down all that divides us, inviting us to live the law of love. That's good news indeed!

Sunday, October 3, 2021
Time after Pentecost

Mark 10:2-16

Teaching on marriage

Some Pharisees came, and to test [Jesus] they asked, "Is it lawful for a man to divorce his wife?" He answered them, "What did Moses command you?" They said, "Moses allowed a man to write a certificate of dismissal and to divorce her." But Jesus said to them, "Because of your hardness of heart he wrote this commandment for you. But from the beginning of creation, 'God made them male and female.'" (Mark 10:2-6)

Psalm

Psalm 8
You adorn us with glory and honor

Additional Readings

Genesis 2:18-24
Created for relationship

Hebrews 1:1-4; 2:5-12
God has spoken by a Son

Hymn: All Are Welcome, ELW 641

Sovereign God, you have created us to live in loving community with one another. Form us for life that is faithful and steadfast, and teach us to trust like little children, that we may reflect the image of your Son, Jesus Christ, our Savior and Lord.

Monday, October 4, 2021
Time after Pentecost

Francis of Assisi, renewer of the church, died 1226
Theodor Fliedner, renewer of society, died 1864

See page 421 for a blessing of pets and animals, often used on or near the October 4 commemoration of Francis of Assisi.

Psalm 112

Happy are those who fear God

Praise the LORD!
>Happy are those who fear the LORD,
>who greatly delight in his commandments.
Their descendants will be mighty in the land;
>the generation of the upright will be blessed.
Wealth and riches are in their houses,
>and their righteousness endures forever.
They rise in the darkness as a light for the upright;
>they are gracious, merciful, and righteous. (Ps. 112:1-4)

Additional Readings
Deuteronomy 22:13-30
Laws about sexual relations

1 Corinthians 7:1-9
Guidance for the married

Hymn: Drawn to the Light, ELW 593

Praise to you, Holy One, for the lives of those who reflect the light of Christ. In your light—and theirs—we are blessed beyond measure. May their lives—and ours—continue to shine.

Tuesday, October 5, 2021
Time after Pentecost

Deuteronomy 24:1-5

Laws about divorce

Suppose a man enters into marriage with a woman, but she does not please him because he finds something objectionable about her, and so he writes her a certificate of divorce, puts it in her hand, and sends her out of his house; she then leaves his house and goes off to become another man's wife. Then suppose the second man dislikes her, writes her a bill of divorce, puts it in her hand, and sends her out of his house (or the second man who married her dies); her first husband, who sent her away, is not permitted to take her again to be his wife. . . .

When a man is newly married, he shall not go out with the army or be charged with any related duty. He shall be free at home one year, to be happy with the wife whom he has married. (Deut. 24:1-4, 5)

Psalm
Psalm 112
Happy are those who fear God

Additional Reading
1 Corinthians 7:10-16
Divorce discouraged

Hymn: Hear Us Now, Our God and Father, ELW 585

Free to be happy! What a dream of joy-filled life you have for us, Loving One. Save us from harm when we fail. Restrain us when we complicate your dream for us. We live only in your love.

Wednesday, October 6, 2021
Time after Pentecost

William Tyndale, translator, martyr, died 1536

Matthew 5:27-36
Teachings about marriage and vow-making

[Jesus said,] "You have heard that it was said, 'You shall not commit adultery.' But I say to you that everyone who looks at a woman with lust has already committed adultery with her in his heart. If your right eye causes you to sin, tear it out and throw it away; it is better for you to lose one of your members than for your whole body to be thrown into hell. And if your right hand causes you to sin, cut it off and throw it away; it is better for you to lose one of your members than for your whole body to go into hell." (Matt. 5:27-30)

Psalm
Psalm 112
Happy are those who fear God

Additional Reading
Jeremiah 3:6-14
God will forgive the unfaithful

Hymn: Chief of Sinners Though I Be, ELW 609

How precious we are to you, faithful God. In our weakness we can contaminate the gift of love in relationships, marriage, and family. Yet you stand with us in our weakness, reminding us of your mercy, new every morning. That's a promise we can live with.

Thursday, October 7, 2021
Time after Pentecost

Henry Melchior Muhlenberg, pastor in North America, died 1787

Psalm 90:12-17
Teach us to number our days

So teach us to count our days
   that we may gain a wise heart.

Turn, O LORD! How long?
   Have compassion on your servants!
Satisfy us in the morning with your steadfast love,
   so that we may rejoice and be glad all our days.
Make us glad as many days as you have afflicted us,
   and as many years as we have seen evil.
Let your work be manifest to your servants,
   and your glorious power to their children.
Let the favor of the Lord our God be upon us,
   and prosper for us the work of our hands—
   O prosper the work of our hands! (Ps. 90:12-17)

Additional Readings
Deuteronomy 5:1-21   **Hebrews 3:7-19**
The ten commandments   *Against disobedience*

Hymn: How Small Our Span of Life, ELW 636

*How long, O Lord! We don't have forever! Bless us now! And even as these
words are in our mouths, your love is with us again this day. All day, every
day, we live in your joy. Forever.*

Friday, October 8, 2021
Time after Pentecost

Deuteronomy 5:22-33

Moses meditates on God's word

The LORD heard your words when you spoke to me, and the LORD said to me: "I have heard the words of this people, which they have spoken to you; they are right in all that they have spoken. If only they had such a mind as this, to fear me and to keep all my commandments always, so that it might go well with them and with their children forever! Go say to them, 'Return to your tents.' But you, stand here by me, and I will tell you all the commandments, the statutes and the ordinances, that you shall teach them, so that they may do them in the land that I am giving them to possess." (Deut. 5:28-31)

Psalm
Psalm 90:12-17
Teach us to number our days

Additional Reading
Hebrews 4:1-11
The rest that God promised

Hymn: Praise, My Soul, the God of Heaven, ELW 864

Your ears, listening God, are open and attentive. You hear the longings, the hopes, and the needs of your creation. You have ordered the days and the seasons of our lives for the good of this beloved creation. For our own good, open our ears!

Saturday, October 9, 2021
Time after Pentecost

Matthew 15:1-9
Jesus teaches true commandments

Then Pharisees and scribes came to Jesus from Jerusalem and said, "Why do your disciples break the tradition of the elders? For they do not wash their hands before they eat." He answered them, "And why do you break the commandment of God for the sake of your tradition? For God said, 'Honor your father and your mother,' and, 'Whoever speaks evil of father or mother must surely die.' But you say that whoever tells father or mother, 'Whatever support you might have had from me is given to God,' then that person need not honor the father. So, for the sake of your tradition, you make void the word of God." (Matt. 15:1-6)

Psalm
Psalm 90:12-17
Teach us to number our days

Additional Reading
Amos 3:13—4:5
Judgment against oppressors

Hymn: Our Father, by Whose Name, ELW 640

Your commandments, loving God, guide us to love you and to love our neighbors. When we use your commandments to justify our self-centered lives, guide us back to loving you and our neighbors.

Sunday, October 10, 2021
Time after Pentecost

Mark 10:17-31
Teaching on wealth and reward

Then Jesus looked around and said to his disciples, "How hard it will be for those who have wealth to enter the kingdom of God!" And the disciples were perplexed at these words. But Jesus said to them again, "Children, how hard it is to enter the kingdom of God! It is easier for a camel to go through the eye of a needle than for someone who is rich to enter the kingdom of God." They were greatly astounded and said to one another, "Then who can be saved?" Jesus looked at them and said, "For mortals it is impossible, but not for God; for God all things are possible." (Mark 10:23-27)

Psalm
Psalm 90:12-17
Teach us to number our days

Additional Readings
Amos 5:6-7, 10-15
Turn from injustice to the poor

Hebrews 4:12-16
Approach the throne of grace

Hymn: Son of God, Eternal Savior, ELW 655

Almighty and ever-living God, increase in us your gift of faith, that, forsaking what lies behind and reaching out to what lies ahead, we may follow the way of your commandments and receive the crown of everlasting joy, through Jesus Christ, our Savior and Lord.

Monday, October 11, 2021
Time after Pentecost

Day of Thanksgiving (Canada)

A Blessing of the Household for Thanksgiving Day is provided on page 359.

Psalm 26
Prayer for acceptance

O Lord, I love the house in which you dwell,
    and the place where your glory abides.
Do not sweep me away with sinners,
    nor my life with the bloodthirsty,
those in whose hands are evil devices,
    and whose right hands are full of bribes.

But as for me, I walk in my integrity;
    redeem me, and be gracious to me.
My foot stands on level ground;
    in the great congregation I will bless the Lord. (Ps. 26:8-12)

Additional Readings
Obadiah 1-9
Those who ate your bread set a trap

Revelation 7:9-17
The nations stand before God's throne

Hymn: We Praise You, O God, ELW 870

Praise to you, God of mercy. In your house we aren't swept out as if we were trash. Instead you sweep us up in your arms. There, right there, we rest in safety.

Tuesday, October 12, 2021
Time after Pentecost

Revelation 8:1-5
The saints' prayers before God

When the Lamb opened the seventh seal, there was silence in heaven for about half an hour. And I saw the seven angels who stand before God, and seven trumpets were given to them.

Another angel with a golden censer came and stood at the altar; he was given a great quantity of incense to offer with the prayers of all the saints on the golden altar that is before the throne. And the smoke of the incense, with the prayers of the saints, rose before God from the hand of the angel. Then the angel took the censer and filled it with fire from the altar and threw it on the earth; and there were peals of thunder, rumblings, flashes of lightning, and an earthquake. (Rev. 8:1-5)

Psalm
Psalm 26
Prayer for acceptance

Additional Reading
Obadiah 10-16
Do not gloat over another's misfortune

Hymn: Evening and Morning, ELW 761

Saving God, when "all hell is breaking loose" around us, where do we stand? In you! Only in you do we stand on level ground. Let the sweet-smelling incense of our prayer rise before you.

Wednesday, October 13, 2021
Time after Pentecost

Obadiah 17-21

The dispossessed shall possess the land

But on Mount Zion there shall be those that escape,
  and it shall be holy;
and the house of Jacob shall take possession of those who dispossessed
      them.
The house of Jacob shall be a fire,
  the house of Joseph a flame,
  and the house of Esau stubble;
they shall burn them and consume them,
  and there shall be no survivor of the house of Esau;
    for the LORD has spoken. (Obad. 17-18)

Psalm
Psalm 26
Prayer for acceptance

Additional Reading
Luke 16:19-31
Lazarus comforted by Abraham

Hymn: To Be Your Presence, ELW 546

God of the nations, our hearts break for those dispossessed of land and home, of dreams and love, of livelihoods and life. Kindle in us the flame of your love for all who are longing for home in you.

Thursday, October 14, 2021
Time after Pentecost

Psalm 91:9-16
The Most High, your refuge

Because you have made the LORD your refuge,
>   the Most High your dwelling place,
no evil shall befall you,
>   no scourge come near your tent.

For he will command his angels concerning you
>   to guard you in all your ways.
On their hands they will bear you up,
>   so that you will not dash your foot against a stone.
You will tread on the lion and the adder,
>   the young lion and the serpent you will trample under foot.
(Ps. 91:9-13)

Additional Readings
Genesis 14:17-24
Abram is blessed by Melchizedek

Romans 15:7-13
The Gentiles glorify God

Hymn: On Eagle's Wings, ELW 787

"Welcome home!" Our hearts quiet at the sound of these words, welcoming God. Hold us secure when we're walking through the fire, when the scourge comes our way, and when we're falling. We are at home in you.

Friday, October 15, 2021
Time after Pentecost

Teresa of Avila, teacher, renewer of the church, died 1582

Isaiah 47:1-9

Throneless nations

Come down and sit in the dust,
     virgin daughter Babylon! . . .
Take the millstones and grind meal,
     remove your veil,
strip off your robe, uncover your legs,
     pass through the rivers.
Your nakedness shall be uncovered,
     and your shame shall be seen.
I will take vengeance,
     and I will spare no one.
Our Redeemer—the Lord of hosts is his name—
     is the Holy One of Israel. (Isa. 47:1, 2-4)

Psalm
Psalm 91:9-16
The Most High, your refuge

Additional Reading
Revelation 17:1-18
Earth's kings conquered

Hymn: If God My Lord Be for Me, ELW 788

Sanctuary God, you will not be silent forever. Rise up as the creatures and creation you love suffer. Open your doors to those searching for refuge, beyond the reach of harm, safe in your loving hands.

Saturday, October 16, 2021
Time after Pentecost

Luke 22:24-30
The greatness of one who serves

A dispute also arose among [the apostles] as to which one of them was to be regarded as the greatest. But [Jesus] said to them, "The kings of the Gentiles lord it over them; and those in authority over them are called benefactors. But not so with you; rather the greatest among you must become like the youngest, and the leader like one who serves. For who is greater, the one who is at the table or the one who serves? Is it not the one at the table? But I am among you as one who serves.

"You are those who have stood by me in my trials; and I confer on you, just as my Father has conferred on me, a kingdom, so that you may eat and drink at my table in my kingdom, and you will sit on thrones judging the twelve tribes of Israel." (Luke 22:24-30)

Psalm
Psalm 91:9-16
The Most High, your refuge

Additional Reading
Isaiah 47:10-15
Futile trust in those who cannot save

Hymn: Lord, Whose Love in Humble Service, ELW 712

Welcoming God, you invite us to your table, with our names written on the place cards in your own hand! No more wrangling about who is most important. You set a place for each of us. You are there serving us. Thanks be to God.

Sunday, October 17, 2021
Time after Pentecost

Ignatius, Bishop of Antioch, martyr, died around 115

Mark 10:35-45

Warnings to ambitious disciples

James and John, the sons of Zebedee, came forward to [Jesus] and said to him, "Teacher, we want you to do for us whatever we ask of you." And he said to them, "What is it you want me to do for you?" And they said to him, "Grant us to sit, one at your right hand and one at your left, in your glory." But Jesus said to them, "You do not know what you are asking. Are you able to drink the cup that I drink, or be baptized with the baptism that I am baptized with?" They replied, "We are able." Then Jesus said to them, "The cup that I drink you will drink; and with the baptism with which I am baptized, you will be baptized; but to sit at my right hand or at my left is not mine to grant, but it is for those for whom it has been prepared." (Mark 10:35-40)

Psalm
Psalm 91:9-16
The Most High, your refuge

Additional Readings
Isaiah 53:4-12
The suffering servant

Hebrews 5:1-10
Through suffering Christ saves

Hymn: O Christ, What Can It Mean for Us, ELW 431

Sovereign God, you turn your greatness into goodness for all the peoples on earth. Shape us into willing servants of your kingdom, and make us desire always and only your will, through Jesus Christ, our Savior and Lord.

Monday, October 18, 2021
Luke, Evangelist

Luke 1:1-4; 24:44-53

Luke witnesses to the ministry of Jesus

Since many have undertaken to set down an orderly account of the events that have been fulfilled among us, just as they were handed on to us by those who from the beginning were eyewitnesses and servants of the word, I too decided, after investigating everything carefully from the very first, to write an orderly account for you, most excellent Theophilus, so that you may know the truth concerning the things about which you have been instructed. (Luke 1:1-4)

Psalm
Psalm 124
Our help is in God

Additional Readings
Isaiah 43:8-13
You are my witness

2 Timothy 4:5-11
The good fight of faith

Hymn: O Christ, the Healer, We Have Come, ELW 610

Almighty God, you inspired your servant Luke to reveal in his gospel the love and healing power of your Son. Give your church the same love and power to heal, and to proclaim your salvation among the nations to the glory of your name, through Jesus Christ, your Son, our healer, who lives and reigns with you and the Holy Spirit, one God, now and forever.

Tuesday, October 19, 2021
Time after Pentecost

1 Samuel 10:17-25
Saul proclaimed king

Then Samuel brought all the tribes of Israel near, and the tribe of Benjamin was taken by lot. He brought the tribe of Benjamin near by its families, and the family of the Matrites was taken by lot. Finally he brought the family of the Matrites near man by man, and Saul the son of Kish was taken by lot. But when they sought him, he could not be found. So they inquired again of the LORD, "Did the man come here?" and the LORD said, "See, he has hidden himself among the baggage." Then they ran and brought him from there. When he took his stand among the people, he was head and shoulders taller than any of them. Samuel said to all the people, "Do you see the one whom the LORD has chosen? There is no one like him among all the people." And all the people shouted, "Long live the king!" (1 Sam. 10:20-24)

Psalm
Psalm 37:23-40
God will exalt the righteous

Additional Reading
Hebrews 6:13-20
The hope of God's promise

Hymn: Give to Our God Immortal Praise! ELW 848

Sovereign God, you set leaders among us, sometimes hidden in plain sight. Give our leaders wisdom and courage to show us the ways to peace. Give us who follow eyes to see your dream for your beloved world.

Wednesday, October 20, 2021
Time after Pentecost

John 13:1-17
Jesus washes the disciples' feet

And during supper Jesus, knowing that the Father had given all things into his hands, and that he had come from God and was going to God, got up from the table, took off his outer robe, and tied a towel around himself. Then he poured water into a basin and began to wash the disciples' feet and to wipe them with the towel that was tied around him. He came to Simon Peter, who said to him, "Lord, are you going to wash my feet?" Jesus answered, "You do not know now what I am doing, but later you will understand." Peter said to him, "You will never wash my feet." Jesus answered, "Unless I wash you, you have no share with me." (John 13:2b-8)

Psalm
Psalm 37:23-40
God will exalt the righteous

Additional Reading
1 Samuel 12:1-25
Israel admonished to fear God

Hymn: Jesu, Jesu, Fill Us with Your Love, ELW 708

Servant God, how easily we confuse clout with true greatness. You are among us as one who serves. Turn us to see you—and join you—where you are on your knees serving your precious creation.

Thursday, October 21, 2021
Time after Pentecost

Psalm 126
Sowing with tears, reaping with joy

Restore our fortunes, O LORD,
    like the watercourses in the Negeb.
May those who sow in tears
    reap with shouts of joy.
Those who go out weeping,
    bearing the seed for sowing,
shall come home with shouts of joy,
    carrying their sheaves. (Ps. 126:4-6)

Additional Readings
Jeremiah 23:9-15
False prophets of hope denounced

Hebrews 7:1-10
The priestly order of Melchizedek

Hymn: Sing to the Lord of Harvest, ELW 694

Turn us, living God, to our hope in Jesus the Christ. Even those living in fields overgrown with tears and weeping can expect a harvest of joy. Cultivate that hope in us as we wait.

Friday, October 22, 2021
Time after Pentecost

Hebrews 7:11-22
Jesus is like Melchizedek

Now if perfection had been attainable through the levitical priesthood—for the people received the law under this priesthood—what further need would there have been to speak of another priest arising according to the order of Melchizedek, rather than one according to the order of Aaron? For when there is a change in the priesthood, there is necessarily a change in the law as well. Now the one of whom these things are spoken belonged to another tribe, from which no one has ever served at the altar. For it is evident that our Lord was descended from Judah, and in connection with that tribe Moses said nothing about priests. (Heb. 7:11-14)

Psalm
Psalm 126
Sowing with tears, reaping with joy

Additional Reading
Jeremiah 26:12-24
Jeremiah threatened with death

Hymn: Soli Deo Gloria, ELW 878

From you, God of promise, come the most unexpected gifts! The crucified Jesus is crowned Melchizedek, "king of righteousness" and "king of peace." In him is our perfection. In him we are made whole.

Saturday, October 23, 2021
Time after Pentecost

James of Jerusalem, martyr, died around 62

Mark 8:22-26

Jesus heals a blind man

[Jesus and the disciples] came to Bethsaida. Some people brought a blind man to [Jesus] and begged him to touch him. He took the blind man by the hand and led him out of the village; and when he had put saliva on his eyes and laid his hands on him, he asked him, "Can you see anything?" And the man looked up and said, "I can see people, but they look like trees, walking." Then Jesus laid his hands on his eyes again; and he looked intently and his sight was restored, and he saw everything clearly. Then he sent him away to his home, saying, "Do not even go into the village." (Mark 8:22-26)

Psalm

Psalm 126
Sowing with tears, reaping with joy

Additional Reading

Jeremiah 29:24-32
A false prophet exposed by Jeremiah

Hymn: Amazing Grace, How Sweet the Sound, ELW 779

Precious Lord, take our hands! Lead us to sites where sight is restored. Lay your loving hands on us. You ask, "Can you see anything?" Yes! We see you and your beloved world with new clarity.

Mark 10:46-52
Christ heals blind Bartimaeus

[Jesus and the disciples] came to Jericho. As [Jesus] and his disciples and a large crowd were leaving Jericho, Bartimaeus son of Timaeus, a blind beggar, was sitting by the roadside. When he heard that it was Jesus of Nazareth, he began to shout out and say, "Jesus, Son of David, have mercy on me!" Many sternly ordered him to be quiet, but he cried out even more loudly, "Son of David, have mercy on me!" Jesus stood still and said, "Call him here." And they called the blind man, saying to him, "Take heart; get up, he is calling you." So throwing off his cloak, he sprang up and came to Jesus. Then Jesus said to him, "What do you want me to do for you?" The blind man said to him, "My teacher, let me see again." Jesus said to him, "Go; your faith has made you well." Immediately he regained his sight and followed him on the way. (Mark 10:46-52)

Psalm

Psalm 126
Sowing with tears, reaping with joy

Additional Readings

Jeremiah 31:7-9
The remnant of Israel is gathered

Hebrews 7:23-28
Christ, the merciful high priest

Hymn: Rise, Shine, You People! ELW 665

Eternal light, shine in our hearts. Eternal wisdom, scatter the darkness of our ignorance. Eternal compassion, have mercy on us. Turn us to seek your face, and enable us to reflect your goodness, through Jesus Christ, our Savior and Lord.

Monday, October 25, 2021
Time after Pentecost

Psalm 119:17-24
Open my eyes

Deal bountifully with your servant,
>so that I may live and observe your word.
Open my eyes, so that I may behold
>wondrous things out of your law.
I live as an alien in the land;
>do not hide your commandments from me.
My soul is consumed with longing
>for your ordinances at all times. (Ps. 119:17-20)

Additional Readings
Exodus 4:1-17
Moses' power from God

1 Peter 2:1-10
Called to a holy priesthood

Hymn: Mine Eyes Have Seen the Glory, ELW 890

Generous God, sometimes like aliens in an unfamiliar land we recognize nothing around us. No familiar landmarks. No friendly faces. Open our eyes to see the wonders of your law in which we live abundant, joy-filled lives.

Tuesday, October 26, 2021
Time after Pentecost

Philipp Nicolai, died 1608; Johann Heermann, died 1647;
Paul Gerhardt, died 1676; hymnwriters

Acts 9:32-35

The healing of Aeneas

Now as Peter went here and there among all the believers, he came
down also to the saints living in Lydda. There he found a man named
Aeneas, who had been bedridden for eight years, for he was paralyzed.
Peter said to him, "Aeneas, Jesus Christ heals you; get up and make your
bed!" And immediately he got up. And all the residents of Lydda and
Sharon saw him and turned to the Lord. (Acts 9:32-35)

Psalm
Psalm 119:17-24
Open my eyes

Additional Reading
2 Kings 6:8-23
Elisha has power over sight

Hymn: Healer of Our Every Ill, ELW 612

*Healing God, where you are, there is life. Where you are there is healing.
We await your invitation to get up from all that holds us down. Make us
whole again!*

Wednesday, October 27, 2021
Time after Pentecost

Matthew 20:29-34

Jesus heals two who are blind

As [Jesus and the disciples] were leaving Jericho, a large crowd followed him. There were two blind men sitting by the roadside. When they heard that Jesus was passing by, they shouted, "Lord, have mercy on us, Son of David!" The crowd sternly ordered them to be quiet; but they shouted even more loudly, "Have mercy on us, Lord, Son of David!" Jesus stood still and called them, saying, "What do you want me to do for you?" They said to him, "Lord, let our eyes be opened." Moved with compassion, Jesus touched their eyes. Immediately they regained their sight and followed him. (Matt. 20:29-34)

Psalm
Psalm 119:17-24
Open my eyes

Additional Reading
Jeremiah 33:1-11
God promises healing

Hymn: We Walk by Faith, ELW 635

God of compassion, hear us when we shout, "Lord, have mercy on us!" In your mercy, you stop. You stand still and ask "What do you want me to do for you?" God of compassion, you hear us!

Thursday, October 28, 2021
Simon and Jude, Apostles

John 14:21-27
Those who love Jesus will keep his word

[Jesus said,] "They who have my commandments and keep them are those who love me; and those who love me will be loved by my Father, and I will love them and reveal myself to them." Judas (not Iscariot) said to him, "Lord, how is it that you will reveal yourself to us, and not to the world?" Jesus answered him, "Those who love me will keep my word, and my Father will love them, and we will come to them and make our home with them. Whoever does not love me does not keep my words; and the word that you hear is not mine, but is from the Father who sent me." (John 14:21-24)

Psalm
Psalm 11
Take refuge in God

Additional Readings
Jeremiah 26:[1-6] 7-16
Jeremiah promises the judgment of God

1 John 4:1-6
Do not believe every spirit of this world

Hymn: Rejoice in God's Saints, ELW 418

O God, we thank you for the glorious company of the apostles, and especially on this day for Simon and Jude. We pray that, as they were faithful and zealous in your mission, so we may with ardent devotion make known the love and mercy of our Savior, Jesus Christ, who lives and reigns with you and the Holy Spirit, one God, now and forever.

Friday, October 29, 2021
Time after Pentecost

Leviticus 19:32-37

Aliens to be treated as fellow citizens

You shall rise before the aged, and defer to the old; and you shall fear your God: I am the LORD.

When an alien resides with you in your land, you shall not oppress the alien. The alien who resides with you shall be to you as the citizen among you; you shall love the alien as yourself, for you were aliens in the land of Egypt: I am the LORD your God.

You shall not cheat in measuring length, weight, or quantity. You shall have honest balances, honest weights, an honest ephah, and an honest hin: I am the LORD your God, who brought you out of the land of Egypt. You shall keep all my statutes and all my ordinances, and observe them: I am the LORD. (Lev. 19:32-37)

Psalm
Psalm 119:1-8
Seeking God with all our hearts

Additional Reading
Romans 3:21-31
Atonement through Christ's blood

Hymn: When the Poor Ones, ELW 725

Lord, you are still speaking to us as you spoke to Moses: Rise for the aged. Love the alien, because you yourself were aliens. Be honest. You are our Lord. And we live well in that confidence.

Saturday, October 30, 2021
Reformation Day (anticipated)

Romans 3:19-28
Justified by God's grace as a gift

But now, apart from law, the righteousness of God has been disclosed, and is attested by the law and the prophets, the righteousness of God through faith in Jesus Christ for all who believe. For there is no distinction, since all have sinned and fall short of the glory of God; they are now justified by his grace as a gift, through the redemption that is in Christ Jesus, whom God put forward as a sacrifice of atonement by his blood, effective through faith. He did this to show his righteousness, because in his divine forbearance he had passed over the sins previously committed; it was to prove at the present time that he himself is righteous and that he justifies the one who has faith in Jesus. (Rom. 3:21-26)

Psalm
Psalm 46
The God of Jacob is our stronghold

Additional Readings
Jeremiah 31:31-34
I will write my law in their hearts

John 8:31-36
The truth will set you free

Hymn: The Church of Christ, in Every Age, ELW 729

Gracious Father, we pray for your holy catholic church. Fill it with all truth and peace. Where it is corrupt, purify it; where it is in error, direct it; where in anything it is amiss, reform it; where it is right, strengthen it; where it is in need, provide for it; where it is divided, reunite it; for the sake of your Son, Jesus Christ, our Savior, who lives and reigns with you and the Holy Spirit, one God, now and forever.

Sunday, October 31, 2021
Time after Pentecost

Reformation Day (transferred to October 30)

Mark 12:28-34

Two commandments: love God and neighbor

One of the scribes came near and heard [some Sadducees] disputing with one another, and seeing that [Jesus] answered them well, he asked him, "Which commandment is the first of all?" Jesus answered, "The first is, 'Hear, O Israel: the Lord our God, the Lord is one; you shall love the Lord your God with all your heart, and with all your soul, and with all your mind, and with all your strength.' The second is this, 'You shall love your neighbor as yourself.' There is no other commandment greater than these." (Mark 12:28-31)

Psalm

Psalm 119:1-8
Seeking God with all our hearts

Additional Readings

Deuteronomy 6:1-9
Keeping the words of God

Hebrews 9:11-14
Redeemed through Christ's blood

Hymn: Lord, Thee I Love with All My Heart, ELW 750

Almighty God, you have taught us in your Son that love fulfills the law. Inspire us to love you with all our heart, our soul, our mind, and our strength, and teach us how to love our neighbor as ourselves, through Jesus Christ, our Savior and Lord.

Prayer List for November

_____

_____

_____

_____

_____

_____

_____

_____

_____

Time after Pentecost
November

The month of November is unique in that it begins with All Saints Day (November 1) and ends with the feast of Christ the King (often the last Sunday of November). The Sunday and daily readings seem to extend the harvest, but in a new way: they speak of God's harvest of human beings into their heavenly home.

Perhaps it is no coincidence that November's scriptural emphasis on the consummation of all things in Christ is reflected in the landscape and the chilling temperatures. Yet in the midst of this turning of the seasons and the reminders of death's presence, Christians hold forth the central feast of the year: the death and resurrection of Christ present in baptism and the holy supper. In these last days of the church's year, Christians are invited to celebrate the reign of Christ, whose death on the cross has transformed our deaths into the gate of everlasting life.

Table Prayer for November

Stay with us, God of life,
as we share the bounty of this food and drink.
We give you thanks for those who have gone before us in faith.
Bring us, with them, to the harvest of everlasting life,
where all people will feast forever at your abundant table.
We ask this through Christ our Lord. Amen.

Remembering Those Who Have Died

Use this prayer in the home or at the grave.

O God, our help in ages past and our hope for years to come:
We give you thanks for all your faithful people
who have followed the light of your word throughout the centuries
into our time and place.

Here individual names may be spoken.

As we remember these people,
strengthen us to follow Christ through this world
until we are carried into the harvest of eternal life,
where suffering and death will be no more.
Hear our prayer in the name of the good and gracious shepherd,
Jesus Christ, our Savior and Lord. Amen.

or

With reverence and affection we remember before you,
O everlasting God,
all our departed friends and relatives.
Keep us in union with them here
through faith and love toward you,
that hereafter we may enter into your presence
and be numbered with those who serve you
and look upon your face in glory everlasting,
through your Son, Jesus Christ our Lord. Amen.

Monday, November 1, 2021
All Saints Day

John 11:32-44
The raising of Lazarus

So [the people] took away the stone. And Jesus looked upward and said, "Father, I thank you for having heard me. I knew that you always hear me, but I have said this for the sake of the crowd standing here, so that they may believe that you sent me." When he had said this, he cried with a loud voice, "Lazarus, come out!" The dead man came out, his hands and feet bound with strips of cloth, and his face wrapped in a cloth. Jesus said to them, "Unbind him, and let him go." (John 11:41-44)

Psalm

Psalm 24
They shall receive a blessing from God

Additional Readings

Isaiah 25:6-9
A feast of rich foods

Revelation 21:1-6a
A new heaven and a new earth

Hymn: Behold the Host Arrayed in White, ELW 425

Almighty God, you have knit your people together in one communion in the mystical body of your Son, Jesus Christ our Lord. Grant us grace to follow your blessed saints in lives of faith and commitment, and to know the inexpressible joys you have prepared for those who love you, through Jesus Christ, our Savior and Lord, who lives and reigns with you and the Holy Spirit, one God, now and forever.

Tuesday, November 2, 2021
Time after Pentecost

Deuteronomy 28:58—29:1
Warnings against disobedience

If you do not diligently observe all the words of this law that are written in this book, fearing this glorious and awesome name, the LORD your God, then the LORD will overwhelm both you and your offspring with severe and lasting afflictions and grievous and lasting maladies. He will bring back upon you all the diseases of Egypt, of which you were in dread, and they shall cling to you. Every other malady and affliction, even though not recorded in the book of this law, the LORD will inflict on you until you are destroyed. Although once you were as numerous as the stars in heaven, you shall be left few in number, because you did not obey the LORD your God. (Deut. 28:58-62)

Psalm
Psalm 51
A contrite heart

Additional Reading
Acts 7:17-29
Moses becomes a resident alien

Hymn: Jesus Loves Me! ELW 595

Awesome God, you give us your laws for the sake of love and liberation for all. Empower us to keep your commands, that we may better love you and our neighbors, bringing health and wholeness to our homes and communities.

Wednesday, November 3, 2021
Time after Pentecost

Martín de Porres, renewer of society, died 1639

Micah 6:1-8

Do justice

"With what shall I come before the LORD,
    and bow myself before God on high?
Shall I come before him with burnt offerings,
    with calves a year old?
Will the LORD be pleased with thousands of rams,
    with ten thousands of rivers of oil?
Shall I give my firstborn for my transgression,
    the fruit of my body for the sin of my soul?"
He has told you, O mortal, what is good;
    and what does the LORD require of you
but to do justice, and to love kindness,
    and to walk humbly with your God? (Micah 6:6-8)

Psalm
Psalm 51
A contrite heart

Additional Reading
John 13:31-35
Commandment to love one another

Hymn: Rise Up, O Saints of God! ELW 669

Merciful God, you sent your begotten one to us as a saving example. Stir our hearts to love justice and kindness, that we may humbly devote ourselves to you for the remainder of our days.

Thursday, November 4, 2021
Time after Pentecost

Psalm 146
God lifts those bowed down

The LORD sets the prisoners free;
    the LORD opens the eyes of the blind.
The LORD lifts up those who are bowed down;
    the LORD loves the righteous.
The LORD watches over the strangers;
    he upholds the orphan and the widow,
    but the way of the wicked he brings to ruin.

The LORD will reign forever,
    your God, O Zion, for all generations.
Praise the LORD! (Ps. 146:7c-10)

Additional Readings
Numbers 36:1-13
Women spared from poverty

Romans 5:6-11
Justified by Christ's blood

Hymn: When Our Song Says Peace, ELW 709

God of the oppressed, you protect the defenseless and aid the abused. Abolish the prisons that confine us and end the separations that divide us, that we may mirror your righteousness and courageously act on behalf of one another.

Friday, November 5, 2021
Time after Pentecost

Deuteronomy 15:1-11
Open your hand to the poor

If there is among you anyone in need, a member of your community in any of your towns within the land that the LORD your God is giving you, do not be hard-hearted or tight-fisted toward your needy neighbor. You should rather open your hand, willingly lending enough to meet the need, whatever it may be. Be careful that you do not entertain a mean thought, thinking, "The seventh year, the year of remission, is near," and therefore view your needy neighbor with hostility and give nothing; your neighbor might cry to the LORD against you, and you would incur guilt. Give liberally and be ungrudging when you do so, for on this account the LORD your God will bless you in all your work and in all that you undertake. Since there will never cease to be some in need on the earth, I therefore command you, "Open your hand to the poor and needy neighbor in your land." (Deut. 15:7-11)

Psalm
Psalm 146
God lifts those bowed down

Additional Reading
Hebrews 9:15-24
The blood of the old covenant

Hymn: Hear I Am, Lord, ELW 574

Generous God, you lavishly provide for all who are in need. Forgive us for our hard-hearted, tight-fisted avarice. Reveal to us the truth of your never-ending abundance, that we may give liberally and ungrudgingly to each other.

Mark 11:12-14, 20-24

Condemnation and blessing

In the morning as [Jesus and the disciples] passed by, they saw the fig tree withered away to its roots. Then Peter remembered and said to him, "Rabbi, look! The fig tree that you cursed has withered." Jesus answered them, "Have faith in God. Truly I tell you, if you say to this mountain, 'Be taken up and thrown into the sea,' and if you do not doubt in your heart, but believe that what you say will come to pass, it will be done for you. So I tell you, whatever you ask for in prayer, believe that you have received it, and it will be yours." (Mark 11:20-24)

Psalm

Psalm 146
God lifts those bowed down

Additional Reading

Deuteronomy 24:17-22
Laws concerning the poor

Hymn: What a Friend We Have in Jesus, ELW 742

God of power, we marvel at your authority. Multiply our faith, dispel our cynicism, deepen our prayers, and spur us to action, that we too may perform miraculous acts that strengthen your reign on earth.

Sunday, November 7, 2021
Time after Pentecost

John Christian Frederick Heyer, died 1873; Bartholomaeus Ziegenbalg, died 1719;
Ludwig Nommensen, died 1918; missionaries

Mark 12:38-44

A widow's generosity

[Jesus] sat down opposite the treasury, and watched the crowd putting money into the treasury. Many rich people put in large sums. A poor widow came and put in two small copper coins, which are worth a penny. Then he called his disciples and said to them, "Truly I tell you, this poor widow has put in more than all those who are contributing to the treasury. For all of them have contributed out of their abundance; but she out of her poverty has put in everything she had, all she had to live on." (Mark 12:41-44)

Psalm

Psalm 146
God lifts those bowed down

Additional Readings

1 Kings 17:8-16
God feeds Elijah and the widow

Hebrews 9:24-28
The sacrifice of Christ

Hymn: Take My Life, That I May Be, ELW 583/685

O God, you show forth your almighty power chiefly by reaching out to us in mercy. Grant us the fullness of your grace, strengthen our trust in your promises, and bring all the world to share in the treasures that come through your Son, Jesus Christ, our Savior and Lord.

Monday, November 8, 2021
Time after Pentecost

Psalm 94
God will vindicate the righteous

Happy are those whom you discipline, O LORD,
> and whom you teach out of your law,
giving them respite from days of trouble,
> until a pit is dug for the wicked.
For the LORD will not forsake his people;
> he will not abandon his heritage;
for justice will return to the righteous,
> and all the upright in heart will follow it. (Ps. 94:12-15)

Additional Readings
Ruth 1:1-22
The widow's poverty

1 Timothy 5:1-8
Widows set their hope on God

Hymn: Let Justice Flow like Streams, ELW 717

Faithful God, you do not forsake or abandon your people. Deepen our love of your law, give us a hunger for your teachings and an eagerness for right relationship, that we may become steadfast in our dealings with you and with each other.

Tuesday, November 9, 2021
Time after Pentecost

1 Timothy 5:9-16

The church assists widows

Let a widow be put on the list if she is not less than sixty years old and has been married only once; she must be well attested for her good works, as one who has brought up children, shown hospitality, washed the saints' feet, helped the afflicted, and devoted herself to doing good in every way. . . . I would have younger widows marry, bear children, and manage their households, so as to give the adversary no occasion to revile us. For some have already turned away to follow Satan. If any believing woman has relatives who are really widows, let her assist them; let the church not be burdened, so that it can assist those who are real widows. (1 Tim. 5:9-10, 14-16)

Psalm
Psalm 94
God will vindicate the righteous

Additional Reading
Ruth 3:14—4:6
The widow's next of kin receive her

Hymn: Will You Let Me Be Your Servant, ELW 659

God our provider, you exhort us to construct safety nets and support for those who society and sinful systems have cast aside. Help us to create policies in line with your laws that uphold those who otherwise would fall through the cracks.

Wednesday, November 10, 2021
Time after Pentecost

Luke 4:16-30
Jesus praises a foreign widow

And [Jesus] said, "Truly I tell you, no prophet is accepted in the prophet's hometown. But the truth is, there were many widows in Israel in the time of Elijah, when the heaven was shut up three years and six months, and there was a severe famine over all the land; yet Elijah was sent to none of them except to a widow at Zarephath in Sidon. There were also many lepers in Israel in the time of the prophet Elisha, and none of them was cleansed except Naaman the Syrian." (Luke 4:24-27)

Psalm
Psalm 94
God will vindicate the righteous

Additional Reading
Ruth 4:7-22
The widow's life restored

Hymn: In Christ There Is No East or West, ELW 650

God of the stranger, you extend your hospitality and healing to immigrants and foreigners. Give encouragement to newcomers and outsiders. Broaden our minds to include new ideas about who is worthy of comfort, relief, and assistance.

Thursday, November 11, 2021
Time after Pentecost

Martin, Bishop of Tours, died 397

Søren Aabye Kierkegaard, teacher, died 1855

Psalm 16
My heart is glad

I bless the LORD who gives me counsel;
>   in the night also my heart instructs me.

I keep the LORD always before me;
>   because he is at my right hand, I shall not be moved.

Therefore my heart is glad, and my soul rejoices;
>   my body also rests secure.

For you do not give me up to Sheol,
>   or let your faithful one see the Pit. (Ps. 16:7-10)

Additional Readings

Daniel 4:4-18
Nebuchadnezzar's dream

1 Timothy 6:11-21
Life that really is life

Hymn: Sing Praise to God, the Highest Good, ELW 871

Mighty Counselor, you go before us to lead and to defend us. You instruct our hearts in wisdom and rescue us from death-dealing forces. We give you thanks for granting rest to our bodies and assurance to our souls.

Friday, November 12, 2021
Time after Pentecost

Daniel 4:19-27
Nebuchadnezzar's dream interpreted

[Daniel said,] "You shall be driven away from human society, and your dwelling shall be with the wild animals. You shall be made to eat grass like oxen, you shall be bathed with the dew of heaven, and seven times shall pass over you, until you have learned that the Most High has sovereignty over the kingdom of mortals, and gives it to whom he will. As it was commanded to leave the stump and roots of the tree, your kingdom shall be re-established for you from the time that you learn that Heaven is sovereign. Therefore, O king, may my counsel be acceptable to you: atone for your sins with righteousness, and your iniquities with mercy to the oppressed, so that your prosperity may be prolonged." (Dan. 4:25-27)

Psalm
Psalm 16
My heart is glad

Additional Reading
Colossians 2:6-15
Christ, the head of every ruler and authority

Hymn: Rise, O Sun of Righteousness, ELW 657

Sovereign God, you dethrone demagogues and drive out tyrants. Liberate us from unjust powers. Transfigure the hearts of our leaders and those in authority, that their governing may center on the needs of the oppressed and not on their own selfish quests for prosperity.

Saturday, November 13, 2021
Time after Pentecost

Mark 12:1-12

The stone which the builders rejected

[Jesus said,] "Have you not read this scripture:

> 'The stone that the builders rejected
> has become the cornerstone;
> this was the Lord's doing,
> and it is amazing in our eyes'?"

When they realized that he had told this parable against them, they wanted to arrest him, but they feared the crowd. So they left him and went away. (Mark 12:10-12)

Psalm
Psalm 16
My heart is glad

Additional Reading
Daniel 4:28-37
Nebuchadnezzar praises God

Hymn: Christ Is Made the Sure Foundation, ELW 645

God of rabble-rousers, your begotten one, Jesus, radically challenged the limitations of our social structures. Bring our focus to those around us who are rejected and despised, that we may deepen our relationships with the people you have put at the center of your kingdom.

Sunday, November 14, 2021
Time after Pentecost

Mark 13:1-8
The end and the coming of the Son

When he was sitting on the Mount of Olives opposite the temple, Peter, James, John, and Andrew asked him privately, "Tell us, when will this be, and what will be the sign that all these things are about to be accomplished?" Then Jesus began to say to them, "Beware that no one leads you astray. Many will come in my name and say, 'I am he!' and they will lead many astray. When you hear of wars and rumors of wars, do not be alarmed; this must take place, but the end is still to come. For nation will rise against nation, and kingdom against kingdom; there will be earthquakes in various places; there will be famines. This is but the beginning of the birth pangs." (Mark 13:3-8)

Psalm
Psalm 16
My heart is glad

Additional Readings
Daniel 12:1-3
God will deliver the people

Hebrews 10:11-14 [15-18] 19-25
The way to God through Christ

Hymn: Through the Night of Doubt and Sorrow, ELW 327

Almighty God, your sovereign purpose brings salvation to birth. Give us faith to be steadfast amid the tumults of this world, trusting that your kingdom comes and your will is done through your Son, Jesus Christ, our Savior and Lord.

Monday, November 15, 2021
Time after Pentecost

Psalm 13
Prayer for salvation

Consider and answer me, O LORD my God!
> Give light to my eyes, or I will sleep the sleep of death,
and my enemy will say, "I have prevailed";
> my foes will rejoice because I am shaken.

But I trusted in your steadfast love;
> my heart shall rejoice in your salvation.
I will sing to the LORD,
> because he has dealt bountifully with me. (Ps. 13:3-6)

Additional Readings

Daniel 8:1-14
A vision of destructive power

Hebrews 10:26-31
Falling into the hands of the living God

Hymn: You Servants of God, ELW 825

Steadfast God, you deal bountifully with your children and answer us when we call upon you. Protect us from harm, that those who seek to destroy us might be transformed by our witness to your life-giving salvation.

Tuesday, November 16, 2021
Time after Pentecost

Hebrews 10:32-39
Call for endurance

But recall those earlier days when, after you had been enlightened, you endured a hard struggle with sufferings, sometimes being publicly exposed to abuse and persecution, and sometimes being partners with those so treated. For you had compassion for those who were in prison, and you cheerfully accepted the plundering of your possessions, knowing that you yourselves possessed something better and more lasting. Do not, therefore, abandon that confidence of yours; it brings a great reward. For you need endurance, so that when you have done the will of God, you may receive what was promised. (Heb. 10:32-36)

Psalm
Psalm 13
Prayer for salvation

Additional Reading
Daniel 8:15-27
Signs of the end times

Hymn: How Firm a Foundation, ELW 796

God of the struggle, you sent your child Jesus in solidarity with all who suffer. Give us compassion for the persecuted in our midst and grant the abused endurance to outlast their oppressors.

Wednesday, November 17, 2021
Time after Pentecost

Elizabeth of Hungary, renewer of society, died 1231

Zechariah 12:1—13:1

The future of Jerusalem

And the Lord will give victory to the tents of Judah first, that the glory of the house of David and the glory of the inhabitants of Jerusalem may not be exalted over that of Judah. On that day the Lord will shield the inhabitants of Jerusalem so that the feeblest among them on that day shall be like David, and the house of David shall be like God, like the angel of the Lord, at their head. And on that day I will seek to destroy all the nations that come against Jerusalem. (Zech. 12:7-9)

Psalm

Psalm 13
Prayer for salvation

Additional Reading

Mark 13:9-23
The coming sufferings

Hymn: Jerusalem, My Happy Home, ELW 628

Victorious one, you have promised to grant the lowliest among us with the same protections afforded to great rulers, and you pledge to safeguard your people from destruction. Uplift those who the world calls feeble and bestow upon them your power.

Thursday, November 18, 2021
Time after Pentecost

Psalm 93
Your throne has been established

The LORD is king, he is robed in majesty;
    the LORD is robed, he is girded with strength.
He has established the world; it shall never be moved;
    your throne is established from of old;
    you are from everlasting.

The floods have lifted up, O LORD,
    the floods have lifted up their voice;
    the floods lift up their roaring.
More majestic than the thunders of mighty waters,
    more majestic than the waves of the sea,
    majestic on high is the LORD! (Ps. 93:1-4)

Additional Readings
Ezekiel 28:1-10
A king pretends to be God

Acts 7:54—8:1a
The Son at God's right hand

Hymn: Blessing and Honor, ELW 854

Everlasting God, the glory of your majesty fills the earth and echoes throughout all creation. We pray for the wellbeing of the waters, that we may live in harmony with your created world and join our voices with the oceans in praising you.

Friday, November 19, 2021
Time after Pentecost

1 Corinthians 15:20-28

That God may be all in all

Then comes the end, when [Christ] hands over the kingdom to God the Father, after he has destroyed every ruler and every authority and power. For he must reign until he has put all his enemies under his feet. The last enemy to be destroyed is death. For "God has put all things in subjection under his feet." But when it says, "All things are put in subjection," it is plain that this does not include the one who put all things in subjection under him. When all things are subjected to him, then the Son himself will also be subjected to the one who put all things in subjection under him, so that God may be all in all. (1 Cor. 15:24-28)

Psalm

Psalm 93
Your throne has been established

Additional Reading

Ezekiel 28:20-26
Israel will be safe

Hymn: Jesus Lives, My Sure Defense, ELW 621

God our ruler, you demolish the powers and principalities that act in defiance of you. Make of us loyal subjects, that we may serve you above any earthly authority.

Saturday, November 20, 2021
Time after Pentecost

John 3:31-36
The one who comes from above

The one who comes from above is above all; the one who is of the earth belongs to the earth and speaks about earthly things. The one who comes from heaven is above all. He testifies to what he has seen and heard, yet no one accepts his testimony. Whoever has accepted his testimony has certified this, that God is true. He whom God has sent speaks the words of God, for he gives the Spirit without measure. The Father loves the Son and has placed all things in his hands. Whoever believes in the Son has eternal life; whoever disobeys the Son will not see life, but must endure God's wrath. (John 3:31-36)

Psalm
Psalm 93
Your throne has been established

Additional Reading
Daniel 7:1-8, 15-18
Daniel's vision of four beasts

Hymn: All Who Believe and Are Baptized, ELW 442

God of life, your truth gives vitality to everyone who experiences it. Strengthen our trust in you, that we may be testimonies to your saving power.

Sunday, November 21, 2021
Christ the King

John 18:33-37
The kingdom of Christ

Then Pilate entered the headquarters again, summoned Jesus, and asked him, "Are you the King of the Jews?" Jesus answered, "Do you ask this on your own, or did others tell you about me?" Pilate replied, "I am not a Jew, am I? Your own nation and the chief priests have handed you over to me. What have you done?" Jesus answered, "My kingdom is not from this world. If my kingdom were from this world, my followers would be fighting to keep me from being handed over to the Jews. But as it is, my kingdom is not from here." Pilate asked him, "So you are a king?" Jesus answered, "You say that I am a king. For this I was born, and for this I came into the world, to testify to the truth. Everyone who belongs to the truth listens to my voice." (John 18:33-37)

Psalm
Psalm 93
Your throne has been established

Additional Readings
Daniel 7:9-10, 13-14
The coming one rules over all

Revelation 1:4b-8
Christ, the ruler of the earth

Hymn: Jesus Shall Reign, ELW 434

Almighty and ever-living God, you anointed your beloved Son to be priest and sovereign forever. Grant that all the people of the earth, now divided by the power of sin, may be united by the glorious and gentle rule of Jesus Christ, our Savior and Lord, who lives and reigns with you and the Holy Spirit, one God, now and forever.

Monday, November 22, 2021
Time after Pentecost

Psalm 76
God is victorious

In Judah God is known,
>   his name is great in Israel.
His abode has been established in Salem,
>   his dwelling place in Zion.
There he broke the flashing arrows,
>   the shield, the sword, and the weapons of war. (Ps. 76:1-3)

Additional Readings

Daniel 7:19-27
The holy ones receive the kingdom

Revelation 11:1-14
The dead are filled with the breath of life

Hymn: A Mighty Fortress Is Our God, ELW 503/504/505

God of peace, you break our bombs, destroy our ammunition, and obliterate our weapons of war. Guide us in the ways of reconciliation. Bring us to the places of harmony and accord where you come to dwell among us.

Tuesday, November 23, 2021
Time after Pentecost

Clement, Bishop of Rome, died around 100
Miguel Agustín Pro, martyr, died 1927

Revelation 11:15-19

God's reign at the end of time

Then the twenty-four elders who sit on their thrones before God fell on their faces and worshiped God, singing,

"We give you thanks, Lord God Almighty,
who are and who were,
for you have taken your great power
and begun to reign.
The nations raged,
but your wrath has come,
and the time for judging the dead,
for rewarding your servants, the prophets
and saints and all who fear your name,
both small and great,
and for destroying those who destroy the earth." (Rev. 11:16-18)

Psalm
Psalm 76
God is victorious

Additional Reading
Ezekiel 29:1-12
Prophecy against Pharaoh

Hymn: Lo! He Comes with Clouds Descending, ELW 435

Eternal God, you reward your saints and prophets and your judgment is against those who decimate the earth. Fortify your people—elders and children, small and great—that we may accomplish the faithful, life-giving work you have called us to do.

Wednesday, November 24, 2021
Time after Pentecost

Justus Falckner, died 1723; Jehu Jones, died 1852; William Passavant,
died 1894; pastors in North America

Ezekiel 30:20-26
I am the Lord

Therefore thus says the Lord GOD: I am against Pharaoh king of Egypt, and will break his arms, both the strong arm and the one that was broken; and I will make the sword fall from his hand. I will scatter the Egyptians among the nations, and disperse them throughout the lands. I will strengthen the arms of the king of Babylon, and put my sword in his hand; but I will break the arms of Pharaoh, and he will groan before him with the groans of one mortally wounded. I will strengthen the arms of the king of Babylon, but the arms of Pharaoh shall fall. And they shall know that I am the LORD, when I put my sword into the hand of the king of Babylon. He shall stretch it out against the land of Egypt, and I will scatter the Egyptians among the nations and disperse them throughout the countries. Then they shall know that I am the LORD. (Ezek. 30:22-26)

Psalm
Psalm 76
God is victorious

Additional Reading
John 16:25-33
I have conquered the world

Hymn: Lead On, O King Eternal! ELW 805

God of promise, you break the sword of the oppressor and scatter the violent. Safeguard us from harm when we are victims of abuse and convict us when we perpetrate bloodshed or cruelty against others.

Blessing of the Household for Thanksgiving Day

We gather this day to give thanks to God for the gifts of this land and its people, for God has been generous to us. As we ask God's blessing upon this food we share, may we be mindful of the lonely and the hungry.

As we prepare to offer thanks to God, let us listen to the words of scripture:

I give thanks to my God always for you because of the grace of God that has been given you in Christ Jesus, for in every way you have been enriched in him, in speech and knowledge of every kind—just as the testimony of Christ has been strengthened among you—so that you are not lacking in any spiritual gift as you wait for the revealing of our Lord Jesus Christ. He will also strengthen you to the end, so that you may be blameless on the day of our Lord Jesus Christ. (1 Cor. 1:4-8)

Let us pray.
God most provident, we join all creation in offering you praise through Jesus Christ. For generations the people of this land have sung of your bounty. With them, we offer you thanksgiving for the rich harvest we have received at your hands. Bless us and this food that we share with grateful hearts. Continue to make our land fruitful, and let our love for you be seen in our pursuit of justice and peace and in our generous response to those in need. We ask this through Christ our Lord. Amen.

May Christ, the living bread, bring us to the feast of eternal life. Amen.

Thursday, November 25, 2021
Time after Pentecost

Day of Thanksgiving (USA)
Isaac Watts, hymnwriter, died 1748

Psalm 25:1-10

To you I lift up my soul

To you, O LORD, I lift up my soul.
O my God, in you I trust;
> do not let me be put to shame;
> do not let my enemies exult over me.
Do not let those who wait for you be put to shame;
> let them be ashamed who are wantonly treacherous. (Ps. 25:1-3)

Additional Readings

Nehemiah 9:6-15
Remembering the exodus

1 Thessalonians 5:1-11
Keep awake

Hymn: O God of Love, O King of Peace, ELW 749

Lover of souls, you are worthy of our trust and praise. Guard us from danger and deception, that your goodness may prevail in our lives and we may glorify your holy name.

Friday, November 26, 2021
Time after Pentecost

1 Thessalonians 5:12-22
Rejoice, pray, give thanks

Rejoice always, pray without ceasing, give thanks in all circumstances; for this is the will of God in Christ Jesus for you. Do not quench the Spirit. Do not despise the words of prophets, but test everything; hold fast to what is good; abstain from every form of evil. (1 Thess. 5:16-22)

Psalm
Psalm 25:1-10
To you I lift up my soul

Additional Reading
Nehemiah 9:16-25
Remembering the exodus

Hymn: God of the Sparrow, ELW 740

God of wisdom, we give you thanks for the lessons of the prophets who teach us to question unjust power. Teach us discernment. Help us to think critically and test everything, that we may hold fast to your goodness.

Luke 21:20-24

A messianic warning

[Jesus said,] "When you see Jerusalem surrounded by armies, then know that its desolation has come near. Then those in Judea must flee to the mountains, and those inside the city must leave it, and those out in the country must not enter it; for these are days of vengeance, as a fulfillment of all that is written. Woe to those who are pregnant and to those who are nursing infants in those days! For there will be great distress on the earth and wrath against this people; they will fall by the edge of the sword and be taken away as captives among all nations; and Jerusalem will be trampled on by the Gentiles, until the times of the Gentiles are fulfilled." (Luke 21:20-24)

Psalm

Psalm 25:1-10
To you I lift up my soul

Additional Reading

Nehemiah 9:26-31
Remembering deliverance from exile

Hymn: Hark! A Thrilling Voice Is Sounding! ELW 246

Majestic God, you sent your begotten one, Jesus Christ, to warn us about coming chaos. Be near to all people caught in the midst of political strife, especially innocent children trapped in places of warfare.

Advent

In the days of Advent, Christians prepare to celebrate the presence of God's Word among us in our own day. During these four weeks, we pray that the reign of God, which Jesus preached and lived, would come among us. We pray that God's justice would flourish in our land, that the people of the earth would live in peace, that the weak and the sick and the hungry would be strengthened, healed, and fed with God's merciful presence.

During the last days of Advent, Christians welcome Christ with names inspired by the prophets: wisdom, liberator of slaves, mighty power, radiant dawn and sun of justice, the keystone of the arch of humanity, and Emmanuel—God with us.

The Advent Wreath

One of the best-known customs for the season is the Advent wreath. The wreath and winter candle-lighting in the midst of growing darkness strengthen some of the Advent images found in the Bible. The unbroken circle of greens is clearly an image of everlasting life, a victory wreath, the crown of Christ, or the wheel of time itself. Christians use the wreath as a sign that Christ reaches into our time to lead us to the light of everlasting life. The four candles mark the progress of the four weeks of Advent and the growth of light. Sometimes the wreath is embellished with natural dried flowers or fruit. Its evergreen branches lead the household and the congregation to the evergreen Christmas tree. In many homes, the family gathers for prayer around the wreath.

An Evening Service of Light for Advent

This brief order may be used on any evening during the season of Advent. If the household has an Advent wreath (one candle for each of the four weeks of Advent), it may be lighted during this service. Alternatively, one simple candle (perhaps a votive candle) may be lighted instead.

Lighting the Advent Wreath

May this candle/these candles be a sign of the coming light of Christ.

One or more candles may be lighted. Use this blessing when lighting the first candle.

Blessed are you, God of Jacob, for you promise to transform weapons of war into implements of planting and harvest and to teach us your way of peace; you promise that our night of sin is far gone and that your day of salvation is dawning.

As we light the first candle on this wreath, wake us from our sleep, wrap us in your light, empower us to live honorably, and guide us along your path of peace.

O house of Jacob, come,
let us walk in the light of the Lord. Amen.

Blessings for the second, third, and fourth weeks of Advent are provided on pages 375, 383, and 391, respectively.

Reading

Read one or more of the scripture passages appointed for the day in the dated pages that follow.

Hymn

One of the following, or the hymn suggested for the day, may be sung. The hymn might be
accompanied by small finger cymbals.

Light One Candle to Watch for Messiah, ELW 240
People, Look East, ELW 248
Savior of the Nations, Come, ELW 263

During the final seven days of the Advent season (beginning on December 17), the
hymn "O Come, O Come, Emmanuel" (ELW 257) is particularly appropriate. The
stanzas of that hymn are also referred to as the "O Antiphons." The first stanza of the
hymn could be sung each day during the final days before Christmas in addition to
the stanza that is specifically appointed for the day.

First stanza
O come, O come, Emmanuel,
and ransom captive Israel,
that mourns in lonely exile here
until the Son of God appear.
Refrain   Rejoice! Rejoice! Emmanuel shall come to you, O Israel.

December 17
O come, O Wisdom from on high,
embracing all things far and nigh:
in strength and beauty come and stay;
teach us your will and guide our way.   *Refrain*

December 18
O come, O come, O Lord of might,
as to your tribes on Sinai's height
in ancient times you gave the law
in cloud, and majesty, and awe.   *Refrain*

December 19
O come, O Branch of Jesse, free
your own from Satan's tyranny;
from depths of hell your people save,
and give them vict'ry o'er the grave.   *Refrain*

December 20

O come, O Key of David, come,
and open wide our heav'nly home;
make safe the way that leads on high,
and close the path to misery.   *Refrain*

December 21

O come, O Dayspring, come and cheer;
O Sun of justice, now draw near.
Disperse the gloomy clouds of night,
and death's dark shadow put to flight.   *Refrain*

December 22

O come, O King of nations, come,
O Cornerstone that binds in one:
refresh the hearts that long for you;
restore the broken, make us new.   *Refrain*

December 23

O come, O come, Emmanuel,
and ransom captive Israel,
that mourns in lonely exile here
until the Son of God appear.   *Refrain*

Text: Psalteriolum Cantionum Catholicarum, Köln, 1710; tr. composite
Text sts. 2, 6, 7 © 1997 Augsburg Fortress

Table Prayer for Advent

For use when a meal follows.

Blessed are you, O Lord our God,
the one who is, who was, and who is to come.
At this table you fill us with good things.
May these gifts strengthen us
to share with the hungry and all those in need,
as we wait and watch for your coming among us
in Jesus Christ our Lord. Amen.

Candles may be extinguished now or after the meal, if one is to follow.

Sunday, November 28, 2021
First Sunday of Advent

Luke 21:25-36

Watch for the coming of the Son of Man

[Jesus said,] "There will be signs in the sun, the moon, and the stars, and on the earth distress among nations confused by the roaring of the sea and the waves. People will faint from fear and foreboding of what is coming upon the world, for the powers of the heavens will be shaken. Then they will see 'the Son of Man coming in a cloud' with power and great glory. Now when these things begin to take place, stand up and raise your heads, because your redemption is drawing near." (Luke 21:25-28)

Psalm

Psalm 25:1-10
To you I lift up my soul

Additional Readings

Jeremiah 33:14-16
A righteous branch springs from David

1 Thessalonians 3:9-13
Strengthen hearts of holiness

Hymn: Wake, Awake, for Night Is Flying, ELW 436

Stir up your power, Lord Christ, and come. By your merciful protection alert us to the threatening dangers of our sins, and redeem us for your life of justice, for you live and reign with the Father and the Holy Spirit, one God, now and forever.

Monday, November 29, 2021
Week of Advent 1

Psalm 90

Prayer for life from God

Lord, you have been our dwelling place
>   in all generations.
Before the mountains were brought forth,
>   or ever you had formed the earth and the world,
>   from everlasting to everlasting you are God.

You turn us back to dust,
>   and say, "Turn back, you mortals."
For a thousand years in your sight
>   are like yesterday when it is past,
>   or like a watch in the night. (Ps. 90:1-4)

Additional Readings

Numbers 17:1-11
The budding of Aaron's rod

2 Peter 3:1-18
Growing in grace

Hymn: O God, Our Help in Ages Past, ELW 632

Life-giving God, in every age you have made a home for your people. Watch over us from the dawn of our mortal lives until the end of our days, that we may testify to your faithfulness throughout the generations.

Tuesday, November 30, 2021
Andrew, Apostle

John 1:35-42
Jesus calls Andrew

One of the two who heard John speak and followed him was Andrew, Simon Peter's brother. He first found his brother Simon and said to him, "We have found the Messiah" (which is translated Anointed). He brought Simon to Jesus, who looked at him and said, "You are Simon son of John. You are to be called Cephas" (which is translated Peter). (John 1:40-42)

Psalm

Psalm 19:1-6
The heavens declare God's glory

Additional Readings

Ezekiel 3:16-21
A sentinel for the house of Israel

Romans 10:10-18
Faith comes from the word of Christ

Hymn: Jesus Calls Us; o'er the Tumult, ELW 696

Almighty God, you gave your apostle Andrew the grace to obey the call of your Son and to bring his brother to Jesus. Give us also, who are called by your holy word, grace to follow Jesus without delay and to bring into his presence those who are near to us, for he lives and reigns with you and the Holy Spirit, one God, now and forever.

Prayer List for December

_____

_____

_____

_____

_____

_____

_____

_____

_____

Wednesday, December 1, 2021
Week of Advent 1

Luke 11:29-32
The coming of the Son of Man

When the crowds were increasing, [Jesus] began to say, "This generation is an evil generation; it asks for a sign, but no sign will be given to it except the sign of Jonah. For just as Jonah became a sign to the people of Nineveh, so the Son of Man will be to this generation. The queen of the South will rise at the judgment with the people of this generation and condemn them, because she came from the ends of the earth to listen to the wisdom of Solomon, and see, something greater than Solomon is here! The people of Nineveh will rise up at the judgment with this generation and condemn it, because they repented at the proclamation of Jonah, and see, something greater than Jonah is here!" (Luke 11:29-32)

Psalm
Psalm 90
Prayer for life from God

Additional Reading
Isaiah 1:24-31
Warning not to wither

Hymn: Mine Eyes Have Seen the Glory, ELW 890

God of revelation, your presence is sometimes hidden, sometimes clear, but always assured. Keep us attentive to your movement around and through us so that we will witness your loving, redeeming power.

Thursday, December 2, 2021
Week of Advent 1

Luke 1:68-79

God's tender compassion

[Zechariah prophesied about John,]
"And you, child, will be called the prophet of the Most High;
for you will go before the Lord to prepare his ways,
to give knowledge of salvation to his people
by the forgiveness of their sins.
By the tender mercy of our God,
the dawn from on high will break upon us,
to give light to those who sit in darkness and in the shadow of death,
to guide our feet into the way of peace." (Luke 1:76-79)

Additional Readings

Malachi 3:5-12
Return to me

Philippians 1:12-18a
Proclaiming Christ

Hymn: Blessed Be the God of Israel, ELW 250

God of new dawns and second chances, you raise us up with tenderness and mercy. Send us the courage and compassion we need to work for the dawning of peace in our hearts, homes, and neighborhoods.

Friday, December 3, 2021
Week of Advent 1

Francis Xavier, missionary to Asia, died 1552

Malachi 3:13-18
Those who serve God

You have spoken harsh words against me, says the LORD. Yet you say, "How have we spoken against you?" You have said, "It is vain to serve God. What do we profit by keeping his command or by going about as mourners before the LORD of hosts?" . . .

Then those who revered the LORD spoke with one another. The LORD took note and listened, and a book of remembrance was written before him of those who revered the LORD and thought on his name. They shall be mine, says the LORD of hosts, my special possession on the day when I act, and I will spare them as parents spare their children who serve them. Then once more you shall see the difference between the righteous and the wicked, between one who serves God and one who does not serve him. (Mal. 3:13-14, 16-18)

Psalm
Luke 1:68-79
God's tender compassion

Additional Reading
Philippians 1:18b-26
Paul rejoices though imprisoned

Hymn: Savior of the Nations, Come, ELW 263

God, you engrave our names in your book of life and you notice everyone who longs for justice. As your people yearn for you like children long for a parent, bring freedom and restoration to all in need.

Saturday, December 4, 2021
Week of Advent 1

John of Damascus, theologian and hymnwriter, died around 749

Luke 9:1-6

The mission of the Twelve

Then Jesus called the twelve together and gave them power and authority over all demons and to cure diseases, and he sent them out to proclaim the kingdom of God and to heal. He said to them, "Take nothing for your journey, no staff, nor bag, nor bread, nor money—not even an extra tunic. Whatever house you enter, stay there, and leave from there. Wherever they do not welcome you, as you are leaving that town shake the dust off your feet as a testimony against them." They departed and went through the villages, bringing the good news and curing diseases everywhere. (Luke 9:1-6)

Psalm

Luke 1:68-79
God's tender compassion

Additional Reading

Malachi 4:1-6
The sun of righteousness shall rise

Hymn: The Son of God, Our Christ, ELW 584

God, you call and send us to be apostles, but we find it difficult to travel light. Help us choose our burdens wisely, leaving behind what does not nourish and carrying only what will help us to share your love.

Lighting the Advent Wreath

Use this blessing when lighting the first two candles.

Blessed are you, God of hope, for you promise to bring forth a shoot from the stump of Jesse who will bring justice to the poor, who will deliver the needy and crush the oppressor, who will stand as a signal of hope for all people.

As we light these candles, turn our wills to bear the fruit of repentance, transform our hearts to live in justice and harmony with one another, and fix our eyes on the root of Jesse, Jesus Christ, the hope of all nations.

O people of hope, come,
let us rejoice in the faithfulness of the Lord. Amen.

Sunday, December 5, 2021
Second Sunday of Advent

Luke 3:1-6

Prepare the way of the Lord

[John the Baptist] went into all the region around the Jordan, proclaiming a baptism of repentance for the forgiveness of sins, as it is written in the book of the words of the prophet Isaiah,

> "The voice of one crying out in the wilderness:
> 'Prepare the way of the Lord,
>> make his paths straight.
> Every valley shall be filled,
>> and every mountain and hill shall be made low,
> and the crooked shall be made straight,
>> and the rough ways made smooth;
> and all flesh shall see the salvation of God.'" (Luke 3:3-6)

Psalm

Luke 1:68-79
God's tender compassion

Additional Readings

Malachi 3:1-4
The messenger refines and purifies

Philippians 1:3-11
A harvest of righteousness

Hymn: On Jordan's Bank the Baptist's Cry, ELW 249

Stir up our hearts, Lord God, to prepare the way of your only Son. By his coming give to all the people of the world knowledge of your salvation; through Jesus Christ, our Savior and Lord, who lives and reigns with you and the Holy Spirit, one God, now and forever.

Monday, December 6, 2021
Week of Advent 2

Nicholas, Bishop of Myra, died around 342

Psalm 126
Prayer for restoration

Restore our fortunes, O LORD,
    like the watercourses in the Negeb.
May those who sow in tears
    reap with shouts of joy.
Those who go out weeping,
    bearing the seed for sowing,
shall come home with shouts of joy,
    carrying their sheaves. (Ps. 126:4-6)

Additional Readings
Isaiah 40:1-11
The earth prepares for God

Romans 8:22-25
All creation waits

Hymn: Oh, That I Had a Thousand Voices, ELW 833

God, you trace the shape of the landscape and set flowing rivers in their courses. Transform our hearts as you renew the face of the earth, restoring everyone to your dreams of healing, justice, and joy.

Tuesday, December 7, 2021
Week of Advent 2

Ambrose, Bishop of Milan, died 397

Isaiah 19:18-25
All nations shall praise God

On that day there will be an altar to the LORD in the center of the land of Egypt, and a pillar to the LORD at its border. It will be a sign and a witness to the LORD of hosts in the land of Egypt; when they cry to the LORD because of oppressors, he will send them a savior, and will defend and deliver them. The LORD will make himself known to the Egyptians; and the Egyptians will know the LORD on that day, and will worship with sacrifice and burnt offering, and they will make vows to the LORD and perform them. The LORD will strike Egypt, striking and healing; they will return to the LORD, and he will listen to their supplications and heal them.

On that day there will be a highway from Egypt to Assyria, and the Assyrian will come into Egypt, and the Egyptian into Assyria, and the Egyptians will worship with the Assyrians. (Isa. 19:19-23)

Psalm
Psalm 126
Prayer for restoration

Additional Reading
2 Peter 1:2-15
Living God's call

Hymn: Prepare the Royal Highway, ELW 264

God, you are steadfast in the midst of crisis and change. Your promise of restoration is a beacon to our hearts. Knit your human family together into one body. Make us a people who love you and one another.

Wednesday, December 8, 2021
Week of Advent 2

Isaiah 35:3-7

God's advent will change everything

Then the eyes of the blind shall be opened,
>and the ears of the deaf unstopped;
then the lame shall leap like a deer,
>and the tongue of the speechless sing for joy.
For waters shall break forth in the wilderness,
>and streams in the desert;
the burning sand shall become a pool,
>and the thirsty ground springs of water;
the haunt of jackals shall become a swamp,
>the grass shall become reeds and rushes. (Isa. 35:5-7)

Psalm
Psalm 126
Prayer for restoration

Additional Reading
Luke 7:18-30
John the Baptist questions Jesus

Hymn: Awake! Awake, and Greet the New Morn, ELW 242

Holy God, you renew life in desolate places, igniting hope against our expectations. Teach us to perceive the preciousness of those who are isolated or abandoned. Equip us to create welcoming spaces of safety and joy.

Thursday, December 9, 2021
Week of Advent 2

Isaiah 12:2-6

In your midst is the Holy One of Israel

With joy you will draw water from the wells of salvation. And you will
say in that day:
Give thanks to the LORD,
    call on his name;
make known his deeds among the nations;
    proclaim that his name is exalted.

Sing praises to the LORD, for he has done gloriously;
    let this be known in all the earth.
Shout aloud and sing for joy, O royal Zion,
    for great in your midst is the Holy One of Israel. (Isa. 12:3-6)

Additional Readings

Amos 6:1-8
Punishment for self-indulgence

2 Corinthians 8:1-15
Encouragement to be generous

Hymn: Rejoice, Rejoice, Believers, ELW 244

*Loving God, you are always among us, even when we worry that you are
far off. Give us words and gestures to proclaim your tireless presence by
embodying your care to the people around us.*

Friday, December 10, 2021
Week of Advent 2

Amos 8:4-12
Do not trample the needy

Hear this, you that trample on the needy,
    and bring to ruin the poor of the land,
saying, "When will the new moon be over
    so that we may sell grain;
and the sabbath,
    so that we may offer wheat for sale?
We will make the ephah small and the shekel great,
    and practice deceit with false balances,
buying the poor for silver
    and the needy for a pair of sandals,
    and selling the sweepings of the wheat."

The LORD has sworn by the pride of Jacob:
Surely I will never forget any of their deeds. (Amos 8:4-7)

Psalm
Isaiah 12:2-6
In your midst is the Holy One of Israel

Additional Reading
2 Corinthians 9:1-15
Generous giving bears fruit

Hymn: Hark, the Glad Sound! ELW 239

God of justice, you remember each person who suffers because of cruelty, carelessness, and neglect. Inspire our memory with yours. Teach us your path of inclusion for the poor, the disenfranchised, and the abandoned.

Saturday, December 11, 2021
Week of Advent 2

Amos 9:8-15

God will set things right

The time is surely coming, says the LORD,
>> when the one who plows shall overtake the one who reaps,
>> and the treader of grapes the one who sows the seed;
> the mountains shall drip sweet wine,
>> and all the hills shall flow with it.
> I will restore the fortunes of my people Israel,
>> and they shall rebuild the ruined cities and inhabit them;
> they shall plant vineyards and drink their wine,
>> and they shall make gardens and eat their fruit.
> I will plant them upon their land,
>> and they shall never again be plucked up
>> out of the land that I have given them,
>>> says the LORD your God. (Amos 9:13-15)

Psalm
Isaiah 12:2-6
In your midst is the Holy One of Israel

Additional Reading
Luke 1:57-66
The birth of John the Baptist

Hymn: People, Look East, ELW 248

God, you call us to rebuild ruined cities and to cultivate abandoned vineyards. Help us tend our frayed connections and neglected relationships so our care will nurture the abundant life rooted in you.

Lighting the Advent Wreath

Use this blessing when lighting three candles.

Blessed are you, God of might and majesty, for you promise to make the desert rejoice and blossom, to watch over the strangers, and to set the prisoners free.

As we light these candles, satisfy our hunger with your good gifts, open our eyes to the great things you have done for us, and fill us with patience until the coming of the Lord Jesus.

O ransomed people of the Lord, come,
let us travel on God's holy way
and enter into Zion with singing. Amen.

Sunday, December 12, 2021
Third Sunday of Advent

Luke 3:7-18

One more powerful is coming

As the people were filled with expectation, and all were questioning in their hearts concerning John, whether he might be the Messiah, John answered all of them by saying, "I baptize you with water; but one who is more powerful than I is coming; I am not worthy to untie the thong of his sandals. He will baptize you with the Holy Spirit and fire. His winnowing fork is in his hand, to clear his threshing floor and to gather the wheat into his granary; but the chaff he will burn with unquenchable fire."

So, with many other exhortations, he proclaimed the good news to the people. (Luke 3:15-18)

Psalm

Isaiah 12:2-6
In your midst is the Holy One of Israel

Additional Readings

Zephaniah 3:14-20
Rejoice in God

Philippians 4:4-7
Rejoice, the Lord is near

Hymn: O Lord, How Shall I Meet You, ELW 241

Stir up the wills of your faithful people, Lord God, and open our ears to the preaching of John that, rejoicing in your salvation, we may bring forth the fruits of repentance; through Jesus Christ, our Savior and Lord, who lives and reigns with you and the Holy Spirit, one God, now and forever.

Monday, December 13, 2021
Week of Advent 3

Lucy, martyr, died 304

Isaiah 11:1-9

A ruler brings justice and peace

A shoot shall come out from the stump of Jesse,
    and a branch shall grow out of his roots.
The spirit of the LORD shall rest on him,
    the spirit of wisdom and understanding,
    the spirit of counsel and might,
    the spirit of knowledge and the fear of the LORD.
His delight shall be in the fear of the LORD.

He shall not judge by what his eyes see,
    or decide by what his ears hear;
but with righteousness he shall judge the poor,
    and decide with equity for the meek of the earth;
he shall strike the earth with the rod of his mouth,
    and with the breath of his lips he shall kill the wicked.
Righteousness shall be the belt around his waist,
    and faithfulness the belt around his loins. (Isa. 11:1-5)

Additional Readings

Numbers 16:1-19
Korah's company rebels

Hebrews 13:7-17
Respect your leaders

Hymn: O Holy Spirit, Enter In, ELW 786

God our wise ruler, you are not distracted or misled. You care for those in need and cannot be moved. Give us wisdom and understanding, counsel and might, knowledge and awe to honor your ways of justice and peace.

Tuesday, December 14, 2021
Week of Advent 3

John of the Cross, renewer of the church, died 1591

Numbers 16:20-35

God destroys Korah's company

As soon as [Moses] finished speaking all these words, the ground under them was split apart. The earth opened its mouth and swallowed them up, along with their households—everyone who belonged to Korah and all their goods. So they with all that belonged to them went down alive into Sheol; the earth closed over them, and they perished from the midst of the assembly. All Israel around them fled at their outcry, for they said, "The earth will swallow us too!" And fire came out from the LORD and consumed the two hundred fifty men offering the incense. (Num. 16:31-35)

Psalm
Isaiah 11:1-9
A ruler brings justice and peace

Additional Reading
Acts 28:23-31
Paul preaches in Rome

Hymn: Lost in the Night, ELW 243

God, you desire engagement and commitment more than lavish offerings or avoidance. Fortify us as we wait for you, giving us the courage to be just and generous on behalf of a world in need.

Wednesday, December 15, 2021
Week of Advent 3

Luke 7:31-35
The Messiah and John the Baptist

[Jesus said,] "To what then will I compare the people of this generation, and what are they like? They are like children sitting in the marketplace and calling to one another,

'We played the flute for you, and you did not dance;
    we wailed, and you did not weep.'

For John the Baptist has come eating no bread and drinking no wine, and you say, 'He has a demon'; the Son of Man has come eating and drinking, and you say, 'Look, a glutton and a drunkard, a friend of tax collectors and sinners!' Nevertheless, wisdom is vindicated by all her children." (Luke 7:31-35)

Psalm
Isaiah 11:1-9
A ruler brings justice and peace

Additional Reading
Micah 4:8-13
God will thresh out the people

Hymn: There's a Voice in the Wilderness, ELW 255

God, you are more than the signs and wonders we expect, but our hearts leap when we catch a glimpse of you. Help us to recognize your wisdom, even where we do not expect it to appear.

Thursday, December 16, 2021
Week of Advent 3

Psalm 80:1-7

Show the light of your countenance

Give ear, O Shepherd of Israel,
    you who lead Joseph like a flock!
You who are enthroned upon the cherubim, shine forth
    before Ephraim and Benjamin and Manasseh.
Stir up your might,
    and come to save us!

Restore us, O God;
    let your face shine, that we may be saved. (Ps. 80:1-3)

Additional Readings

Jeremiah 31:31-34
A new covenant written on the heart

Hebrews 10:10-18
New priest, new sacrifice once for all

Hymn: Come, Thou Long-Expected Jesus, ELW 254

God, we turn to you with longing like plants growing toward the sun. Your mercy restores us. Shine your care on all who have come to the end of their strength. Renew the whole world with your daily dawning.

Friday, December 17, 2021
Week of Advent 3

Hebrews 10:32-39

Confidence that rewards

But recall those earlier days when, after you had been enlightened, you endured a hard struggle with sufferings, sometimes being publicly exposed to abuse and persecution, and sometimes being partners with those so treated. For you had compassion for those who were in prison, and you cheerfully accepted the plundering of your possessions, knowing that you yourselves possessed something better and more lasting. Do not, therefore, abandon that confidence of yours; it brings a great reward. For you need endurance, so that when you have done the will of God, you may receive what was promised. (Heb. 10:32-36)

Psalm
Psalm 80:1-7
Show the light of your countenance

Additional Reading
Isaiah 42:10-18
Sing to God a new song

Hymn: All Earth Is Hopeful, ELW 266

Compassionate God, you endured humiliation and death on behalf of the poor and oppressed. Send us the courage and strength we need to persist in your ways of peace, love, and gentleness.

Saturday, December 18, 2021
Week of Advent 3

Isaiah 66:7-11

God as a nursing mother

Before she was in labor
    she gave birth;
before her pain came upon her
    she delivered a son. . . .
Shall I open the womb and not deliver?
    says the LORD;
shall I, the one who delivers, shut the womb?
    says your God.
Rejoice with Jerusalem, and be glad for her,
    all you who love her;
rejoice with her in joy,
    all you who mourn over her—
that you may nurse and be satisfied
    from her consoling breast;
that you may drink deeply with delight
    from her glorious bosom. (Isa. 66:7, 9-11)

Psalm

Psalm 80:1-7
Show the light of your countenance

Additional Reading

Luke 13:31-35
Jesus as mother hen laments over Jerusalem

Hymn: Love Divine, All Loves Excelling, ELW 631

Laboring God, you open new pathways that no one can block. Give us joy in the wideness of your love and a faith prepared to follow you as you refresh everyone hungering for your compassion.

Lighting the Advent Wreath

Use this blessing when lighting all four candles.

Blessed are you, God of hosts, for you promised to send a son, Emmanuel, who brought your presence among us; and you promise through your Son Jesus to save us from our sin.

As we light these candles, turn again to us in mercy; strengthen our faith in the word spoken by your prophets; restore us and give us life that we may be saved.

O house of David, come,
let us rejoice, for the Son of God, Emmanuel,
comes to be with us. Amen.

Sunday, December 19, 2021
Fourth Sunday of Advent

Luke 1:39-45 [46-55]

Blessed are you among women

In those days Mary set out and went with haste to a Judean town in the hill country, where she entered the house of Zechariah and greeted Elizabeth. When Elizabeth heard Mary's greeting, the child leaped in her womb. And Elizabeth was filled with the Holy Spirit and exclaimed with a loud cry, "Blessed are you among women, and blessed is the fruit of your womb. And why has this happened to me, that the mother of my Lord comes to me? For as soon as I heard the sound of your greeting, the child in my womb leaped for joy. And blessed is she who believed that there would be a fulfillment of what was spoken to her by the Lord." (Luke 1:39-45)

Psalm

Luke 1:46b-55
My soul magnifies the Lord

Additional Readings

Micah 5:2-5a
From Bethlehem comes a ruler

Hebrews 10:5-10
I have come to do your will

Hymn: O Come, O Come, Emmanuel, ELW 257

Stir up your power, Lord Christ, and come. With your abundant grace and might, free us from the sin that binds us, that we may receive you in joy and serve you always, for you live and reign with the Father and the Holy Spirit, one God, now and forever.

Monday, December 20, 2021
Week of Advent 4

Katharina von Bora Luther, renewer of the church, died 1552

Psalm 113
Praise to God, who lifts up the lowly

Who is like the LORD our God,
>who is seated on high,

who looks far down
>on the heavens and the earth?

He raises the poor from the dust,
>and lifts the needy from the ash heap,

to make them sit with princes,
>with the princes of his people.

He gives the barren woman a home,
>making her the joyous mother of children.

Praise the LORD! (Ps. 113:5-9)

Additional Readings

Genesis 25:19-28
Rebekah bears Jacob and Esau

Colossians 1:15-20
Jesus Christ, the firstborn of creation

Hymn: Each Winter As the Year Grows Older, ELW 252

God of change and renewal, you plant seeds of spring in the heart of winter as you lift the lowly and provide for the poor. Open our hearts to greet your reign among us, welcoming the stranger and embracing the outcast.

Tuesday, December 21, 2021
Week of Advent 4

Romans 8:18-30

The whole creation is in labor

We know that the whole creation has been groaning in labor pains until now; and not only the creation, but we ourselves, who have the first fruits of the Spirit, groan inwardly while we wait for adoption, the redemption of our bodies. For in hope we were saved. Now hope that is seen is not hope. For who hopes for what is seen? But if we hope for what we do not see, we wait for it with patience. (Rom. 8:22-25)

Psalm

Psalm 113
Praise to God, who lifts up the lowly

Additional Reading

Genesis 30:1-24
Leah and Rachel bear their sons

Hymn: Fling Wide the Door, ELW 259

God of our past, present, and future, you remind us that no change comes without effort. Give us patience and teach us the labor of hope as we look toward your new creation—a world of safety, justice, and equity for all.

Wednesday, December 22, 2021
Week of Advent 4

Isaiah 42:14-21

God is like a woman in labor

For a long time I have held my peace,
>I have kept still and restrained myself;
now I will cry out like a woman in labor,
>I will gasp and pant.
I will lay waste mountains and hills,
>and dry up all their herbage;
I will turn the rivers into islands,
>and dry up the pools.
I will lead the blind
>by a road they do not know,
by paths they have not known
>I will guide them.
I will turn the darkness before them into light,
>the rough places into level ground.
These are the things I will do,
>and I will not forsake them. (Isa. 42:14-16)

Psalm
Psalm 113
Praise to God, who lifts up the lowly

Additional Reading
Luke 1:5-25
Elizabeth will bear a child

Hymn: Comfort, Comfort Now My People, ELW 256

Eternal God, you are near to us even in times of change and upheaval. When we are lost or confused, help us to trust in you, even if we cannot envision the future you have in store

Thursday, December 23, 2021
Week of Advent 4

Micah 4:6-8

Dominion shall return to Zion

In that day, says the LORD,
　　I will assemble the lame
and gather those who have been driven away,
　　and those whom I have afflicted.
The lame I will make the remnant,
　　and those who were cast off, a strong nation;
and the LORD will reign over them in Mount Zion
　　now and forevermore.

And you, O tower of the flock,
　　hill of daughter Zion,
to you it shall come,
　　the former dominion shall come,
　　the sovereignty of daughter Jerusalem. (Micah 4:6-8)

Psalm
Luke 1:46b-55
My soul gives glory to God

Additional Reading
2 Peter 1:16-21
Making known the coming of Christ

Hymn: Come Now, O Prince of Peace, ELW 247

God of faithfulness and hope, where the world sees weakness, you see worth and strength. Show us the importance and dignity of each human being. Open our hearts to welcome strangers and friends as your Son draws near.

Christmas

Over the centuries, various customs have developed which focus the household on welcoming the light of Christ: the daily or weekly lighting of the Advent wreath, the blessing of the lighted Christmas tree, the candle-lit procession of Las Posadas, the flickering lights of the luminaria, the Christ candle at Christmas.

The Christian household not only welcomes the light of Christ at Christmas, but celebrates the presence of that light throughout the Twelve Days, from Christmas until the Epiphany, January 6. In the Christmas season, Christians welcome the light of Christ that is already with us through faith. In word and gesture, prayer and song, in the many customs of diverse cultures, Christians celebrate this life-giving Word and ask that it dwell more deeply in the rhythm of daily life.

Table Prayer for the Twelve Days of Christmas

With joy and gladness we feast upon your love, O God.
You have come among us in Jesus, your Son,
and your presence now graces this table.
May Christ dwell in us that we might bear his love to all the world,
for he is Lord forever and ever. Amen.

Lighting the Christmas Tree

Use this prayer when you first illumine the tree or when you gather at the tree.

Holy God,
we praise you as we light this tree.
It gives light to this place
as you shine light into darkness through Jesus,
the light of the world.

God of all,
we thank you for your love,
the love that has come to us in Jesus.
Be with us now as we remember that gift of love,
and help us to share that love with a yearning world.

Creator God,
you made the stars in the heavens.
Thank you for the light that shines on us in Jesus,
the bright morning star.
Amen.

Blessing of the Nativity Scene

This blessing may be used when figures are added to the nativity scene and throughout the days of Christmas.

Bless us, O God, as we remember a humble birth. With each angel and shepherd we place here before you, show us the wonder found in a stable. In song and prayer, silence and awe, we adore your gift of love, Christ Jesus our Savior.
Amen.

Friday, December 24, 2021

Nativity of Our Lord
Christmas Eve

Luke 2:1-14 [15-20]

God with us

In those days a decree went out from Emperor Augustus that all the world should be registered. This was the first registration and was taken while Quirinius was governor of Syria. All went to their own towns to be registered. Joseph also went from the town of Nazareth in Galilee to Judea, to the city of David called Bethlehem, because he was descended from the house and family of David. He went to be registered with Mary, to whom he was engaged and who was expecting a child. While they were there, the time came for her to deliver her child. And she gave birth to her firstborn son and wrapped him in bands of cloth, and laid him in a manger, because there was no place for them in the inn. (Luke 2:1-7)

Psalm

Psalm 96
Let the earth be glad

Additional Readings

Isaiah 9:2-7
A child is born for us

Titus 2:11-14
The grace of God has appeared

Hymn: O Little Town of Bethlehem, ELW 279

Almighty God, you made this holy night shine with the brightness of the true Light. Grant that here on earth we may walk in the light of Jesus' presence and in the last day wake to the brightness of his glory; through your Son, Jesus Christ our Lord, who lives and reigns with you and the Holy Spirit, one God, now and forever.

Saturday, December 25, 2021
Nativity of Our Lord
Christmas Day

John 1:1-14
The Word became flesh

In the beginning was the Word, and the Word was with God, and the Word was God. He was in the beginning with God. All things came into being through him, and without him not one thing came into being. What has come into being in him was life, and the life was the light of all people. The light shines in the darkness, and the darkness did not overcome it. . . .

And the Word became flesh and lived among us, and we have seen his glory, the glory as of a father's only son, full of grace and truth. (John 1:1-5, 14)

Psalm
Psalm 98
The victory of our God

Additional Readings
Isaiah 52:7-10
Heralds announce God's salvation

Hebrews 1:1-4 [5-12]
God has spoken by a son

Hymn: Let All Together Praise Our God, ELW 287

Almighty God, you gave us your only Son to take on our human nature and to illumine the world with your light. By your grace adopt us as your children and enlighten us with your Spirit, through Jesus Christ, our Redeemer and Lord, who lives and reigns with you and the Holy Spirit, one God, now and forever.

Sunday, December 26, 2021

First Sunday of Christmas

Stephen, Deacon and Martyr (transferred to December 29)

Luke 2:41-52

Jesus increased in favor with all

When [Jesus'] parents saw him [in the temple] they were astonished; and his mother said to him, "Child, why have you treated us like this? Look, your father and I have been searching for you in great anxiety." He said to them, "Why were you searching for me? Did you not know that I must be in my Father's house?" But they did not understand what he said to them. Then he went down with them and came to Nazareth, and was obedient to them. His mother treasured all these things in her heart.

And Jesus increased in wisdom and in years, and in divine and human favor. (Luke 2:48-52)

Psalm

Psalm 148
God's splendor is over earth and heaven

Additional Readings

1 Samuel 2:18-20, 26
Samuel grew in favor with all

Colossians 3:12-17
Clothe yourselves in love

Hymn: Once in Royal David's City, ELW 269

Shine into our hearts the light of your wisdom, O God, and open our minds to the knowledge of your word, that in all things we may think and act according to your good will and may live continually in the light of your Son, Jesus Christ, who lives and reigns with you and the Holy Spirit, one God, now and forever.

Monday, December 27, 2021
John, Apostle and Evangelist

John 21:20-25
The beloved disciple remains with Jesus

Peter turned and saw the disciple whom Jesus loved following them; he was the one who had reclined next to Jesus at the supper and had said, "Lord, who is it that is going to betray you?" When Peter saw him, he said to Jesus, "Lord, what about him?" Jesus said to him, "If it is my will that he remain until I come, what is that to you? Follow me!" So the rumor spread in the community that this disciple would not die. Yet Jesus did not say to him that he would not die, but, "If it is my will that he remain until I come, what is that to you?"

This is the disciple who is testifying to these things and has written them, and we know that his testimony is true. But there are also many other things that Jesus did; if every one of them were written down, I suppose that the world itself could not contain the books that would be written. (John 21:20-25)

Psalm
Psalm 116:12-19
The death of faithful servants

Additional Readings
Genesis 1:1-5, 26-31
Humankind is created by God

1 John 1:1—2:2
Jesus, the Word of life

Hymn: Love Has Come, ELW 292

Merciful God, through John the apostle and evangelist you have revealed the mysteries of your Word made flesh. Let the brightness of your light shine on your church, so that all your people, instructed in the holy gospel, may walk in the light of your truth and attain eternal life, through Jesus Christ, our Savior and Lord, who lives and reigns with you and the Holy Spirit, one God, now and forever.

Tuesday, December 28, 2021
The Holy Innocents, Martyrs

Matthew 2:13-18
Herod kills innocent children

Now after [the wise men] had left, an angel of the Lord appeared to Joseph in a dream and said, "Get up, take the child and his mother, and flee to Egypt, and remain there until I tell you; for Herod is about to search for the child, to destroy him." Then Joseph got up, took the child and his mother by night, and went to Egypt, and remained there until the death of Herod. This was to fulfill what had been spoken by the Lord through the prophet, "Out of Egypt I have called my son."

When Herod saw that he had been tricked by the wise men, he was infuriated, and he sent and killed all the children in and around Bethlehem who were two years old or under, according to the time that he had learned from the wise men. (Matt. 2:13-16)

Psalm
Psalm 124
We have escaped like a bird

Additional Readings
Jeremiah 31:15-17
Rachel weeps for her children

1 Peter 4:12-19
Continue to do good while suffering

Hymn: Lo, How a Rose E'er Blooming, ELW 272

We remember today, O God, the slaughter of the innocent children of Bethlehem by order of King Herod. Receive into the arms of your mercy all innocent victims. By your great might frustrate the designs of evil tyrants and establish your rule of justice, love, and peace, through Jesus Christ, our Savior and Lord, who lives and reigns with you and the Holy Spirit, one God, now and forever.

Wednesday, December 29, 2021
Stephen, Deacon and Martyr (transferred)

Matthew 23:34-39

Jesus laments that Jerusalem kills her prophets

[Jesus said,] "Therefore I send you prophets, sages, and scribes, some of whom you will kill and crucify, and some you will flog in your synagogues and pursue from town to town, so that upon you may come all the righteous blood shed on earth, from the blood of righteous Abel to the blood of Zechariah son of Barachiah, whom you murdered between the sanctuary and the altar. Truly I tell you, all this will come upon this generation.

"Jerusalem, Jerusalem, the city that kills the prophets and stones those who are sent to it! How often have I desired to gather your children together as a hen gathers her brood under her wings, and you were not willing! See, your house is left to you, desolate. For I tell you, you will not see me again until you say, 'Blessed is the one who comes in the name of the Lord.'" (Matt. 23:34-39)

Psalm

Psalm 17:1-9, 15
I call upon you, O God

Additional Readings

2 Chronicles 24:17-22
Zechariah is stoned to death

Acts 6:8—7:2a, 51-60
Stephen is stoned to death

Hymn: What Child Is This, ELW 296

We give you thanks, O Lord of glory, for the example of Stephen the first martyr, who looked to heaven and prayed for his persecutors. Grant that we also may pray for our enemies and seek forgiveness for those who hurt us, through Jesus Christ, our Savior and Lord, who lives and reigns with you and the Holy Spirit, one God, now and forever.

Thursday, December 30, 2021
Week of Christmas 1

2 Chronicles 1:7-13
Solomon's prayer for wisdom

That night God appeared to Solomon, and said to him, "Ask what I should give you." Solomon said to God, "You have shown great and steadfast love to my father David, and have made me succeed him as king. O LORD God, let your promise to my father David now be fulfilled, for you have made me king over a people as numerous as the dust of the earth. Give me now wisdom and knowledge to go out and come in before this people, for who can rule this great people of yours?" (2 Chron. 1:7-10)

Psalm
Psalm 147:12-20
Praise God in Zion

Additional Reading
Mark 13:32-37
Keep awake

Hymn: Let Our Gladness Have No End, ELW 291

God of wisdom, you teach us to turn to you in prayer in all seasons of life. Help us to discern what we truly need to be your faithful people, living into the purpose to which you have called us.

Friday, December 31, 2021
Week of Christmas 1

Psalm 147:12-20
Praise God in Zion

Praise the LORD, O Jerusalem!
    Praise your God, O Zion!
For he strengthens the bars of your gates;
    he blesses your children within you.
He grants peace within your borders;
    he fills you with the finest of wheat.
He sends out his command to the earth;
    his word runs swiftly.
He gives snow like wool;
    he scatters frost like ashes. (Ps. 147:12-16)

Additional Readings
1 Kings 3:5-14
God grants a discerning mind

John 8:12-19
I am the light

Hymn: Cold December Flies Away, ELW 299

God, we turn to you at year's end with these prayers: for children to be safe, for peace to reign, and for hunger to be satisfied. We trust your wisdom and your word, for you are endless love.

Lesser Festivals and Commemorations

Interested in enriching your prayer life further and in learning more about the people included among the festivals and commemorations? See Gail Ramshaw's *More Days for Praise: Festivals* and *Commemorations in Evangelical Lutheran Worship* (Augsburg Fortress, 2016; 320 pages; ISBN 9781451496215). Each day's entry includes a brief chronology of the person's life; a summary of why the person is remembered by the church; an image of, or related to, the commemoration; a quote from the person, where possible; and devotional hymn and prayer suggestions for the day.

January 1—Name of Jesus Every Jewish boy was circumcised and formally named on the eighth day of his life. Already in his infancy, Jesus bore the mark of a covenant that he made new through the shedding of his blood on the cross.

January 2—Johann Konrad Wilhelm Loehe Wilhelm Loehe was a pastor in nineteenth-century Germany. From the small town of Neuendettelsau he sent pastors to North America, Australia, New Guinea, Brazil, and the Ukraine.

January 15—Martin Luther King Jr. Martin Luther King Jr. is remembered as an American prophet of justice among races and nations. Many churches hold commemorations near Dr. King's birth date of January 15, in conjunction with the American civil holiday honoring him.

January 17—Antony of Egypt Antony was one of the earliest Egyptian desert fathers. He became the head of a group of monks who lived in a cluster of huts and devoted themselves to communal prayer, worship, and manual labor.

January 17—Pachomius Another of the desert fathers, Pachomius was born in Egypt about 290. He organized hermits into a religious community in which the members prayed together and held their goods in common.

January 18—Confession of Peter; *Week of Prayer for Christian Unity begins* The Week of Prayer for Christian Unity is framed by two commemorations, the Confession of Peter and the Conversion of Paul. On this day the church remembers that Peter was led by God's grace to acknowledge Jesus as "the Christ, the Son of the living God" (Matt. 16:16).

January 19—Henry When Erik, king of Sweden, determined to invade Finland for the purpose of converting the people there to Christianity, Henry went with him. Henry is recognized as the patron saint of Finland.

January 21—Agnes Agnes was a girl of about thirteen living in Rome, who had chosen a life of service to Christ as a virgin, despite the Roman emperor Diocletian's ruling that had outlawed all Christian activity. She gave witness to her faith and was put to death as a result.

January 25—Conversion of Paul; *Week of Prayer for Christian Unity ends* As the Week of Prayer for Christian Unity comes to an end, the church remembers how a man of Tarsus named Saul, a former persecutor of the early Christian church, was led to become one of its chief preachers.

January 26—Timothy, Titus, Silas On the two days following the celebration of the Conversion of Paul, his companions are remembered. Timothy, Titus, and Silas were missionary coworkers with Paul.

January 27—Lydia, Dorcas, Phoebe On this day the church remembers three women who were companions in Paul's ministry.

January 28—Thomas Aquinas Thomas Aquinas was a brilliant and creative theologian who immersed himself in the thought of Aristotle and worked to explain Christian beliefs in the philosophical culture of the day.

February 2—Presentation of Our Lord Forty days after the birth of Christ, the church marks the day Mary and Joseph presented him in the temple in accordance with Jewish law. Simeon greeted Mary and Joseph, responding with the canticle that begins "Now, Lord, you let your servant go in peace."

February 3—Ansgar Ansgar was a monk who led a mission to Denmark and later to Sweden. His work ran into difficulties with the rulers of the day, and he was forced to withdraw into Germany, where he served as a bishop in Hamburg.

February 5—The Martyrs of Japan In the sixteenth century, Jesuit missionaries, followed by Franciscans, introduced the Christian faith in Japan. By 1630, Christianity was driven underground. This day commemorates the first martyrs of Japan, twenty-six missionaries and converts, who were killed by crucifixion.

February 14—Cyril, Methodius These brothers from a noble family in Thessalonika in northeastern Greece were priests who are regarded as the founders of Slavic literature. Their work in preaching and worshiping in the language of the people is honored by Christians in both East and West.

February 18—Martin Luther On this day Luther died at the age of sixty-two. For a time, he was an Augustinian monk, but it is primarily for his work as a biblical scholar, translator of the Bible, reformer of the liturgy, theologian, educator, and father of German vernacular literature that he is remembered.

February 23—Polycarp Polycarp was bishop of Smyrna and a link between the apostolic age and the church at the end of the second century. At the age of eighty-six he was martyred for his faith.

February 25—Elizabeth Fedde Fedde was born in Norway and trained as a deaconess. Among her notable achievements is the establishment of the Deaconess House in Brooklyn and the Deaconess House and Hospital of the Lutheran Free Church in Minneapolis.

March 1—George Herbert Herbert was ordained a priest in 1630 and served the little parish of St. Andrew Bremerton until his death. He is best remembered, however, as a writer of poems and hymns, such as "Come, My Way, My Truth, My Life" and "The King of Love My Shepherd Is."

March 2—John Wesley, Charles Wesley The Wesleys were leaders of a revival in the Church of England. Their spiritual methods of frequent communion, fasting, and advocacy for the poor earned them the name "Methodists."

March 7—Perpetua, Felicity In the year 202 the emperor Septimius Severus forbade conversions to Christianity. Perpetua, a noblewoman; Felicity, a slave; and other companions were all catechumens at Carthage in North Africa, where they were imprisoned and sentenced to death.

March 10—Harriet Tubman, Sojourner Truth Harriet Tubman helped about three hundred slaves to escape via the Underground Railroad until slavery was abolished in the United States. After slavery was abolished in New York in 1827, Sojourner Truth became deeply involved in Christianity, and in later life she was a popular speaker against slavery and for women's rights.

March 12—Gregory the Great Gregory held political office and at another time lived as a monk, all before he was elected to the papacy. He also established a school to train church musicians; thus Gregorian chant is named in his honor.

March 17—Patrick Patrick went to Ireland from Britain to serve as a bishop and missionary. He made his base in the north of Ireland and from there made many missionary journeys, with much success.

March 19—Joseph The Gospel of Luke shows Joseph acting in accordance with both civil and religious law by returning to Bethlehem for the census and by presenting the child Jesus in the temple on the fortieth day after his birth.

March 21—Thomas Cranmer Cranmer's lasting achievement is contributing to and overseeing the creation of the Book of Common Prayer, which remains (in revised form) the worship book of the Anglican Communion. He was burned at the stake under Queen Mary for his support of the Protestant Reformation.

March 22—Jonathan Edwards Edwards was a minister in Connecticut and has been described as the greatest of the New England Puritan preachers. Edwards carried out mission work among the Housatonic Indians of Massachusetts and became president of the College of New Jersey, later to be known as Princeton University.

March 24—Oscar Arnulfo Romero Romero is remembered for his advocacy on behalf of the poor in El Salvador, though it was not a characteristic of his early priesthood. After several years of threats to his life, Romero was assassinated while presiding at the eucharist.

March 25—Annunciation of Our Lord Nine months before Christmas, the church celebrates the annunciation. In Luke the angel Gabriel announces to Mary that she will give birth to the Son of God, and she responds, "Here am I, the servant of the Lord."

March 29—Hans Nielsen Hauge Hans Nielsen Hauge was a layperson who began preaching in Norway and Denmark after a mystical experience that he believed called him to share the assurance of salvation with others. At the time, itinerant preaching and religious gatherings held without the supervision of a pastor were illegal, and Hauge was arrested several times.

March 31—John Donne This priest of the Church of England is commemorated for his poetry and spiritual writing. Most of his poetry was written before his ordination and is sacred and secular, intellectual and sensuous.

April 4—Benedict the African Although Benedict was illiterate, his fame as a confessor brought many visitors to him, and he was eventually named superior of a Franciscan community. A patron saint of African Americans, Benedict is remembered for his patience and understanding when confronted with racial prejudice and taunts.

April 6—Albrecht Dürer, Matthias Grünewald, Lucas Cranach These great artists revealed through their work the mystery of salvation and the wonder of creation. Though Dürer remained a Roman Catholic, at his death Martin Luther wrote to a friend, "Affection bids us mourn for one who was the best." Several religious works are included in Grünewald's small surviving corpus, the most famous being the Isenheim Altarpiece. Lucas Cranach was widely known for his woodcuts, some of which illustrated the first German printing of the New Testament.

April 9—Dietrich Bonhoeffer In 1933, and with Hitler's rise to power, Bonhoeffer became a leading spokesman for the Confessing Church, a resistance movement against the Nazis. After leading a worship service on April 8, 1945, at Schönberg prison, he was taken away to be hanged the next day.

April 10—Mikael Agricola Agricola began a reform of the Finnish church along Lutheran lines. He translated the New Testament, the prayer book, hymns, and the mass into Finnish and through this work set the rules of orthography that are the basis of modern Finnish spelling.

April 19—Olavus Petri, Laurentius Petri These two brothers are commemorated for their introduction of the Lutheran movement to the Church of Sweden after studying at the University of Wittenberg. Together the brothers published a complete Bible in Swedish and a revised liturgy in 1541.

April 21—Anselm This eleventh-century Benedictine monk stands out as one of the greatest theologians between Augustine and Thomas Aquinas. He is perhaps best known for his "satisfaction" theory of atonement, in which God takes on human nature in Jesus Christ in order to make the perfect payment for sin.

April 23—Toyohiko Kagawa Toyohiko Kagawa's vocation to help the poor led him to live among them. He was arrested for his efforts to reconcile Japan and China after the Japanese attack of 1940.

April 25—Mark Though Mark himself was not an apostle, it is likely that he was a member of one of the early Christian communities. The gospel attributed to him is brief and direct and is considered by many to be the earliest gospel.

April 29—Catherine of Siena Catherine of Siena was a member of the Order of Preachers (Dominicans), and among Roman Catholics she was the first woman to receive the title Doctor of the Church. She also advised popes and any uncertain persons who told her their problems.

May 1—Philip, James Philip and James are commemorated together because the remains of these two saints were placed in the Church of the Apostles in Rome on this day in 561.

May 2—Athanasius At the Council of Nicea in 325 and when he himself served as bishop of Alexandria, Athanasius defended the full divinity of Christ against the Arian position held by emperors, magistrates, and theologians.

May 4—Monica Almost everything known about Monica comes from Augustine's *Confessions*, his autobiography. Her dying wish was that her son remember her at the altar of the Lord, wherever he was.

May 8—Julian of Norwich Julian was most likely a Benedictine nun living in an isolated cell attached to the Carrow Priory in Norwich, England. When she was about thirty years old, she reported visions that she later compiled into a book, *Sixteen Revelations of Divine Love*, which is a classic of medieval mysticism.

May 9—Nicolaus Ludwig von Zinzendorf Drawn from an overly intellectual Lutheran faith to Pietism, at the age of twenty-two Count Zinzendorf permitted a group of Moravians to live on his lands. Zinzendorf participated in worldwide missions emanating from this community and is also remembered for writing hymns characteristic of his Pietistic faith.

May 14—Matthias After Christ's ascension, the apostles met in Jerusalem to choose a replacement for Judas. Though little is known about him, Matthias had traveled among the disciples from the time of Jesus' baptism until his ascension.

May 18—Erik Erik, long considered the patron saint of Sweden, ruled there from 1150 to 1160. He is honored for efforts to bring peace to the nearby pagan kingdoms and for his crusades to spread the Christian faith in Scandinavia.

May 21—Helena Helena was the mother of Constantine, a man who later became the Roman emperor. Helena is remembered for traveling through Palestine and building churches on the sites she believed to be where Jesus was born, where he was buried, and from which he ascended.

May 24—Nicolaus Copernicus, Leonhard Euler Copernicus formally studied astronomy, mathematics, Greek, Plato, law, medicine, and canon law and is chiefly remembered for his work as an astronomer and his idea that the sun, not the earth, is the center of the solar system. Euler is regarded as one of the founders of the science of pure mathematics and made important contributions to mechanics, hydrodynamics, astronomy, optics, and acoustics.

May 27—John Calvin Having embraced the views of the Reformation by his mid-twenties, John Calvin was a preacher in Geneva, was banished once, and later returned to reform the city with a rigid, theocratic discipline. Calvin is considered the father of the Reformed churches.

May 29—Jiří Tranovský Jiří Tranovský is considered the "Luther of the Slavs" and the father of Slovak hymnody. He produced a translation of the Augsburg Confession and published his hymn collection *Cithara Sanctorum* (Lyre of the Saints), also known as the Tranoscius, which is the foundation of Slovak Lutheran hymnody.

May 31—Visit of Mary to Elizabeth Sometime after the annunciation, Mary visited her cousin Elizabeth, who greeted Mary with the words "Blessed are you among women," and Mary responded with her famous song, the Magnificat.

June 1—Justin Justin was a teacher of philosophy and engaged in debates about the truth of the Christian faith. Having been arrested and jailed for practicing an unauthorized religion, he refused to renounce his faith, and he and six of his students were beheaded.

June 3—The Martyrs of Uganda King Mwanga of Uganda was angered by Christian members of the court whose first allegiance was not to him but to Christ. On this date in 1886, thirty-two young men were burned to death for refusing to renounce Christianity. Their persecution led to a much stronger Christian presence in the country.

June 3—John XXIII Despite the expectation upon his election that the seventy-seven-year-old John XXIII would be a transitional pope, he had great energy and spirit. He convened the Second Vatican Council in order to open the windows of the church. The council brought about great changes in Roman Catholic worship and ecumenical relationships.

June 5—Boniface Boniface led large numbers of Benedictine monks and nuns in establishing churches, schools, and seminaries. Boniface was preparing a group for confirmation on the eve of Pentecost when he and others were killed by a band of pagans.

June 7—Seattle The city of Seattle was named after Noah Seattle against his wishes. After Chief Seattle became a Roman Catholic, he began the practice of morning and evening prayer in the tribe, a practice that continued after his death.

June 9—Columba, Aidan, Bede These three monks from the British Isles were pillars among those who kept alive the light of learning and devotion during the Middle Ages. Columba founded three monasteries, including one on the island of Iona, off the coast of Scotland. Aidan, who helped bring Christianity to the Northumbria area of England, was known for his pastoral style and ability to stir people to charity and good works. Bede was a Bible translator and scripture scholar who wrote a history of the English church and was the first historian to date events anno Domini (AD), the "year of our Lord."

June 11—Barnabas Though he was not among the Twelve mentioned in the gospels, the book of Acts gives Barnabas the title of apostle. When Paul came to Jerusalem after his conversion, Barnabas took him in over the fears of the other apostles who doubted Paul's discipleship.

June 14—Basil the Great, Gregory of Nyssa, Gregory of Nazianzus, Macrina The three men in this group are known as the Cappadocian fathers; all three explored the mystery of the Holy Trinity. Basil's Longer Rule and Shorter Rule for monastic life are the basis for Eastern monasticism to this day, and express a preference for communal monastic life over that of hermits. Gregory of Nazianzus defended Orthodox trinitarian and christological doctrine, and his preaching won over the city of Constantinople. Gregory of Nyssa is remembered as a writer on spiritual life and the contemplation of God in worship and sacraments. Macrina was the older sister of Basil and Gregory of Nyssa, and her teaching was influential within the early church.

June 17—Emanuel Nine On June 17, 2015, Clementa C. Pinckney, Cynthia Marie Graham Hurd, Susie Jackson, Ethel Lee Lance, DePayne Middleton-Doctor, Tywanza Sanders, Daniel Lee Simmons, Sharonda Coleman-Singleton, and Myra Thompson were murdered by a self-professed white supremacist while they were gathered for Bible study and prayer at the Emanuel African Methodist Episcopal Church (often referred to as Mother Emanuel) in Charleston, South Carolina. A resolution to commemorate June 17 as a day of repentance for the martyrdom of the Emanuel Nine was adopted by the Churchwide Assembly of the Evangelical Lutheran Church in America on August 8, 2019.

June 21—Onesimos Nesib Onesimos, an Ethiopian, was captured by slave traders and taken from his homeland to Eritrea, where he was bought, freed, and educated by Swedish missionaries. He translated the Bible into Oromo and returned to his homeland to preach the gospel there.

June 24—John the Baptist The birth of John the Baptist is celebrated exactly six months before Christmas Eve. For Christians in the Northern Hemisphere, these two dates are deeply symbolic, since John said that he must decrease as Jesus increased. John was born as the days are longest and then steadily decrease, while Jesus was born as the days are shortest and then steadily increase.

June 25—Presentation of the Augsburg Confession On this day in 1530 the German and Latin editions of the Augsburg Confession were presented to Emperor Charles of the Holy Roman Empire. The Augsburg Confession was written by Philipp Melanchthon and endorsed by Martin Luther and consists of a brief summary of points in which the reformers saw their teaching as either agreeing with or differing from that of the Roman Catholic Church of the time.

June 25—Philipp Melanchthon Though he died on April 19, Philipp Melanchthon is commemorated today because of his connection with the Augsburg Confession. Colleague and co-reformer with Martin Luther, Melanchthon was a brilliant scholar, known as "the teacher of Germany."

June 27—Cyril Remembered as an outstanding theologian, Cyril defended the Orthodox teachings about the person of Christ against Nestorius, who was at that time bishop of Constantinople. Eventually it was decided that Cyril's interpretation, that Christ's person included both divine and human natures, was correct.

June 28—Irenaeus Irenaeus believed that only Matthew, Mark, Luke, and John were trustworthy gospels. As a result of his battles with the Gnostics, he was one of the first to speak of the church as "catholic," meaning that congregations did not exist by themselves but were linked to one another throughout the whole church.

June 29—Peter, Paul One of the things that unites Peter and Paul is the tradition that says they were martyred together on this date in AD 67 or 68. What unites them even more closely is their common confession of Jesus Christ.

July 1—Catherine Winkworth, John Mason Neale Many of the most beloved hymns in the English language are the work of these gifted poets. Catherine Winkworth devoted herself to the translation of German hymns into English, while John Mason Neale specialized in translating many ancient Latin and Greek hymns.

July 3—Thomas Alongside the doubt for which Thomas is famous, the Gospel according to John shows Thomas moving from doubt to deep faith. Thomas makes one of the strongest confessions of faith in the New Testament, "My Lord and my God!" (John 20:28).

July 6—Jan Hus Jan Hus was a Bohemian priest who spoke against abuses in the church of his day in many of the same ways Luther would a century later. The followers of Jan Hus became known as the Czech Brethren and later became the Moravian Church.

July 11—Benedict of Nursia Benedict is known as the father of Western monasticism. Benedict encouraged a generous spirit of hospitality. Visitors to Benedictine communities are to be welcomed as Christ himself.

July 12—Nathan Söderblom In 1930 this Swedish theologian, ecumenist, and social activist received the Nobel Prize for peace. Söderblom organized the Universal Christian Council on Life and Work, which was one of the organizations that in 1948 came together to form the World Council of Churches.

July 17—Bartolomé de Las Casas Bartolomé de Las Casas was a Spanish priest and a missionary in the Western Hemisphere. Throughout the Caribbean and Central America, he worked to stop the enslavement of native people, to halt the brutal treatment of women by military forces, and to promote laws that humanized the process of colonization.

July 22—Mary Magdalene The gospels report Mary Magdalene was one of the women of Galilee who followed Jesus. As the first person to whom the risen Lord appeared, she returned to the disciples with the news and has been called "the apostle to the apostles" for her proclamation of the resurrection.

July 23—Birgitta of Sweden Birgitta's devotional commitments led her to give to the poor and needy all that she owned while she began to live a more ascetic life. She founded an order of monks and nuns, the Order of the Holy Savior (Birgittines), whose superior was a woman.

July 25—James James was one of the sons of Zebedee and is counted as one of the twelve disciples. James was the first of the Twelve to suffer martyrdom and is the only apostle whose martyrdom is recorded in scripture.

July 28—Johann Sebastian Bach, Heinrich Schütz, George Frederick Handel These three composers did much to enrich the worship life of the church. Johann Sebastian Bach drew on the Lutheran tradition of hymnody and wrote about two hundred cantatas, including at least two for each Sunday and festival day in the Lutheran calendar of his day. George Frederick Handel was not primarily a church musician, but his great work *Messiah* is a musical proclamation of the scriptures. Heinrich Schütz wrote choral settings of biblical texts and paid special attention to ways his composition would underscore the meaning of the words.

July 29—Mary, Martha, Lazarus of Bethany Mary and Martha are remembered for the hospitality and refreshment they offered Jesus in their home. Following the characterization drawn by Luke, Martha represents the active life, and Mary, the contemplative.

July 29—Olaf Olaf is considered the patron saint of Norway. While at war in the Baltic and in Normandy, he became a Christian; then he returned to Norway and declared himself king, and from then on Christianity was the dominant religion of the realm.

August 8—Dominic Dominic believed that a stumbling block to restoring heretics to the church was the wealth of clergy, so he formed an itinerant religious order, the Order of Preachers (Dominicans), who lived in poverty, studied philosophy and theology, and preached against heresy.

August 10—Lawrence Lawrence was one of seven deacons of the congregation at Rome and, like the deacons appointed in Acts, was responsible for financial matters in the church and for the care of the poor.

August 11—Clare At age eighteen, Clare of Assisi heard Francis preach a sermon. With Francis's help she and a growing number of companions established a women's Franciscan community called the Order of Poor Ladies, or Poor Clares.

August 13—Florence Nightingale, Clara Maass Nightingale led a group of thirty-eight nurses to serve in the Crimean War, where they worked in appalling conditions. She returned to London as a hero and there resumed her work for hospital reform. Clara Maass was born in New Jersey and served as a nurse in the Spanish-American War, where she encountered the horrors of yellow fever. Later responding to a call for subjects in research on yellow fever, Maass contracted the disease and died.

August 14—Maximilian Kolbe, Kaj Munk Confined in Auschwitz, Father Kolbe was a Franciscan priest who gave generously of his meager resources and finally volunteered to be starved to death in place of another man who was a husband and father. Kaj Munk, a Danish Lutheran pastor and playwright, was an outspoken critic of the Nazis. His plays frequently highlighted the eventual victory of the Christian faith despite the church's weak and ineffective witness.

August 15—Mary, Mother of Our Lord The honor paid to Mary as mother of our Lord goes back to biblical times, when Mary herself sang, "From now on all generations will call me blessed" (Luke 1:48). Mary's song speaks of reversals in the reign of God: the mighty are cast down, the lowly are lifted up, the hungry are fed, and the rich are sent away empty-handed.

August 20—Bernard of Clairvaux Bernard was a Cistercian monk who became an abbot of great spiritual depth. Through translation his several devotional writings and hymns are still read and sung today.

August 24—Bartholomew Bartholomew is mentioned as one of Jesus' disciples in Matthew, Mark, and Luke. Except for his name on these lists of the Twelve, little is known.

August 28—Augustine As an adult, Augustine came to see Christianity as a religion appropriate for a philosopher. Augustine was baptized by Ambrose at the Easter Vigil in 387, was made bishop of Hippo in 396, and was one of the greatest theologians of the Western church.

August 28—Moses the Black A man of great strength and rough character, Moses the Black was converted to Christian faith toward the close of the fourth century. The change in his heart and life had a profound impact on his native Ethiopia.

September 2—Nikolai Frederik Severin Grundtvig Grundtvig was a prominent Dan-

ish theologian of the nineteenth century. From his university days, he was convinced that poetry spoke to the human spirit better than prose, and he wrote more than a thousand hymns.

September 9—Peter Claver Peter Claver was born into Spanish nobility and was persuaded to become a Jesuit missionary. He served in Cartagena (in what is now Colombia) by teaching and caring for the slaves.

September 13—John Chrysostom John was a priest in Antioch and an outstanding preacher. His eloquence earned him the nickname Chrysostom ("golden mouth"), but he also preached against corruption among the royal court, whereupon the empress sent him into exile.

September 14—Holy Cross Day The celebration of Holy Cross Day commemorates the dedication of the Church of the Resurrection in 335 on the location believed to have been where Christ was buried.

September 16—Cyprian During Cyprian's time as bishop, many people had denied the faith under duress. In contrast to some who held the belief that the church should not receive these people back, Cyprian believed they ought to be welcomed into full communion after a period of penance.

September 17—Hildegard, Abbess of Bingen Hildegard lived virtually her entire life in convents yet was widely influential. She advised and reproved kings and popes, wrote poems and hymns, and produced treatises in medicine, theology, and natural history.

September 18—Dag Hammarskjöld Dag Hammarskjöld was a Swedish diplomat and humanitarian who served as secretary general of the United Nations. The depth of Hammarskjöld's Christian faith was unknown until his private journal, *Markings*, was published following his death.

September 21—Matthew Matthew was a tax collector, an occupation that was distrusted, since tax collectors were frequently dishonest and worked as agents for the Roman occupying government; yet it was these outcasts to whom Jesus showed his love. Since the second century, tradition has attributed the first gospel to him.

September 29—Michael and All Angels The scriptures speak of angels who worship God in heaven, and in both testaments angels are God's messengers on earth. Michael is an angel whose name appears in Daniel as the heavenly being who leads the faithful dead to God's throne on the day of resurrection, while in the book of Revelation, Michael fights in a cosmic battle against Satan.

September 30—Jerome Jerome translated the scriptures into the Latin that was spoken and written by the majority of people in his day. His translation is known as the Vulgate, which comes from the Latin word for "common."

October 4—Francis of Assisi Francis renounced wealth and future inheritance and devoted himself to serving the poor. Since Francis had a spirit of gratitude for all of God's creation, this commemoration has been a traditional time to bless pets and animals, creatures Francis called his brothers and sisters.

October 4—Theodor Fliedner Fliedner's work was instrumental in the revival of the ministry of deaconesses among Lutherans. Fliedner's deaconess motherhouse in Kaiserswerth, Germany, inspired Lutherans all over the world to commission deaconesses to serve in parishes, schools, prisons, and hospitals.

October 6—William Tyndale Tyndale's plan to translate the scriptures into English met opposition from Henry VIII. Though Tyndale completed work on the New Testament in 1525 and worked on a portion of the Old Testament, he was tried for heresy and burned at the stake.

October 7—Henry Melchior Muhlenberg Muhlenberg was prominent in setting the course for Lutheranism in the United States by helping Lutheran churches make the transition from the state churches of Europe to independent churches of America. Among other things, he established the first Lutheran synod in America and developed an American Lutheran liturgy.

October 15—Teresa of Avila Teresa of Avila (also known as Teresa de Jesús) chose the life of a Carmelite nun after reading the letters of Jerome. Teresa's writings on devotional life are widely read by members of various denominations.

October 17—Ignatius Ignatius was the second bishop of Antioch in Syria. When his own martyrdom approached, he wrote in one of his letters, "I prefer death in Christ Jesus to power over the farthest limits of the earth.... Do not stand in the way of my birth to real life."

October 18—Luke Luke, as author of both Luke and Acts, was careful to place the events of Jesus' life in both their social and religious contexts. Some of the most loved parables and canticles are found only in this gospel.

October 23—James of Jerusalem James is described in the New Testament as the brother of Jesus, and the secular historian Josephus called James, the brother of Jesus, "the so-called Christ." Little is known about James, but Josephus reported that the Pharisees respected James for his piety and observance of the law.

October 26—Philipp Nicolai, Johann Heermann, Paul Gerhardt These three outstanding hymnwriters all worked in Germany in the seventeenth century during times of war and plague. Philipp Nicolai's hymns "Wake, Awake, for Night Is Flying" and "O Morning Star, How Fair and Bright!" were included in a series of meditations he wrote to comfort his parishioners during the plague. The style of Johann Heermann's hymns (including "Ah, Holy Jesus") moved away from the more objective style of Reformation hymnody toward expressing the emotions of faith. Paul Gerhardt, whom some have called the greatest of Lutheran hymnwriters, lost a preaching position at St. Nicholas's Church in Berlin because he refused to sign a document stating he would not make theological arguments in his sermons.

October 28—Simon, Jude Little is known about Simon and Jude. In New Testament lists of the apostles, Simon the "zealot" or Cananaean is mentioned, but he is never mentioned apart from these lists. Jude, sometimes called Thaddaeus, is also mentioned in lists of the Twelve.

October 31—Reformation Day By the end of the seventeenth century, many Lutheran churches celebrated a festival commemorating Martin Luther's posting of the 95 Theses, a summary of abuses in the church of his time. At the heart of the reform movement was the gospel, the good news that it is by grace through faith that we are justified and set free.

November 1—All Saints Day The custom of commemorating all of the saints of the church on a single day goes back at least to the third century. All Saints Day celebrates the baptized people of God, living and dead, who make up the body of Christ.

November 3—Martín de Porres Martín was a lay brother in the Order of Preachers (Dominicans) and engaged in many charitable works. He is recognized as an advocate for Christian charity and interracial justice.

November 7—John Christian Frederick Heyer, Bartholomaeus Ziegenbalg, Ludwig Nommensen Heyer was the first missionary sent out by American Lutherans, and he became a missionary in the Andhra region of India. Ziegenbalg was a missionary to the Tamils of Tranquebar on the southeast coast of India. Nommensen worked among the Batak people, who had previously not seen Christian missionaries.

November 11—Martin of Tours In 371 Martin was elected bishop of Tours. As bishop he developed a reputation for intervening on behalf of prisoners and heretics who had been sentenced to death.

November 11—Søren Aabye Kierkegaard Kierkegaard, a nineteenth-century Danish theologian whose writings reflect his Lutheran heritage, was the founder of modern existentialism. Kierkegaard's work attacked the established church of his day—its complacency, its tendency to intellectualize faith, and its desire to be accepted by polite society.

November 17—Elizabeth of Hungary This Hungarian princess gave away large sums of money, including her dowry, for relief of the poor and sick. She founded hospitals, cared for 392 orphans, and used the royal food supplies to feed the hungry.

November 23—Clement Clement is best remembered for a letter he wrote to the Corinthian congregation still having difficulty with divisions in spite of Paul's canonical letters. Clement's letter is also a witness to early understandings of church government and the way each office in the church works for the good of the whole.

November 23—Miguel Agustín Pro Miguel Agustín Pro grew up amid oppression in Mexico and worked on behalf of the poor and homeless. Miguel and his two brothers were arrested, falsely accused of throwing a bomb at the car of a government official, and executed by a firing squad.

November 24—Justus Falckner, Jehu Jones, William Passavant Not only was Falckner the first Lutheran pastor to be ordained in North America, but he published a catechism that was the first Lutheran book published on the continent. Jones was the Lutheran Church's first African American pastor and carried out missionary work in Philadelphia, which led to the formation there of the first African American Lutheran congregation (St. Paul's). William Passavant helped to establish hospitals and orphanages in a number of cities and was the first to introduce deaconesses to the work of hospitals in the United States.

November 25—Isaac Watts Watts wrote about six hundred hymns, many of them in a two-year period beginning when he was twenty years old. When criticized for writing hymns not taken from scripture, he responded that if we can pray prayers that are not from scripture but written by us, then surely we can sing hymns that we have made up ourselves.

November 30—Andrew Andrew was the first of the Twelve. As a part of his calling, he brought other people, including Simon Peter, to meet Jesus.

December 3—Francis Xavier Francis Xavier became a missionary to India, Southeast Asia, Japan, and the Philippines. Together with Ignatius Loyola and five others, Francis formed the Society of Jesus (Jesuits).

December 4—John of Damascus John left a career in finance and government to become a monk in an abbey near Jerusalem. He wrote many hymns as well as theological works, including *The Fount of Wisdom,* a work that touches on philosophy, heresy, and the orthodox faith.

December 6—Nicholas Nicholas was a bishop in what is now Turkey. Legends that surround Nicholas tell of his love for God and neighbor, especially the poor.

December 7—Ambrose Ambrose was baptized, ordained, and consecrated a bishop all on the same day. While bishop, he gave away his wealth and lived in simplicity.

December 13—Lucy Lucy was a young Christian of Sicily who was martyred during the persecutions under Emperor Diocletian. Her celebration became particularly important in Sweden and Norway, perhaps because the feast of Lucia (whose name means "light") originally fell on the shortest day of the year.

December 14—John of the Cross John was a monk of the Carmelite religious order who met Teresa of Avila when she was working to reform the Carmelite Order and return it to a stricter observance of its rules. His writings, like Teresa's, reflect a deep interest in mystical thought and practice.

December 20—Katharina von Bora Luther Katharina took vows as a nun, but around age twenty-four she and several other nuns who were influenced by the writings of Martin Luther left the convent. When she later became Luther's wife, she proved herself a gifted household manager and became a trusted partner.

December 26—Stephen Stephen, a deacon and the first martyr of the church, was one of those seven upon whom the apostles laid hands after they had been chosen to serve widows and others in need. Later, Stephen's preaching angered the temple authorities, and they ordered him to be put to death by stoning.

December 27—John John, a son of Zebedee, was a fisherman and one of the Twelve. Tradition has attributed authorship of the gospel and the three epistles bearing his name to the apostle John.

December 28—The Holy Innocents The infant martyrs commemorated on this day were the children of Bethlehem, two years old and younger, who were killed by Herod, who worried that his reign was threatened by the birth of a new king named Jesus.

Anniversary of Baptism (abbreviated)

This order is intended for use in the home. It may be adapted for use in another context, such as a Christian education setting. When used in the home, a parent or sponsor may be the leader. A more expanded version of this order appears in *Evangelical Lutheran Worship Pastoral Care* (pp. 128–135).

A bowl of water may be placed in the midst of those who are present.

Gathering

A baptismal hymn or acclamation (see Evangelical Lutheran Worship #209–217, 442–459) may be sung.

The sign of the cross may be made by all in remembrance of their baptism as the leader begins.

In the name of the Father, and of the + Son, and of the Holy Spirit.
Amen.

The candle received at baptism or another candle may be used. As it is lighted, the leader may say:

Jesus said, I am the light of the world.
Whoever follows me will have the light of life.

Reading

One or more scripture readings follow. Those present may share in reading.

A reading from Mark: People were bringing little children to Jesus in order that he might touch them; and the disciples spoke sternly to them. But when Jesus saw this, he was indignant and said, "Let the little children come to me; do not stop them; for it is to such as these that the kingdom of God belongs." And he took them up in his arms, laid his hands on them, and blessed them. *(Mark 10:13-14, 16)*

A reading from Second Corinthians: If anyone is in Christ, there is a new creation: everything old has passed away; see, everything has become new! *(2 Corinthians 5:17)*

A reading from First John: Beloved, let us love one another, because love is from God; everyone who loves is born of God and knows God. *(1 John 4:7)*

Those present may share experiences related to baptism and their lives as baptized children of God. A portion of the Small Catechism (Evangelical Lutheran Worship, pp. 1160–1167) may be read as part of this conversation.

A baptismal hymn or acclamation may be sung.

Baptismal Remembrance

A parent or sponsor may trace a cross on the forehead of the person celebrating a baptismal anniversary. Water from a bowl placed in the midst of those present may be used. These or similar words may be said.

Name, when you were baptized, you were marked with the cross of Christ forever.
Remember your baptism with thanksgiving and joy.

Prayers

Prayers may include the following or other appropriate prayers. Others who are present may place a hand on the head or shoulder of the one who is celebrating the anniversary.

Let us pray.
Gracious God, we thank you for the new life you give us through holy baptism. Especially, we ask you to bless *name* on the anniversary of *her/his* baptism. Continue to strengthen *name* with the Holy Spirit, and increase in *her/him* your gifts of grace: the spirit of wisdom and understanding, the spirit of counsel and might, the spirit of knowledge and the fear of the Lord, the spirit of joy in your presence; through Jesus Christ, our Savior and Lord.
Amen.

Other prayers may be added. Those present may offer petitions and thanksgivings.

The prayers may conclude with the Lord's Prayer.

Our Father in heaven,
> **hallowed be your name, your kingdom come,**
> **your will be done, on earth as in heaven.**

Give us today our daily bread.
Forgive us our sins
> **as we forgive those who sin against us.**

Save us from the time of trial and deliver us from evil.
For the kingdom, the power, and the glory are yours,
> **now and forever. Amen.**

Blessing

The order may conclude with this or another suitable blessing.

Almighty God, who gives us a new birth by water and the Holy Spirit and forgives us all our sins, strengthen us in all goodness and by the power of the Holy Spirit keep us in eternal life through Jesus Christ our Lord.

Amen.

The greeting of peace may be shared by all.

Other suggested readings for this service:
John 3:1-8: *Born again from above*
Romans 6:3-11: *Raised with Christ in baptism*
Galatians 3:26-28: *All are one in Christ*
Ephesians 4:1-6: *There is one body and one Spirit*
Colossians 1:11-13: *Claimed by Christ, heirs of light*
1 Peter 2:2-3: *Long for spiritual food*
1 Peter 2:9: *Chosen in baptism to tell about God*
Revelation 22:1-2: *The river of the water of life*

Prayers for Various Situations

A prayer to begin the work day

May the graciousness of the Lord our God be upon us;
prosper the work of our hands. (Ps. 90:17, *ELW*)
Generous God, you call us to lives of service.
In my words and actions this day, move me to serve in Christ's name.
When I lack energy, inspire me. When I lack courage, strengthen me.
When I lack compassion, be merciful to me.

You may make the sign of the cross.

In all things, O God, you are our way, our truth, and our life. Reveal through
me your life-giving work, that I love my neighbors as myself. I ask this in Jesus'
name. Amen.

A prayer to begin the school day

Show me your ways, O Lord, and teach me your paths. (Ps. 25:4, *ELW*)
Christ be with me: in you I am never alone.
Christ within me: your Spirit is at work in me.
Christ behind me: reassure me when I struggle.
Christ before me: lead me when I am uncertain.
Christ beneath me: support me when I am weak.
Christ above me: encourage me to do my best.
Christ in quiet: I listen for the sound of your voice.
Christ in danger: I will not fear, for you are with me.

You may make the sign of the cross.

In all things, O God, you are our way, our truth, and our life.
Teach me to love you and my neighbors as myself.
I ask this in Jesus' name. Amen.

(Based on the Prayer of St. Patrick)

Blessing for pets and animals

Use this prayer on St. Francis Day, October 4, or whenever it is appropriate.

Gracious God,
in your love you created us in your image
and made us stewards of the animals
that live in the skies, the earth, and the sea.
Bless us in our care for our *pet/s (animal/s)* (names may be added here).
Help us recognize your power and wisdom
in the variety of creatures that live in our world,
and hear our prayer for all that suffer overwork, hunger, and ill-treatment.
Protect your creatures and guard them from all evil, now and forever. Amen.

Time of conflict, crisis, disaster

O God, where hearts are fearful and constricted, grant courage and hope. Where anxiety is infectious and widening, grant peace and reassurance. Where impossibilities close every door and window, grant imagination and resistance. Where distrust twists our thinking, grant healing and illumination. Where spirits are daunted and weakened, grant soaring wings and strengthened dreams. All these things we ask in the name of Jesus Christ, our Savior and Lord. Amen.

Health of body and soul

By your power, great God, our Lord Jesus healed the sick and gave new hope to the hopeless. Though we cannot command or possess your power, we pray for those who want to be healed. Mend their wounds, soothe fevered brows, and make broken people whole again. Help us to welcome every healing as a sign that, though death is against us, you are for us, and have promised renewed and risen life in Jesus Christ the Lord. Amen.

Those in affliction

Lord Christ, you came into the world as one of us, and suffered as we do. As we go through the trials of life, help us to realize that you are with us at all times and in all things; that we have no secrets from you; and that your loving grace enfolds us for eternity. In the security of your embrace we pray. Amen.

Those in trouble or bereavement

Almighty God, your love never fails, and you can turn the shadow of death into daybreak. Help us to receive your word with believing hearts, so that, confident in your promises, we may have hope and be lifted out of sorrow into the joy and peace of your presence; through Jesus Christ our Savior and Lord. Amen.

Those suffering from addiction

O blessed Jesus, you ministered to all who came to you. Look with compassion upon all who through addiction have lost their health and freedom. Restore to them the assurance of your unfailing mercy; remove the fears that attack them; strengthen those who are engaged in the work of recovery; and to those who care for them, give honesty, understanding, and persevering love; for your mercy's sake. Amen.

The chronically ill and those who support them

Loving God, your heart overflows with compassion for your whole creation. Pour out your Spirit on all people living with illness for which there is no cure, as well as their families and loved ones. Help them to know that you claim them as your own and deliver them from fear and pain; for the sake of Jesus Christ, our healer and Lord. Amen.

Caregivers and others who support the sick

God, our refuge and strength, our present help in time of trouble, care for those who tend the needs of *name*. Strengthen them in body and spirit. Refresh them when weary; console them when anxious; comfort them in grief; and hearten them in discouragement. Be with us all, and give us peace at all times and in every way; through Christ our peace. Amen.

Recovery from sickness

Almighty and merciful God, you are the only source of health and healing; you alone can bring calmness and peace. Grant to us, your children, an awareness of your presence and a strong confidence in you. In our pain, our weariness, and our anxiety, surround us with your care, protect us by your loving might, and permit us once more to enjoy health and strength and peace; through Jesus Christ, our Savior and Lord. Amen.

A prayer attributed to Francis of Assisi

Lord, make us instruments of your peace. Where there is hatred, let us sow love; where there is injury, pardon; where there is discord, union; where there is doubt, faith; where there is despair, hope; where there is darkness, light; where there is sadness, joy. Grant that we may not so much seek to be consoled as to console; to be understood as to understand; to be loved as to love. For it is in giving that we receive; it is in pardoning that we are pardoned; and it is in dying that we are born to eternal life. Amen.

A prayer of Catherine of Siena

Power of the eternal Father, help me. Wisdom of the Son, enlighten the eye of my understanding. Tender mercy of the Holy Spirit, unite my heart to yourself. Eternal God, restore health to the sick and life to the dead. Give us a voice, your own voice, to cry out to you for mercy for the world. You, light, give us light. You, wisdom, give us wisdom. You, supreme strength, strengthen us. Amen.

A prayer of Julian of Norwich

In you, Father all-mighty, we have our preservation and our bliss. In you, Christ, we have our restoring and our saving. You are our mother, brother, and savior. In you, our Lord the Holy Spirit, is marvelous and plenteous grace. You are our clothing; for love you wrap us and embrace us. You are our maker, our lover, our keeper. Teach us to believe that by your grace all shall be well, and all shall be well, and all manner of things shall be well. Amen.

A prayer of Martin Luther

Behold, Lord, an empty vessel that needs to be filled. My Lord, fill it. I am weak in the faith; strengthen me. I am cold in love; warm me and make me fervent, that my love may go out to my neighbor. I do not have a strong and firm faith; at times I doubt and am unable to trust you altogether. O Lord, help me. Strengthen my faith and trust in you. In you I have sealed the treasure of all I have. I am poor; you are rich and came to be merciful to the poor. I am a sinner; you are upright. With me, there is an abundance of sin; in you is the fullness of righteousness. Therefore I will remain with you, of whom I can receive, but to whom I may not give. Amen.

Prayers on pages 420–423 from *Evangelical Lutheran Worship* and *Sundays and Seasons 2020*.

Morning Blessing

You may make the sign of the cross.

I am a beloved child of God, marked with the cross of Christ forever.

Your mercies are new every morning. *(Based on Lam. 3:23)*

Thank you, gracious God, for the gift of this new day.
Awaken me to your abiding presence;
open my eyes to your creation;
open my ears to your promises;
open my heart to the needs of others.
Fill me with your Spirit and guide me this day
in works of kindness, justice, and mercy.
I ask this in the name of Jesus, the light and life of the world.
Amen.

A Simplified Form for Morning Prayer

Opening

O Lord, open my lips,
and my mouth shall proclaim your praise.
Glory to the Father, and to the Son,
and to the Holy Spirit:
as it was in the beginning, is now,
and will be forever. Amen.

The alleluia is omitted during Lent.

[Alleluia.]

Psalmody

The psalmody may begin with Psalm 63, Psalm 67, Psalm 95, Psalm 100, or another psalm appropriate for morning. Psalms provided in this book for each week may be used instead of or in addition to the psalms mentioned.

A time of silence follows.

A hymn may follow (see the suggested hymn for each day).

Readings

One or more readings for each day may be selected from those provided in this book. The reading of scripture may be followed by silence for reflection.

The reflection may conclude with these or similar words.

Long ago God spoke to our ancestors
in many and various ways by the prophets,
but in these last days God has spoken to us by the Son.

Gospel Canticle

The song of Zechariah may be sung or said.

Blessed are you, Lord, the God of Israel,
you have come to your people and set them free.
You have raised up for us a mighty Savior,
born of the house of your servant David.
Through your holy prophets, you promised of old
to save us from our enemies,
from the hands of all who hate us,
to show mercy to our forebears,
and to remember your holy covenant.
This was the oath you swore to our father Abraham:
to set us free from the hands of our enemies,
free to worship you without fear,
holy and righteous before you, all the days of our life.
And you, child, shall be called the prophet of the Most High,
for you will go before the Lord to prepare the way,
to give God's people knowledge of salvation
by the forgiveness of their sins.
In the tender compassion of our God
the dawn from on high shall break upon us,
to shine on those who dwell in darkness and the shadow of death,
and to guide our feet into the way of peace.

Prayers

Various intercessions may be spoken at this time. The prayer provided in this book for each day may also be used.

The following prayer is especially appropriate for morning.

Almighty and everlasting God,
you have brought us in safety to this new day.
Preserve us with your mighty power,
that we may not fall into sin
nor be overcome in adversity.

In all we do, direct us to the fulfilling of your purpose;
through Jesus Christ our Lord.
Amen.

The Lord's Prayer

Our Father in heaven,
   hallowed be your name,
   your kingdom come,
   your will be done, on earth as in heaven.
Give us today our daily bread.
Forgive us our sins
   as we forgive those who sin against us.
Save us from the time of trial
   and deliver us from evil.
For the kingdom, the power, and the glory are yours,
   now and forever. Amen.

Blessing

Let us bless the Lord.
Thanks be to God.

Almighty God,
the Father, + the Son, and the Holy Spirit,
bless and preserve us.
Amen.

Additional materials for daily prayer are available in Evangelical Lutheran Worship
(pp. 295–331) and may supplement this simple order.

A Simplified Form for Evening Prayer

Opening

Jesus Christ is the light of the world,
the light no darkness can overcome.
Stay with us, Lord, for it is evening,
and the day is almost over.
Let your light scatter the darkness
and illumine your church.

Psalmody

The psalmody may begin with Psalm 141, Psalm 121, or another psalm appropriate for evening. Psalms provided in this book for each week may be used instead of or in addition to the psalms mentioned.

A time of silence follows.

A hymn may follow (see the suggested hymn for each day).

Readings

One or more readings for each day may be selected from those provided in this book. The reading of scripture may be followed by silence for reflection.

The reflection may conclude with these or similar words.

Jesus said, I am the light of the world.
Whoever follows me will never walk in darkness.

Gospel Canticle

The song of Mary may be sung or said.

My soul proclaims the greatness of the Lord,
my spirit rejoices in God my Savior,
for you, Lord, have looked with favor on your lowly servant.
From this day all generations will call me blessed:
you, the Almighty, have done great things for me,
and holy is your name.
You have mercy on those who fear you,
from generation to generation.
You have shown strength with your arm
and scattered the proud in their conceit,
casting down the mighty from their thrones
and lifting up the lowly.
You have filled the hungry with good things
and sent the rich away empty.
You have come to the aid of your servant Israel,
to remember the promise of mercy,
the promise made to our forebears,
to Abraham and his children forever.

Prayers

*Various intercessions may be spoken at this time. The prayer provided in this book for
each day may also be used.*

The following prayer is especially appropriate for evening.

We give thanks to you, heavenly Father,
through Jesus Christ your dear Son,
that you have graciously protected us today.
We ask you to forgive us all our sins, where we have done wrong,
and graciously to protect us tonight.

For into your hands we commend ourselves:
our bodies, our souls, and all that is ours.
Let your holy angels be with us,
so that the wicked foe may have no power over us.
Amen.

The Lord's Prayer

Our Father in heaven,
hallowed be your name,
your kingdom come,
your will be done, on earth as in heaven.
Give us today our daily bread.
Forgive us our sins
as we forgive those who sin against us.
Save us from the time of trial
and deliver us from evil.
For the kingdom, the power, and the glory are yours,
now and forever. Amen.

Blessing

Let us bless the Lord.
Thanks be to God.

The peace of God,
which surpasses all understanding,
keep our hearts and our minds in Christ Jesus.
Amen.

Additional materials for daily prayer are available in Evangelical Lutheran Worship
(pp. 295–331) and may supplement this simple order.

Evening Blessing

You may make the sign of the cross.

I am a beloved child of God, marked with the cross of Christ forever.
Come to me, all you that are weary . . . and I will give you rest.
(Matt. 11:28)

Thank you, gracious God, for the gift of this coming night.
Restore me with your right spirit. Calm my mind. Quiet my heart.
Enfold me with your bountiful mercy.
Protect me from all harm,
that I sleep assured of the peace found in you alone.
I ask this in the name of Jesus, who gives us rest. Amen.

Night Prayers with Children

Dear Jesus, as a hen covers her chicks with her wings to keep them safe,
protect us this night under your golden wings; for your mercy's sake.
Amen.

We bless you, God, for the day just spent,
for laughter, tears, and all you've sent.
Grant us, Good Shepherd, through this night,
a peaceful sleep till morning light.

A parent or caregiver may trace the cross on the child's forehead or heart and say one of these blessings:

God the Father, Son, and Holy Spirit watch over you.
May God protect you through the night.
May the Lord Jesus keep you in his love.

Suggestions for Daily Reflection

God's word for me this day is:

God's word will shape my day by:

I will share God's word with others through:

My prayers today will include:

- The church universal, its ministry, and the mission of the gospel

- The well-being of creation

- Peace and justice in the world, the nations and those in authority, the community

- The poor, oppressed, sick, bereaved, lonely

- All who suffer in body, mind, or spirit

- Special concerns